MAN IS NOT LOST

MAN IS NOT LOST

The Log of a Pioneer RAF Pilot/Navigator 1933–1946

Group Captain 'Dickie' Richardson

Airlife
England

Copyright © 1997 F C Richardson

First published in the UK in 1997
by Airlife Publishing Ltd

British Library Cataloguing-in-Publication Data
A catalogue record for this book
is available from the British Library

ISBN 1 85310 868 5

Typeset by Servis Filmsetting Ltd, Manchester
Printed and bound in Great Britain by MPG Books Ltd, Bodmin, Cornwall

Airlife Publishing Ltd
101 Longden Road, Shrewsbury, SY3 9EB, England

Contents

Preface

This autobiography by a master air navigator brings to life the RAF of the 1930s when its aircraft ranged freely over Imperial routes in Africa and the Middle East; it recounts how a classic treatise on air navigation was written and published in the desperate early years of the Second World War; and it records the grim struggle of aircraft versus U-boats in the bitterly fought Battle of the Atlantic.

It tells all these stories through the pen (or word processor) and memories of Frederick Charles Richardson – always known as Dickie – who was commissioned into the RAF in 1933, trained to fly in Egypt and by 1943 had become a Group Captain in charge of navigation at Coastal Command Headquarters.

Dickie died on 12 October 1995 at the age of 83, having completed his autobiography, to which he gave the title *Man Is Not Lost*. Two Air Marshals (themselves no longer with us) commended it: in a Preface Sir Edward Chilton wrote that Dickie's 'contributions to the advancement of air navigation and of the air navigators themselves continued unabated during and after the war'. Sir Charles Ness referred to the pages which follow as 'a remarkable journal written by a remarkable man', noting that Dickie's accounts of his 'Arabian and African odysseys reflect another world – a world of great hardship, great privileges and great adventure'.

In a measured obituary tribute in the *Journal* of the Royal Institute of Navigation, of which Dickie was a Fellow, his old friend and distinguished contemporary Air Vice-Marshal Wilf Oulton wrote that he made 'many valuable contributions to the science . . . and practice of air navigation' – notably with the 'world-famous' *Manual of Air Navigation*, the Royal Air Force *Air Publication 1234*; that he 'played an important role in . . . pioneering . . . the air reinforcement route from Takoradi . . . to Cairo'; and that he 'so distinguished himself' in command of No 502 (Ulster) Auxiliary Air Force Squadron that he was 'promoted to Group Captain, to be the Command Navigation Officer at Headquarters Coastal Command', where he 'played a major part in our ultimate success in the Battle of the Atlantic'.

Dickie subsequently helped to set up the Empire Air Navigation School at RAF Shawbury, being appointed Assistant Commandant. One of the students at Shawbury on No 2 Specialist Navigation Course was a young Dutchman who in 1944–45 had flown B-25 Mitchells with No 320 (Dutch Naval) Squadron and who later became Netherlands Defence Attaché in London and was a member of the Aries Association. In 1975, as retired Commodore Hans van der Kop, he visited the MoD Air Historical Branch (AHB). As a result, I wrote about him in the *Royal Air Forces Quarterly* and helped to get his autobiography published in the UK. The Commodore introduced me to Dickie (with whom he used to attend the Aries Association Reunions at the RAF College, Cranwell) in the hope that I might be able to help him similarly.

Sadly, this was not achieved before Dickie died; but having got to know him and admired him for all he had achieved in the RAF, and for the perceptive and articulate way in which he has set it down, I am grateful to have had the opportunity of helping to put his story into print, and salute his memory.

I would like to record my thanks to his son Richard for his help and co-operation, to Group Captain Tony Stephens of the AHB for his able assistance with navigational queries, and to Alastair Simpson and Peter Coles of Airlife for putting *Man Is Not Lost* into book form.

H.W.

Introduction

Dickie Richardson – formally Group Captain F. C. Richardson CBE FRIN but always known as Dickie – was the genius who wrote the words which gave thousands of wartime pilots and navigators their first instruction in finding their way about the skies: he was the author of what was forbiddingly called by the Air Ministry *AP (Air Publication) 1234 Air Navigation*, a masterly treatise which he wrote in 1940–41 while the Battle of Britain and the *Blitz* were raging in the skies above London and the Home Counties. How he did it will be described hereafter in his own words; but how did he come to be chosen to do it?

He was born on 24 January 1912 at Streatham, south London, and remembered the Zeppelin raids of 1915 in the first German air attacks on Britain and the terror they caused. His first school was the 'pretentiously named' Pendennis College; then he and his brother Jack (both C of E) went to St Joseph's (RC) College, Beulah Hill. They spent holidays in Belgium (still littered with the horrendous devastation of the First World War), Jersey, Cornwall, Wales and Scotland. They cycled in France, Germany and Austria, even riding over the 9,080ft Col de l'Iseran, Europe's highest road – Jack riding a tandem with their 26-year-old sister Mary.

Dickie matriculated when only 15, which delayed his enrolment for London University until 1928, when he was 16: he entered for a three-year degree course at the London School of Economics and Political Science – which happened to be next door to Adastral House, the Air Ministry building in Kingsway, which he was destined to come to know well during the war years. He always stoutly defended LSE from its 'stigma of radicalism' as inapplicable to the 'vast majority of hard-working, normally oriented, level-headed students'.

To 'save pennies and travelling time' he cycled daily the seven miles from Streatham on a racing bike, and could reach the Aldwych in 30 minutes; then after a shower and change he was ready for lectures.

He rowed for the LSE Boat Club and was also elected joint secretary of the Students' Union. He 'came down' in 1931 – only to discover that 'a commerce degree and an athletic and social record [were] no magic key to an executive job in trade or industry during the prevailing, terrible worldwide depression'. So he went back to LSE for a fourth, post-graduate year in the new Department of Business Administration. He was awarded a Bursary and his work involved studying case histories and travelling round the country looking at companies' methods and problems.

Dickie had more success in rowing than in motoring – he won the University winter sculls in 1932 and was selected for the University VIII, but he was fined for speeding down the Mall, at 3 mph over the 20 mph limit, and had to abandon his open sports Austin Seven after a fire under the bonnet in Park Lane. In 1932 he was awarded a post-graduate diploma in business administration.

By mid-1932, with three million unemployed in the UK, there were few job vacancies. Dickie earned pocket-money by trying to sell a new line of milk for Clover Dairies, based in Clapham. His job was to go round 'knocking on doors' – one day ahead of the delivery-man, hopefully booking orders for him. His pay – £4 a week – was 'good money' in 1932; but he was far too sorry for his customers – mostly London dockers who had been on and off the dole – to be really persuasive.

He tried unsuccessfully for a job in Paris as assistant to the General Secretary of the International Rubber Growers' Association, being rejected because, despite his paper qualifications, he was still only 20, had no practical business experience and was up against an older applicant who had everything.

Then he had a taste of the fish-and-chip trade, having met a Mr Bell, a civil servant who worked in the Patent Office but also dabbled in shop speculations and had an idea of building up a fried-fish empire in London. Mr Bell liked the look of Dickie, who got a glowing report from the LSE Department of Business Administration, but who knew nothing of the trade apart from its end product and had to brief himself by contacting the editor of the *Fried Fish Trade's Gazette*, who referred him to John Dory's – by repute London's leading fried fish emporium. The location where Dickie began – and ended – his work lay on one corner of an Islington cross-roads, the three other corners being occupied by pubs.

His first task was to become the 'chips king', handling four tons of potatoes each week. These came from the Borough market, were dumped on the pavement and had to be carried through to the rear premises. Every single one then passed through his hands for five dif-

10

ferent processes – in one of which each spud had to be held long-way upwards on the sharp chipper knives, while he pulled down a lever with his right hand to push it through them. He spent his mornings in the near-freezing out-house, cutting these long fingers of raw potato which were then stored in bins of water.

For the rest of the day he stood over vats of oil, boiling at 360°F, into which the chips were dunked until they were a light golden brown and crisp enough to snap between his fingers. He concluded that to shovel the last penn'orth of chips into a grease-proof bag for the night's last hungry customer gave him a real sense of achievement. But his 18-hr day, six-days-a-week career in the fish-and-chip trade was to be cut short by two accidents of fortune.

When involved in the hunt for new shop sites – which brought him into contact with both local authorities and agents, both of whom had strong views on the fish-frying trade – Dickie encountered a smooth and suave character called Mr Jones, who he understood was the London 'rep' for Ford's, a leading Lancashire manufacturer of fish-frying stoves. Clearly he knew the London trade like the back of his hand, and the first accident was that Dickie introduced him to Mr Bell. The second was that Dickie himself fell victim to a severe attack of 'flu', having taken too much out of himself with all the hard work he had put in.

Mr Bell called to see Dickie while he was laid up, and even took a cup of tea with Mrs Richardson. But his apparent concern for Dickie's welfare took a sour turn when he rang up a few days later to say that he had had doubts about Dickie's suitability for the job and was going into partnership with Mr Jones.

Dickie ruefully decided that he was not cut out for big business: he put all his smelly, oily, fishy clothes into the dustbin, bought himself a new suit and took a long look at the future from his penniless situation, for he had earned nothing from Mr Bell, except some hard lessons.

Much to his parents' dismay, he responded to an advertisement in *The Times*, applying for a short-term, six-year commission in the Royal Air Force. It would end with a £500 gratuity and a four-year Reserve commission.

Although in 1933 the European dictators had begun to rise and Japan had invaded Manchuria, the RAF had only 30 squadrons worldwide (all detailed in the *Air Force List* and Service diaries), and the threat of actual confrontation then seemed fairly remote.

Dickie was summoned to undergo a tough medical check-up, but had no qualms about it; with all his cycling exploits he never felt fitter in his life. His personal interview was another matter, for he feared that his LSE pedigree might arouse some ill-informed prejudice; but all was well, and after an anxious two-week wait he received an Air Ministry letter instructing him to report to the RAF Depot at Uxbridge for further assessment as a temporarily commissioned Acting Pilot Officer on probation, for flying duties. He had to be there, with full civilian kit including his dinner jacket and sports gear, at 10 o'clock sharp on 6 June 1933.

I
Per Ardua

THE TRAIN leaving Baker Street early that morning was pretty full, but at each stop it shed some of its suburban load. By the time it reached Rayners Lane there was only one other male passenger left in my carriage – a young man wearing a fashionable 'pork pie' hat and a smart tweed suit. Like me, he had a suitcase on the rack.

We eyed each other warily and simultaneously decided to break the ice. He was Alan Theed, who in 1932 had left the 6th form at Merchant Taylors, where he had played rugby and boxed as a welterweight. He too was now heading for the RAF depot. We became friends for life.

We were both 21, and as we walked into the warm sunshine up the road from the Metropolitan Railway terminus to the depot, I found myself quite literally treading on air. At long last I seemed to have landed a real job of work: I was actually going somewhere to learn to fly!

Little did we know what a pregnant date 6 June was to be. Six years later, to the day, we were both granted permanent commissions. On 6 June 1940, in the midst of the Battle of France, Winston Churchill issued his famous Directive to the Joint Chiefs of Staff to mount a 'rigorous, enterprising and ceaseless offensive against the whole German-occupied coastline'.[1] On 6 June 1941 my own *Air Navigation* (Air Publication 1234) was ready for the printers. Most importantly of all, on 6 June 1944 the Allies invaded Europe.

But back in 1933, 6 June was a momentous enough day for each of us. Our own immediate fate was about to be sealed. The remote future would just have to look after itself, for we were both only too eager to seize the present.

We walked into the Guard Room together and were directed to the Officers' Mess where elderly civilian batmen took our bags and showed us to our rooms. Then, with several other young men, we were assembled in an ante-room and addressed by a rather 'wet-looking' Adjutant – considering that the Station Commander, Gp Capt. F. L. Robinson DSO MC DFC, was almost as highly decorated as his

13

namesake, the fabled scourge of the Zeppelins.[2] We received the exciting news that we were going to Egypt for our flying training.

We gathered that the next two weeks would be spent being chased around the barrack square by a former Guards Warrant Officer of very imposing stature, stentorian voice and purple language. Mr Nightingirl was not someone to be trifled with. We would also attend lectures, keep-fit sessions and be quickly kitted-out by West End tailors of our choice, several having been summoned the very next day to measure us for our uniforms.

Because we were going abroad, we were also greeted by a Medical Officer, armed to the teeth with vaccines, serums and fairly blunt needles which he proceeded to jab into our left arms bared at the ready and offered to him in one long line for instant inoculation.

After that, we had a rather subdued lunch and were at once ordered to change into singlets and shorts to jog seven miles round the perimeter of the depot, as fast as we could go; tough going on a hot summer afternoon! There were several empty chairs at dinner in the Mess that night: we were all running post-jab high temperatures and some had fallen by the wayside.

Apart from a lot of boring marching and arms drill which we absorbed mainly through our hands and feet, we were taught some basic Service etiquette – saluting and all that. Mess life involved innumerable negative injunctions, such as a complete taboo on all political discussions – as if we wanted any! Somewhat inexplicably, we were never to mention ladies by name in the Mess. We were also warned not to talk shop – but if the hangar doors had to be kept shut, there really didn't seem to be much left for us to talk about. Above all, we must never wear uniform when off duty in public, no doubt a vestige of anti-Cromwellian reaction from England's Restoration past.

One of the more fascinating lectures dealt with the proper maintenance of our bank accounts – into which our salaries of 11 shillings and sixpence (57p) a day would shortly be paid – and the related miracles of a cheque book. This facility was evidently something of a red-hot potato if we were careless and wrote a cheque that bounced, for it could involve our instant dismissal. We wondered how often that happened.

While waiting impatiently for the fitting and arrival of our uniforms and of a green camp-roll containing a canvas bed, wash basin and bath, a mosquito net, pillow and ground-sheet and also of an imposing stout tin trunk for our gear, all bearing our stencilled names and ranks, we were forever changing out of one costume into another to suit the activities of the passing day.

The arrival of our uniforms added to these charades and in next to no time we became quick-change artists, able to turn a silk double-ended black dress tie into a neat bow with our eyes shut or in the dark, an invaluable skill for later life.

We also learned to jump at every bark from the 'staff' coming in our direction and 'got fell-in' as a squad at speed for every conceivable task or relaxation. We were paraded for meals, lectures, PT, drill, games – even for sleep! Only the calls of nature were excluded from a daily timetable that completely filled our every waking moment.

But the prospect of ten days nirvana as first-class passengers onboard the P & O liner *Ranchi* to far away Port Said enabled the diet of intensive 'bull' to be swallowed with indifference by thirteen young bloods who had long since discovered that no one gets anything for nothing in this world.

Our numbers included Ozzy bush-whacker John McNab Newman, shot down two years later in Iraq; merchant marine officer Derek Atkinson; and permanently laid-back Pat Meagher, son of a Surgeon Rear-Admiral – an amusingly sarcastic and potentially priceless asset to his colleagues.

One cadet had joined a day or two ahead of us and was appointed to be our prefect on the grounds of this brief seniority, a distinction we others silently resented, making his job all the more onerous, poor fellow. To make matters worse, he was a natural martinet and quickly found we were inclined to be unco-operative.

But in the end it made very little difference to our enjoyment of life. If our monitor became too officious for our liking, we took pains to make him squirm by excessively indulging his latent bossiness. He had a lot to learn about man-management and we were there to help him.

At last the July day dawned when we embarked at Tilbury for our luxury cruise, to be waited on hand and foot, lotus-eating our way to Egypt. We were instantly transported to a state of suspended reality as the great ship glided effortlessly across a calm Bay of Biscay and on past Gibraltar into a placid Mediterranean of indescribable hue.

The only fly in the ointment was a compulsory dawn parade for half an hour of energetic PT up on the boat deck while all our fellow shipmates were still happily tucked up in their bunks – or in someone else's! Our uncouth physical activity briefly broke the magic spell each day, but the all-pervading charisma of the voyage was soon restored by a hearty breakfast and an inviting smile from one or two of the 'lovelies' with whom our shipborne lives were being shared.

At Marseille *Ranchi* waited for a day and a night for her more affluent passengers from London to catch her up overland by train *via* Paris. We naturally speculated on what new female talent might be arriving onboard for our future delectation and, as it turned out, we were not to be disappointed.

Short leave ashore in port was the order of the day and the nearby Riviera resorts, not to mention the shops and the notorious stews of the Rue Canabière, received our urgent attention. A howling cold mistral had quite spoilt our outing along the coast but we made up for it in the evening.

By the time we had found our bearings and had also become a little tamed, some having shed a virginity they were only too keen to lose – even at the possible chance of a few anxious visits to the MO – *Ranchi* was once more on her languid way, through seas of deepest blue, at night trailing a sparkling wake of phosphorescence.

Aboard again, a surge of self-confidence and new-found male maturity seemed suddenly to be inexplicably attractive to our fair companions. It was perhaps lucky for us that, after passing through the Straits of Messina and having left Malta behind, there were no other exotic visits to distract us from our favourite quarries, most of whom turned out to be on their way to India and beyond. We were all in it together and the chase was on: it was now or never!

Four days after leaving France, thirteen 'sprogs' and their rather out-manoeuvred conducting Flight Lieutenant disembarked at Port Said. All were now dressed in tropical khaki kit and some had aching hearts under their tunics. Then, in the blinding July heat of mid-morning, we set off for our desert destination, 80 miles away to the south-west.

This last two-hour hot and thirsty trek by fly-blown, dusty train, running alongside the Suez Canal south to Ismailia and then westwards to Abu Sueir, shattered our brief and charmed idyll of life on the ocean wave. We had come down to earth with a horrible bump; little did we realise that our troubles were only just beginning. In truth, we really didn't know what on earth to expect. It was strange and quite intriguing.

Twice a year since the early 'twenties, a dozen or so adventurous young men had sailed out from England to No 4 Flying Training School (FTS) at the godforsaken Royal Air Force station of Abu Sueir, situated alongside a scruffy little Egyptian peasant village in the desert west of the Suez Canal. Their camp was remote from the bright lights of civilisation; but they had come to take advantage of the reliably good desert flying conditions, invaluable for basic pilot training and so very much better than the unsettled weather in England where poor visibility interrupted training programmes.

16

The camp's isolation fostered *esprit de corps*. The climate was briefly pleasant in spring and autumn but extremely hot in summer and cold enough to need coal fires in winter. The cadets found themselves in a reasonably comfortable officers' mess but were ostentatiously segregated from the staff officers who had their own ante-room.

Local distractions included a social club frequented by wives of the few married officers, two clay tennis courts, an open-air squash court, a swimming pool, gravel football pitch and a concrete cricket table.

Ismailia, 12 miles east, had small shops, a one-eyed Greek hotel and a French Club reserved for staff of the Suez Canal Company. The Canal joined Lake Timsah at Ferry Point beach, much patronised by No 4 FTS and No 6 Squadron, whose nearby airfield had an un-used airship mooring mast, a forlorn monument to the ill-fated R101 that had crashed at Beauvais in 1930 *en route* for India.

Beyond the barbed wire boundaries of Abu Sueir camp lay a large undulating gravel desert, absolutely perfect for the Other Ranks' land-yacht club. Their wheeled sail-craft had been ingeniously cobbled together from bits and pieces of crashed aeroplanes and were capable of fast cruising speeds in the strong sea breeze which arrived from the Med like clockwork at noon every day. One intrepid club crew had reputedly reached the sandy outskirts of Cairo, 80 miles away to the west, in a day.

Alas, these basic diversions could be used by the cadets only on sufferance, as it was policy to treat us on arrival as less than dust, until we were able to show our mettle. Then, little by little, we would be grudgingly accorded a rather less servile human status. Hence, for the best part of a year and until we had won our spurs, we were called 'Bog Rats', the lowest form of life.

Holding probationary commissions as acting pilot officers, we knew we could be summarily dismissed if we ever failed to come up to scratch for any reason before we had been awarded those much-coveted Wings.

Unlike our peers at Cranwell, we were destined for only six-year commissions, unless we were able to gain preferment through stiff competitive exams and be awarded permanent commissions and become regular officers before our active service time ran out. In the small Air Force,[3] starved of money as it then was, the odds on having such a full career were calculably very slim indeed. Alternatively, we might be offered a rather dead-end extension to ten years.

It was pretty demanding to arrive in the dehydrating desert of Egypt in mid-July, with a shade temperature of 114°F – and precious little shade in sight. After our first breakfast, we were paraded in the open forecourt of Station Headquarters, each waiting to be interviewed individually by the Station Commander.

Dressed in full tropical uniform of topee, khaki breeches, boots and puttees, it was unpleasantly gruelling to wait in the unaccustomed and relentlessly blazing sun – seldom could the order to 'Stand at Ease!' have been more meaningless.

Our unrehearsed replies to the Station Commander's queries were surprisingly rational, considering the physical distress we were enduring. Each was asked why he had joined the Royal Air Force and each had spontaneously given the identically true but ingenuous answer: 'There was nothing better to do, Sir!'

We had thereby in all innocence put up a communal 'black'. Far from being taken as highly complimentary, our candour branded us as being extremely offensive in the eyes of the pathetically inept Group Captain, who carried a grudge against us for months to come. Evidently, he had not yet heard that we had left behind us in the United Kingdom more than three million unemployed. Unwittingly, he forfeited our respect for him.

Work at the school started at 5.30 am, when it was just light enough to see. A very welcome cup of tea, known locally as 'shai', brought by the Egyptian batman assigned to each pair of cadets, was then rapidly gulped down while overalls, flying boots and leather helmets were hastily pulled over pyjamas, bare feet and sleepy heads.

There followed an awkward stumble across 200 yards of soft sand to the hangars, to pick up parachutes and then head for the appointed aeroplanes and flying instructors, who were very shortly to become admired as demi-gods in their pupils' eyes.

There was a scent of excitement in the air, for from all quarters came the sound of aircraft engines starting and being revved up against the chocks. Avro 504N groundcrews had to swing their propellers by hand to get their Lynx engines started; but round the corner of another hangar was a line of Atlases, presenting their noses to a Hucks Starter, a modified T-model Ford with a mobile overhead shaft fitted on a gantry and connected by sprocket and chain to the car's propeller shaft. This grappled with the hooked bosses protruding from the aircraft engines, one by one as it worked along the line.[4]

To relieve air congestion at base, the junior and senior flights were allotted separate landing grounds from which to do their morning flying exercises. Moreover, for lack of aircraft, only half the cadets could fly at any one time; the others had to clamber into the backs of three-ton tarpaulin-covered trucks to lumber in low gear over 15 miles of desert tracks to a dispersed landing area, its corners marked by whitewashed empty four-gallon petrol cans.

Clouds of dust poured in relentlessly upon the unhappy passengers, jolting uncomfortably on hard wooden benches. By the time they had been going for half-an-hour they were covered from head to foot in fine yellow powder.

Their journey ended just as the sun was coming up and they needed several mugs of very sweet shai to slake their sanded throats. First the tea had to be brewed over a fire kindled in a hole in the sand by ever-resourceful accompanying 'erks', as airmen were always familiarly called. Rags soaked in old engine oil provided the fuel and the water-filled four-gallon petrol can was soon boiling. Into the tea went such heaps of sugar that a spoon would almost stand up in our mugs.

While this was going on, a wind-sock was hastily hoisted to indicate the direction for take-offs and landings. The dawn air in summer was delightfully cool, but in winter it felt bitterly cold and we were glad of our fur-lined Sidcot suits.[5]

The five-month initial training phase for novices was conducted on low-powered Avro 504Ns which were biplanes made of wood, canvas and string. Any squeamishness we might have secretly felt about our flying future was completely removed in the first few minutes of the first 'lesson', a dazzling flying display by our instructors. They proceeded to turn their aircraft upside-down and throw them all over the sky while we crouched behind, securely strapped into the rear cockpits. All we sensed was an enormous exhilaration – a thrill which was to last us to the end of our days.

Flying practices lasted a short 30 minutes and woe betide the bog rat who overstayed his allotted period! From then on we learnt to judge the passage of time without a watch.

Waiting for our turn at the flying controls, swilling shai, smoking 'fags', swapping yarns and watching critically the aerial antics of our comrades, we learnt the jargon and distinctive intonation of Service speech – wizard, prang, buy it, flat spin (something you seldom got out of), flap, dicing (with Death) – hence dicey or split (a derivation of split-arse, a shortened version of the Cavalry's split-arse gallop, a hazardous and rather uncontrolled manoeuvre). Every contingency was covered, from putting up a good show, rewarded by a brown mark, to putting up a black and being torn off a strip.

Listening to our flying instructors whom we were anxious to copy, we quickly picked up the special 'speak' of our new profession. Reprimanded for denigrating aeroplanes by calling them machines or kites, we had to cringe whenever the proud Royal Air Force was vulgarly referred to as the 'raf' – which sounded uncomfortably like 'riff-raff' and was terribly non-U: only Ar Aye Eff would do. It took a Second World War of jarring popular misuse to overwhelm this pedantry.

Eventually, the inactivity of the 'dusty section' ended and the waiting bog rats eagerly changed places with the lucky ones who had flown out from camp and had arrived after their flying lesson, still fresh and enviably clean. After two hours the trucks would crawl back to camp the way they had come, duly baptising their latest load of trainee pilots from head to foot with dust. First or last, you could never win both ways!

After that, it was showers and shaves, rapid scrambles into uniform and gobbled breakfasts of more tea or coffee, cereals, bacon, pigeon-sized eggs (from the under-fed Egyptian fowls), fried bread, toast and marmalade – we were hungry. But there was no time for snatched glances at newspapers or letters from home – the 9 am working parade was already assembling.

Off we went for four solid hours of lectures, marching smartly under the eagle eyes of the ex-RM adjutant, Flight Lieutenant H. M. A. 'Pricky' Day AM (later, better known as 'Wings' Day and awarded a DSO for his services as a PoW). Long before we could fall out for lunch, the heat became so overpowering we found it almost impossible to keep our eyes open. Not surprisingly, lunch was usually followed by a collapse into a weary 'snurge' in our bedrooms.

At 5 pm the batmen again broke into our slumbers with more shai, just in time for a quick swim or game of tennis or squash, before the light faded. One afternoon, mistaking it for daybreak, I started out for the hangars in full flying kit before realising that it was evening – the light was the same but it felt much hotter when I stopped to think about it!

After an hour's play we climbed into our 'DJs': black ties and starched shirts were donned for the formal meal which punctuated every weekday evening. Any time left over was spent reading or writing – hard to credit in a radio and TV age.

Music came from portable gramophones – not necessarily to everyone's taste. Gambling was strictly forbidden but bridge was encouraged at a penny a hundred and the small gains and losses were recorded in a book which was scrutinised monthly by the Station Commander. Fortunately, the bog rat's days were so long and tiring we always found bed very welcome. Sleep also helped time to slip by more quickly.

As an evening diversion, we would sometimes stroll out of camp, cross the railway lines and wait for the train to arrive from Port Said on its way to Cairo. We were not train-watchers but bird-watchers. There were always a few interesting female visitors to ogle at as they stared out of their Pullman cars at the incongruous sight of young Englishmen staring in at them. In winter we were muffled up to the ears against the cold and this must have come as a quite a nasty surprise to the scantily-dressed tourists who had so recently been living in cruise-ship luxury and had obviously not been briefed to expect Egypt to be so cold.

Alternatively, a Sunday walk in mufti could break our deadly, daily work routine. It was interesting to watch the 'fellahin' toiling in the fields, allegedly for a mere pittance, working and irrigating even by moonlight. Simple and unspoilt, these peasants formed unforgettable tableaux as they waded along the ditches in grey cotton 'galabiyahs' tucked above the knees, wielding their hoes against a backdrop of archaic water-wheels, camels, water buffaloes, donkeys, doves, egrets and all the other, more familiar livestock of their rural life. How little had life changed since first being depicted on the walls of the Pharaonic tombs all those millennia ago. These peasants were uncannily identifiable with their ancestors.

Abu Sueir lay in the biblical Land of Goshen, of Genesis and the Exodus. Crossing over the local 'sweet water' canal, itself of great antiquity, we explored heaps of unimpressive broken shards and faun-grey mud-brick walls, all that was left of Pithom, one of Joseph's famous granaries.

We discovered comradeship and amusement from within our own resources and grew into a collection of dedicated, individual but kindred souls, ready for whatever might befall. Our daily lot was beset by constant hard work and strict discipline but always spiced and tempered by light-hearted asides.

There was always something to poke fun at, perhaps rather scornfully. Thus, the inventories of furnishings on the Forms 22 hanging behind the doors of our bedrooms were good for a laugh when we read the official description of a certain ornate piece of earthenware as 'Pot, Chamber, Grade 1 Officer, for the use of'. Our minds boggled at the thought of what Grades 2 or 3 would be like. The interior decoration was said to increase with rank but we suspected that this was perhaps a bit of 'duff gen'!

Life had become a great adventure and a devastating war still seemed far too remote for any accounts of upheavals in distant parts of the world to be taken too seriously. After all, we were urgently learning to fly and there were many more immediate hazards demanding our daily undistracted attention than a few minor colonial wars or rumours of war.

For the first five months we bog rats were subjected to endless indignities. We had few freedoms and even these were ironically called 'privileges'. Thus constrained, a sense of achievement was felt when the next intake arrived from home and we found we had become the senior course and were then accorded a rather more tolerable existence, a crude psychology that worked quite well, judging by the ranks eventually reached by many former bog rats.

A surprise softening of the régime was the kind-hearted offer from middle-aged Squadron Leader 'Papa' Damant and his motherly wife. They invited Pat Meagher, Alan Theed and myself to a Saturday dinner and dance at Port Said's Eastern Exchange Hotel, riding the 80 miles each way on the back seat of their open tourer.

The entertainment was most enjoyable and the night sped by until finally we set off homewards in the pale grey dawn, tired and somewhat 'tiddly'. The road from Port Said followed the Suez canal and ran as straight as a die for 35 miles to El Kantara and then bent very slightly to run for another 25 miles to Ismailia. Down a steep stone embankment on our left lay the Suez Canal and on our right, across a narrow grass verge, the so-called 'sweet water' canal taking Nile water for Port Said to drink.

From the draughty back of the car we three bog rats kept a very wary eye on the Squadron Leader nodding off at the wheel. In the half-light of dawn, the slightest turn to left or right would have had most undesirable consequences for all of us.

After a while, we halted to 'shed a tear for Nelson' and, leaving Mrs Damant dozing in the front, the four men lined up unsteadily on the edge of the 'sweet water' canal just where a bloated dead donkey happened to be floating by.

It may have been this gruesome sight that caused him to lose control, but Pat's own weavings became so wild that he toppled in and had to be pulled out, to sit shivering and dripping between us while Alan and I, sitting in his puddles, had visions of contracting bilharzia through our sterns as we both grew steadily wetter and wetter by capillary action.

Pat, our amusing laid-back friend and brilliant pilot, won a DSO on the Arakan Front in Burma in 1945. Afterwards, he went to work in Civil Aviation, but Nemesis caught up with him in Lagos, Nigeria. He was drowned one dark and rainy night when being driven as a passenger in a car which went over the quayside into the deep docks whose ill-marked brink had been indistinguishable in the myriad of wet reflections.

After five months and 75 hours' flying, we had, to some extent, mastered the vice-free Avro 504N, with an accent on stalls, spinning, stall turns, forced landings and basic aerobatics. We then progressed to the front-line Armstrong-Whitworth Atlas, a two-seater Army co-operation biplane whose massive air-cooled 450 bhp radial Jaguar engine blotted out all forward vision.

The Atlas had a propensity to fall out of the sky; in fact it flew like a lump of lead! It was reputedly the home of gremlins and dingbats, against whose malevolence and mischief even friendly phagocytes[6] were said to be powerless. After 88 hours of heaving these nasty brutes around, with more spinning, forced landings, advanced aerobatics and formation flying, we went off on solo tours to the Nile Delta and were sent on a height test which took ages to reach 16,000ft. Lack of oxygen up there induced tunnel vision and, judging by its final reluctance to climb any further, it also seemed to be the operational ceiling of the Atlas itself!

Our navigation exercises were extremely primitive, flown over the fairly empty desert area contained between the Mediterranean to the north, the edge of Nile cultivation on the west, the Gebel Ataqah and the Red Sea hills on the south and the Suez Canal to the east. We made comparatively useless pre-flight plans from badly-forecast winds, had only inefficient compasses and no way, without banking the aircraft, of seeing the ground directly below to check our progress. At our comparatively slow flying speeds, the effect of wind was considerable, but as our sorties were never flown in poor visibility it was difficult to get lost, though we very seldom knew exactly where we were.

At last we were awarded pilot's flying badges and proudly had them sewn on to tunics and flying overalls. One of our number had 'bought it' by stalling his Atlas and spinning-in while on a final approach to land, a sad event laconically and correctly attributed to 'pilot error'.

Two others on the course who lacked flying aptitude were suspended for the good of their health, one then accepting a commission in the Rolls-Royce-powered RAF Armoured Cars, helping to control the mandated territories of Iraq, Palestine and Transjordan. The other drop-out returned disconsolately to the anonymity of 'Civvy Street'.

The AOC Middle East, Air Vice-Marshal Sir Cyril Newall, Lord Trenchard's highly-favoured disciple, came to grace our passing-out parade and to witness individual aerobatics which I had been ordered to display, in company with our Senior Cadet, Ben Boult. We each had to do a sequence of a stall turn, slow roll, loop and recovery from a spin in our Atlases and then execute a forced landing over a dummy fence with a 'dead' prop from 1,000ft.

What I remember most about his visit was Newall's fatuous address to our Course in which he strongly advised us against marrying ex-patriots. Perhaps he was rueing his own private folly, for his wife was known as 'Lady Foot and Mouth' in Cairo society on account of her notorious verbal indiscretions.

As Chief of the Air Staff (1937–40), Newall later perpetrated his own species of 'gaffes' and has been blamed for his failure in the Spanish Civil War and again in 1939/40 to recognise the basic contribution of air power to Hitler's *Blitzkriegs*, which he denounced as 'a gross misuse of air forces'. An exponent of the famous doctrine of the 'knock-out blow', he inadvertently overlooked the First Principle of War – to ensure the security of the Base. Ignoring his advice about 'ex-pats', four years later I married the long-suffering Cairo-born English daughter of a former Director of Mines of the Egyptian Government. But that is another story.

Our training as 'Drivers, airframe' had been of a standard beyond compare. The embryonic treatment of air navigation reflected the common oversight of this crucial activity by the RAF, a defect that was not very obvious to us in 1933. Recognition of the dire consequences of such neglect was unfortunately still light years away. Little did we know that there were in 1933 only 14 navigationally-conscious staff officers in the entire Service and that their influence was accordingly minimal.

The all-pervading voluntary discipline we encountered at all levels was a clear earnest of the reliability of our young and, to us, highly-esteemed Service. We may have appeared slack and irreverent to the Senior Services but beneath the surface there was a dedication to efficiency second-to-none. We could not have wished for better colleagues and we purred with satisfaction at being able to indulge our new-found obsession with flying.

As bemused spectators, we had watched while our instructors coped with a staff colleague who had evidently earned their displeasure. Returning from a weekend furlough, he had found his bedroom occupied by a donkey which had been well fed and watered during his absence. An awful lot of mucking-out was needed but a nod was as good as a wink and he became a reformed character.

We had likewise worn off quite a few prickles and rough edges among ourselves to meet the demands of our communal life. But most importantly, in the process of winning our Wings, we had acquired the priceless and life-long habit of making quick and positive decisions. Our safety in the air would afterwards often depend on this mental prowess and in later years we found it applied equally well to many non-flying but potentially traumatic situations.

We were now home and dry and raring to get started as half-fledged members of our future operational squadrons. We were happily on the threshold of an élite and far-flung club called the RAF which operated across a world that was red all over the atlas and where passports would seldom be required.

Wherever we went, there would always be a warm, familiar welcome. Sixty years later, the same goodwill would still abound, though now the map would scarcely be coloured red anywhere. In fact we had ourselves only just been hatched! We no longer had to accept the implied indignity of being 'acting pilot officers (on probation)' but were now the proud recipients of a personal scroll of parchment from the Monarch naming us among his trusty servants as pilot officers.

During our training, one name had always been on the lips of our seniors and mentioned with great reverence: that of our Founding Father, 'Boom' Trenchard. He became what Nelson had been to the Royal Navy – an apocalyptic idol. But his hallowed doctrine that 'the bomber will always get through' was only true after the achievement of air supremacy. Without asserting that pre-condition, the RAF fell into grave error.

Appointed by Winston Churchill and Jan Smuts in the gloom of 1918 to form the world's first independent air force, able to develop its full potential untrammelled by the often hidebound traditions of both the Senior Services, Boom's powerful personal drive carried his vision to its ultimate fruition. He lived to be 83 and by 1946 had the satisfaction of seeing the dominant role played from the air in titanic struggles across the world. The inspiration passed to his immediate colleagues had been handed down, perhaps rather dangerously unquestioned in detail and embellished like the sacred scrolls. We in 1934 could all plainly see the same beckoning light ahead.

Notes to Chapter I

1 'PM to Gen Ismay: "... I look to the Joint Chiefs of the Staff to propose me measures for a rigorous, enterprising and ceaseless offensive against the whole German-occupied coast-line"' (6 June 1940, quoted in Winston Churchill's *The Second World War, Vol II Their Finest Hour*; Cassell & Co, 1949).

2 Lt (later Capt.) W. Leefe Robinson VC.

3 So small that it used to be said that, if you waited for a week in the long bar of the RAF Club, you would be bound to meet every officer serving in the UK.

4 It was named after its inventor, B. C. ('Benny') Hucks, who did maintenance work for Claude Grahame-White in return for flying lessons and later became a test and display pilot with Robert Blackburn.

5 Named after their originator, Sidney Cotton.

6 'Leucocyte capable of guarding the system against infection by absorbing microbes' (OED).

II

Sun City and Victorias

I PASSED OUT top from No 4 FTS, not by being rated an exceptional pilot but because ground studies came easily to me. I was also probably judged to have a safe pair of hands.

I then spent nine June days of my month's home leave with brother Jack on a tandem in the snowbound Pyrénées. Leaving the bike at Barèges, we hired wiry little Mr Fortine, a Basque guide, to help us up to the Observatory on the summit of 9,440ft Pic du Midi de Bigorre, a demanding 25-mile, 14 hours' scramble. Next day, riding up the Col du Tourmalet, the last mile of our road disconcertingly disappeared under a thick bank of winter snow, so we lugged the bike over a white slope to the col and luckily found the road again on the far side. We then free-wheeled for 30 miles at speeds up to 60 mph, knowing there would be nothing coming up!

On another day, riding and hiking 20 miles from Luchon up to the wild Spanish frontier at the Port de Picarde, we were caught in an alarming and dangerous violent-thunderstorm while exposed on the bare Maladeta mountainside. Finally, an initiating lunch of snails in garlic at Carcassonne brought this exacting tour to an end. Jack then caught a 'rapide' back to Calais, while I caught another one for Marseille and the SS *Narkunda*. For the last time in my life, in June 1934, I was actually athletically fit!

In July, 'Ben' Boult and I reported from Abu Sueir to RAF Heliopolis,[1] for duty with the prestigious No 216 bomber/transport Squadron. Pre-war Cairo was noted for its glamorous splendour and our good fortune had been envied by our brother bog rats. Our chums went to Ismailia to fly Fairey Gordons, or Westland Wapitis and Fairey IIIFs from the arid environs of Amman or from Mosul, a turbulent Kurdish mountain fastness with its strategic oil-field.

The worst fate of all seemed to befall laid-back Pat Meagher, the Surgeon Admiral's son, who was sent to No 84 Sqn at Shaibah, a desert outpost on the Iraq/Kuwait border, its only saving grace being gin at 1d a tot! It was likely to be two years of absolute hell. Yet he had been our star pilot: was there no justice in life? In fact, he liked it there so much that he put in for and was granted a third year's extension. There's no accounting for taste.

Our arrival at Heliopolis coincided with the 35th birthday of grey-haired 'Poppa' Watt of No 216 – our squadron – whose rank reflected the prevailing terribly slow rate of promotion, for he was wearing 1914–18 medal ribbons and after 16 years was still only a Flight Lieutenant, looking old enough to be my Dad.

As new boys, we were not allowed to buy any drinks that evening but a party was already brewing up. Poppa had been given an unusual cocktail shaker. It had two circular sliding sections by which the ingredients of every known knock-out concoction were revealed by twisting the parts around. Its extensive repertoire was fully tested during two hours before dinner, and by the time we two 'sprogs' were allowed to drift off to hit the hay I had to hang on for dear life when my bed began to spin out of control as I laid my head on the pillow.

Ben and I suffered severe after-effects and vowed we would not willingly repeat the recipe. But that reception by our first operational squadron had not been our first baptism by alcohol and its lessons would not always stand up to the test of time either!

We took several weeks to suss out the chaff from the wheat in what our surroundings had to offer. On the camp doorstep was the Heliopolis Sporting Club, with its large open-air pool where, every afternoon, exponents of the high diving board grandly took to the air in macho displays of leaps and bounds. Others attacked the tennis courts or sipped tea, dallying with pretty young ladies from the local, mainly Levantine community.

No vestiges of On, its Pharaonic predecessor, were evident in Heliopolis; but nearby, across a polo pitch, stood the ornate 'Hell' Palace Hotel, asking more for refreshments than young officers could afford. We were to discover much later that its grandiose marble halls were absolutely perfect for all-Service winter balls, when the Cairo garrison dined and danced in resplendent multi-coloured regimental mess kits. These local facilities were manifestly impressive, but Ben and I turned instinctively towards Cairo and to Gezira Island for choice.

Our camp lay round two sides of an airfield, a finger of soft sandy desert intruding into the suburban township from the south. On the west side, facing the domestic area, were three large hangars for No 216 Squadron's Vickers Victoria biplanes; on the south were the hangars and huts of No 208 Army Co-operation Squadron and of Middle East Communications Flight.

There were no married quarters; the few officers with wives and families in tow had to make do with somewhat indifferent furnished flats hired in nearby private apartment blocks. The families of the Other Ranks were conspicuously absent. Consequently, life on the camp centred on the messes which all had well-tended gardens, wide verandahs and cool stone floors, easy to wash and sweep. The communal rooms in the Officers' and NCOs' Messes and the NAAFI itself had been built with coal fireplaces against the cold winter nights; but all other areas were left to freeze except in the near vicinity of coal-burning stoves.

A rough undulating desert on the south rose gently up to the crests of the Moqattam hills and stretched on out of sight, coming to an abrupt end on the west where a geological fault marked the great Nile valley. Seen from Heliopolis, Saladin's Citadel and Mohammed Ali's tall minarets, with countless spiky neighbours, stood out like sentinels on the western skyline.

North lay the verdant, fertile Delta with its myriads of water channels and ditches, the life-blood of a teeming peasant population that filled Egyptian bread baskets with cereals. Here grew the finest long-staple cotton, luscious dates, figs, mangoes, citrus fruits, water melons, succulent small bananas and strawberries. Early potatoes and superb onions were shipped to Europe. Vegetables of every kind thrived in the dark alluvial soil, re-fertilised since before recorded time by the annual Nile floods which cut a razor-sharp edge between barren, yellow desert and the lush, green cultivation.

Transport is always an important consideration of life in a camp. Motorcycles were not greatly favoured, owing to the chaos on the Cairo roads; but even very old jalopies were beyond the reach of a junior officer's pay, already mostly pre-empted for unavoidable social activities. A car was definitely a luxury in 1934. Happily, only ten minutes walk away from camp was a halt for the Belgian-built electric light railway, whose brown trams, so familiar in Belgium, made short work of the run into Cairo's European shopping centre, for a very small outlay of piastres, of which there were then 97 in a £ sterling.

From the Cairo tram terminus, other destinations were easily reached, either on foot or by a 'garry' drawn by an emaciated horse, which its unfeeling driver whipped far too frequently. Local trams and buses in Cairo were too packed by the native populace to be useful, though a tram to the Pyramids ten miles west was an experience well worth the discomfort. Gezira Sporting Club occupied a large part of a luxuriant island separating Cairo from its western suburbs. It was a leisure Mecca, an oasis of green spaciousness and quietude, offering polo, golf, tennis, cricket, croquet, squash, bowls and swimming; with swings, roundabouts and swings for the kids.

There was horse racing on Saturdays and a bridge 'school' seemingly played all day and every day. Barbers and beauticians were on tap and excellent cuisine and liquid refreshments were served by attentive Nubian *saffragis*, gliding around silently in their red-sashed ankle-length white cotton *galabiyahs*.

Standing in gardens ablaze with flame trees, jacarandas, bougainvillaea, graceful eucalyptus and exotic imported sub-tropical shrubs and trees, the Club maintained high Victorian standards through the enthusiasm of an elected committee. Membership was by no means exclusively European but a preponderance of expatriate British regularly used its amenities which were carefully designed to meet all tastes. Perhaps this slight national imbalance offered a possible opening for some Egyptian resentment, but it was certainly never apparent and tension was unknown: after all, the British had many good Egyptian friends. Harmony was the rule of the day in Gezira.

We from Heliopolis could meet our opposite numbers serving in No 45 Sqn at RAF Helwan, 18 miles south of Cairo. We befriended Army officers and many civilians who lived and worked in Cairo. The Club engulfed us in a swirl of picnics, parties and dances and the ever-reliable climate favoured a grand open-air life. For a change, it was pleasant to relax at the historic Shepheard's Hotel, sitting on its raised verandah and scanning the passing crowds. Here the earliest travellers from Europe and the Orient had broken their coach journeys between Alexandria and Suez, having to change ships before the Canal was opened in 1869. The hotel had been left almost high and dry on the shores of Old Cairo when the new city, begun by the Khedive Ismail in mid-19th century, advanced steadily west towards the Nile. By 1934 Shepheard's was overlooking Clot Bey, a very seedy 'red light' district, out of bounds to British troops.

Ever since the 'thirties, the tide of Egyptianisation has swept on, ever westwards – but so has Shepheard's, now re-built on the east bank of the Nile, having been ruthlessly torched in 1952 in one of Cairo's many anti-European, bloodthirsty riots.

The finest dishes of king prawns in mayonnaise could be had at Jimmy's Bar, a favourite open-air restaurant in a little back street which, once found, was never forgotten. Another rendezvous for gourmets was Torino's pavement trattoria, in the Midan Suarez. The chicken à la king was a poem. For the sweet tooth, it was impossible to beat the fabulous displays of the Italian-Swiss Groppi patisseries. However, for the purist seeking genuine traditional sweetmeats, nothing could compare with Turkish delight and hallowha from Hadji Bakir's at the bottom end of Sharia Kasr el Nil. No matter

29

where, good Stella beer was always served chilled, accompanied by ample side-dishes called 'mezzes'. Food was cheap and we took our fill of the fleshpots of Cairo whenever we could.

But life in the Officers' Mess was also very tolerable. We each had a large cool room in one of the two-storey blocks flanking the Mess proper, with its spotless ante-room, dining room, ladies' room, billiard room and library. We shared it with 208 Sqn, natural rivals who were mostly ex-Cranwell, secure with permanent commissions, while we in 216 Sqn, with few exceptions, held only tenuously short-term commissions. Nevertheless, we felt slightly superior because our tasks of bombing and transport seemed so much more interesting than their stereotyped Army co-operation role. Until re-equipped with Hawker Audaxes, 208 Sqn pilots had to cope with Atlases, which we had so gladly left behind at FTS. As a pilot, I always felt rather sorry for them. Their escutcheon was a winged Egyptian eye, known colloquially as the 'Flying Shufti'.

We also shared life with pilots of the small Communication Flight whose Fairey IIIFs and a Gordon offered self-drive or taxi services for Command HQ staff in Cairo. This mixed bag of Mess-mates, cross-fertilised by their varied experiences, made for more fun than tears and many a lifelong friendship sprang up. We lived under the benign discipline of 'Henry' Ford, the suave senior Flight Lieutenant PMC.[2] Henry was a born master of ceremonies to whom one spoke at breakfast only at grave personal peril. Silence at such an unspeakable hour was his golden rule – and not a bad one either. Things were always lively if 'Baron' Worrall, 'Larry' Ling – later a hero of Habbaniyah, 'Hetty' Hyde, 'Tubby' Parselle, 'Fanny' Adnams or 'EJ' Edwardes-Jones were around.

No 216 Sqn's residents were prosaic by comparison – our star performers were mostly married and living out. Top of the list came the Adjutant, Flight Lieutenant 'Paddy' the Earl of Bandon. Known as 'the Abandoned Earl', he was always up to mischief. There was also Geoffrey Wood who had created a sensation as a bog rat at Abu Sueir by marrying the 'school marm' at RAF Ismailia. Before joining the RAF, he had crossed the Rockies on horseback one winter, grizzly bears *et al*. His wife Ann's claim to fame was her sister Lydia Sherwood, then a leading West End actress.

Malin and Bunny Sorsbie also held the stage. Malin had joined the RAF after a commission in the Canadian Mounties and could spellbind anybody with stories of the Wild West. Females were easy prey to his dazzling blue eyes, flaxen hair and handsome tall stature, a fact that often led to marital friction. One day Malin arrived for duty with three fresh deep nail scratches down each cheek.

Our bosses stupidly judged him to be 'not quite the right material' for a permanent commission and he wasn't even allowed to sit for the annual competitive exam. But at the end of his five-year commission, Malin left to fly for Wilson Airways in Kenya; became an Overseas Operations Director of BOAC; built up East African Airways; was air adviser to Jomo Kenyatta; was knighted in 1965 and, helped by a new wife, acted as Chairman for the Munitalp Foundation, an East African wild life protection society. His book *Dragonfly*, published by Hamish Hamilton in 1971, paints life in 216 Sqn and Heliopolis and makes a very good read. So much for certain senior officers' character assessment!

If not detailed for earlier flying, our days began at 0530 with a cuppa, a shave and shower, a five-minute stumble across the sand to No 216 Sqn's flight offices, to study manuals, practise Morse and watch the aircraft maintenance, to get to know the aircraft and the erks, especially our own crew. It would soon be 0800 hours and time for a bite back in the Mess, where a substantial English breakfast awaited, served by self-effacing, bare-footed, white-uniformed native staff, the best of whom were dark Berberines from Upper Egypt. There was a harsh mess rule that if any waiter smelled of garlic – a staple item of ethnic diet – he was in danger of dismissal. Anglo-Saxon abomination of that marvellous highly pungent vegetable has softened with the passing years; but in 1934 it was a fiercely-upheld British culinary taboo. The PMC was obviously unaware that the world's earliest recorded case of an industrial dispute concerned the builders of one of the Great Pyramids at Giza, who went on strike for larger garlic supplies to match their ration of bread!

After another cup of coffee, we would resume our ground tasks, purposefully killing time till 1300 hours when we knocked off for the day. Back in the Mess for a long, cool John Collins, we ate lunch, read our mail, glanced through the *Egyptian Gazette* and faced out to the world of recreation and amusement. This meant changing into mufti and going off to Gezira by brown tram and 'garry' to play squash or swim or perhaps just to laze in the sun. We could sit under the trees to watch polo or in the summer a cricket match, sometimes against touring sides from England, like Martineau's XI.

Then a pot of tea and a Groppi cake or two was indicated, hopefully in the company of young unattached females of whom there was no shortage in winter. All too soon it would be twilight, but as soon as the sun sank below the yard-arm it was time for drinks, accompanied by baked salted peanuts, an irresistible local speciality. Unless we had 'warned out' for lack of cash, we rushed back to camp to change into a dinner jacket, in time to greet the senior officer formally in the ante-room and take a glass of sherry before dinner. Smoking was forbidden during this half-hour to preserve our palates, really quite a good rule; but in the days when smoking was in such general vogue, the restriction seemed irksome.

Every fourth Friday, a guest night was held, to return hospitality and to entertain Service and civilian contacts: an all-male affair and an excuse for high jinks after dinner, wearing our expensive, uncomfortably tight, albeit glamorous mess kit. The horse-play was good-humoured and usually physically demanding. 'High Cockaloram' required an anchor-man standing with his back to the wall, facing two others in line, bending down from the waist, braced against each other's hips. The opposing side had to jump, one by one, on top of the two bent backs, piling higher and higher until they all toppled over with a crash to the floor – the winning side being the one which made the highest heap before collapsing.

A great trial of strength was to try to go round the ante-room, hanging on by fingertips from the picture rail – very few could manage to turn the first corner! In 'Are you there, Moriarty?' two blindfold opponents lay face down on the carpet, holding each other's left hand and taking turns to ask the question. Then, armed with a tight roll of newspaper in the free hand, the questioner tried to whack the place from whence the reply had come. After shouting 'Yes! ', the player replying twisted away from the oncoming blow. In one spirited encounter, someone's hand was accidentally cut by a broken tumbler. Help was instantly available in the shape of a rather inebriated MO, while the patient was marched off to sick quarters to be stitched up. Weeks later, a sizeable chunk of glass emerged from the scar. Finally, a rather rough house game involved our cotton dress shirts being torn from our backs without being unbuttoned: one Flight Lieutenant, who had married money, was nearly strangled when his silk shirt refused to tear.

When we were exhausted, those still in the mood gathered round a budding pianist, of whom there always seemed to be plenty, albeit few as competent as 'Tiddly' Powell of 208 Sqn. Sometimes I dug out the old clarinet I had played in my youth. There followed a rollicking sing-song of mostly bawdy but tuneful ditties, the folklore of generations of sex-starved Anglo-Saxons, many from WWI and some attributable to the Royal Flying Corps. We had easy access to alcohol but there was a golden rule: 'No drinking before flying'. Despite popular belief, I never once saw this ukase deliberately transgressed.

As already related, a leading light in our gaiety was 'Paddy, the

Abandoned Earl'. Then in his early thirties, 'Paddy', a round-faced, dark-haired, urbane, married Flight Lieutenant with twinkling brown eyes, eventually reached the dizzy rank of Air Chief Marshal. A more amusing comrade would be hard to imagine and he was up to every prank. One winter guest night, when a welcoming fire was burning in the anteroom grate and the jollity had reached its peak, Paddy climbed unseen up to the flat roof and popped a red smoke candle down the chimney. This was a pyrotechnic we sometimes dropped from the air to mark a place on the ground. The effect was spectacular, taking several fire extinguishers to smother the choking fumes; nobody was hurt – we were only covered in soot!

One day, when our CO had gone on home leave for a month, Paddy had a fleeting offer of an empty seat (for free) in an Imperial Airways flying-boat to Marseille, from where he could catch a train and be in the RAF Club the next day. The journey normally took a week to ten days and for this reason home leave was rigidly rationed.

This was a chance in a million, to be seized with both hands and he quickly appointed a stand-in to 'hold the fort' for a few days. On the following morning he was happily ensconced in the Long Bar of the Club busily planning details for his stolen long weekend, when in walked Wing Commander Bill Mackey, who was amazed to find the Adjutant he thought he'd left behind on duty in Heliopolis. Paddy was aghast to see his truancy collapse like a pricked balloon and had to catch the next flight back to Cairo, setting himself back a pretty penny.

Mess life was well ordered but never dull, the catering first-class, our rooms comfortable, the company amusing and friendly. As there was no escape till we were 30 and free to marry, or, even less likely, had become Squadron Leaders with marriage allowances, the Mess was our only haven and rest. The native servants contributed greatly to our personal contentment. Faithful, hard-working, long-suffering and efficient, they were delightfully simple and easy to amuse. No account of mess life would be complete without paying them sincere compliments.

Displayed in a glass case over our anteroom door was a silver-gilt plaque which had been presented to 216 Sqn by a grateful Spaniard for the rescue of his son from the desert. Upon the table on dining-in nights stood the squadrons' sporting trophies, outshone by 2ft-long solid silver replicas of a Victoria and, in 1936, of a Valentia, presented by Vickers. Similarly, silver scale models of an Armstrong Whitworth Atlas and a Hawker Audax belonging to 208 Sqn completed this display.

Those trophies were fine reminders of past glories; but my own reference to their present whereabouts, on the occasion of the short-lived revival of 216 Sqn as a 'Strike' squadron at RAF Honington in 1986, led me to conclude that they had become victims of endless squadron wartime movements. According to the new CO, no trace had been found of any silver model aeroplanes, languishing unrecognised in dusty corners of some remote storage depot. Sadly, they all seem to have disappeared.

Apart from being the squadron's God-given joker, Paddy was also a qualified flying instructor. Soon after my arrival, he was detailed to give me dual instruction in one of No 216 Sqn's Victorias – a process known as 'conversion to type'. Having first shown me what to expect by way of gliding the cumbersome and unfamiliar monster, Paddy handed over to me to taxi downwind, turn around and head off into the sky. The huge plane behaved like a bird and the roar of the two Napier Lion engines close behind the open cockpit was quite thrilling.

As we approached Cairo Citadel, I made a turn back towards Heliopolis and, on arrival at the aerodrome, a flat piece of desert, turned acrosswind, throttled back and started my first-ever glide in a Victoria. It was only then that I noticed the wind was stronger than I had expected; but it didn't occur to me that I was too far away to reach the airfield boundary.

In those days of unreliable engines, every landing had to be made without power so as to be ready for the real thing, if and when it happened. Once we had cut the throttles back, we were never allowed to open them up again as a second thought. So I persevered, turned on to the final leg and looked hopefully at the distant boundary, flattening my glide path to squeeze the last foot out of the remaining height.

Paddy had been sitting, not uttering a word. Suddenly he came to life, seized the controls, shouted 'Christ! I can hear the angels singing!' and banged on full throttles, to zoom away for a second try. In urging the aircraft to glide at too shallow an angle, I had allowed our airspeed to fall almost to the point of losing all lateral control with the wing slots automatically wide open. A stall at 200 feet above the ground was definitely not to be recommended.

The Victoria stalled at an amazing 45 mph and at that slow airspeed only a pair of sharp ears were needed to know what was about to happen. In normal powered flight, the din was so loud, nothing could be heard above the roar of the engines. When these were idling in a glide, the air made a musical hum passing through the forest of struts and mesh of flying and landing wires bracing the wings and holding them on. The humming died away as gliding speed slowed and disappeared altogether at stalling speed, when there would be an ominous silence.

Paddy had heard the celestial voices calling and he made it an unforgettable lesson for me. I learnt how to 'hear' the correct gliding speed without glancing at the airspeed indicator. It became instinctive to listen to the humming and enabled the pilot to concentrate on the approaching landing area. This was known as 'flying by the seat of your pants'.

We also always fine-tuned our twin-engines by ear to eliminate annoying audible 'beats' from unsynchronised revs. The return of 'beats' also gave warning of engine trouble.

On another memorable occasion, Paddy demonstrated how a show of bravado was often the best way to respond to a tricky situation. In late 1934, three Victorias went off on a six-week cruise to Cape Town and back, a major undertaking in those days. The lead aircraft carried the AOC Middle East together with his wife; and as the regular bucket seats of folding canvas were too uncomfortable for VIPs to endure for weeks on end in the tropics, the squadron engineer officer applied himself to making a few local modifications.

Two Lloyd Loom wicker chairs were lashed to the floor of the VIPs' Victoria. At the rear of the cabin, a small area was curtained off to contain an Elsan and a pedestal wash-basin installed for convenience in flight. To complete these niceties, four packets of 'Bronco' were provided.

The cruise had early been marred by tragedy at Tororo in Uganda, where one Victoria, taxying to take off, became stuck in the deep dried footprints left by elephants on the edge of the airfield. Flying Officer 'Mary' Moore, a very popular captain in the squadron, got out to inspect his problem at close quarters and tripped up into his own propeller.

In due course, the cruise had continued, flying mostly through British territory, the visitors being received rapturously at every stop. 'Showing the Flag' was always fun. The colonials, no less than the African natives, were touchingly pleased to meet a visit from the outside world – it broke their isolation. Visitors from the skies were ambassadors from a civilisation that so many of their hosts had long since relinquished.

All three aircraft returned to Cairo without further mishap, though to a rather muted reception. In due course, other new and more daring aerial exploits would take centre stage and the 1934 RAF bomber/transport cruise to South Africa passed quietly into history, soon to be almost completely forgotten. But not entirely so. Beavering away in the Command HQ audit office was a little gnome, scrutinising the accounts of every penny spent during the six-week journey. It must be recalled that promotion was so slow in 1934 that even the slightest recorded blemish might mean consignment to the Styx[3]: an auditor's 'observation' could certainly do untold harm.

When Paddy examined the Adjutant's mail one morning, he was perturbed to find a letter from the Middle East auditor asking to know why public funds had been used to buy four packets of Bronco for the cruise, when Army Form X – which had the texture and appearance of sandpaper – was in free supply from stores?

He considered this for a moment and then let out a guffaw that could be heard all over the squadron. Ringing for his Orderly Room clerk, he sent him over to the NAAFI shop with £E1 to buy four packets of Bronco. He then dictated a dutiful reply saying that he:

'had the honour to refer to the audit observation Number . . .
Herewith the four packets of Bronco.
You know what you can do with them.

I have the honour to be,
Sir,
Your Obedient Servant, etc.'

End of story. Audacity! That was another lesson for us to learn.

Notes to Chapter II

1 Plt Off. N. de W. Boult. Heliopolis was 'the city of the sun'.
2 President of the Messing Committee.
3 In Greek legend, the river surrounding the Underworld.

III

Bearing Gifts[1]

I T WOULD be utterly misleading to suggest that life was all
cakes and ale. In 216 Sqn we had our work cut out coping with
our two military tasks of bombing and of transporting passengers and freight, but first we had to become adept in flying our
ungainly giants to their design limits in many different circumstances.

Compared with a single-engined aircraft, an empty Victoria V
weighed a ponderous 11,942lb and fully-loaded was 18,000lb, so it
felt more like a shire horse than a bucking pony. Depending on air
temperature and altitude, it came unstuck at 65 mph, climbed slowly
at 75, cruised at 100, reached 105 flat out, glided at 70 and, as already
recorded, stalled at 45 mph. It was so badly underpowered, I once
took half an hour to climb 1,000ft after leaving Atbara at midday,
struggling in the very bumpy hot air with a load of passengers bound
for Khartoum. One horror story related how an over-laden 'Vic' had
surmounted a steadily rising part of the Sinai desert only by riding
on the cushion of air trapped between the ground and its lower
mainplanes.

The fuel was calculated for each payload and stops to refuel were
in turn dictated by the resulting endurance, a topsy-turvy procedure
as seen from today. Sometimes we had to trim our payload for lack
of refuelling facilities *en route*! We could carry 405 gallons of fuel
but calculated what was needed, plus an hour for safety: at 7lb a
gallon and 180lb per person, at sea-level and air at 70°F only 55
gallons were permissible and 250-mile stages were normal. Away
from RAF stations, fuel from four-gallon cans had to be carefully
strained through chamois leather while being poured by hand
through a large funnel into the top tank.

When landing, a foot-wide cast-iron tail-skid tore up the ground
and acted as an anchor and our leaky water-cooled Napier Lions,
when hot, refused to re-start after endless hand-cranking. In 1934
Victoria VIs, with four-bladed propellers and air-cooled Bristol
Pegasus engines, were very warmly welcomed; and in 1935 Valentias
began to appear and, wonder of wonders, had a tailwheel and

differential brakes for steering from the cockpit! No more erks having to jump out to hang on to a wingtip when turning on the ground. The brakes were priceless for making the most of small clearings bordered by scrub, which were typical of many African airfields. The Valentias couldn't come fast enough.

Cruising at 110 mph, their reliable air-cooled radials gave a reassuring throaty roar as we flew across the wilder parts of our 'parish'. At night our exhaust manifolds glowed red-hot, showering carbon sparks like tiny shooting stars into the dark slipstream. Effective inertia engine starters also saved us time at every stop for fuel, sparing our erks an awful lot of sweaty cranking. The engines usually fired first go.

The top mainplanes had slots that opened automatically at low speeds to improve aileron control when landing over hurdles like 60ft date palms, when height and speed had to be shed at the very last moment by deft sideslips and tail-swishing, unseemly manoeuvres for big aircraft and mastered only after much practice. Our frankest critics were naturally our own crew: a fitter, rigger and wireless operator, each having a personal interest in their two pilots' skill and sitting in judgment on anything less than perfection.

Squadron training never stopped. Thus, for weeks on end it would concentrate on bombing, starting with dummy runs over a 'camera obscura' at Base. The bomb-aiming pilot, lying prone in the nose, signalled the simulated moment of bomb release, the two pilots' efforts being later evaluated rather unconvincingly back at Base. But it was a useful lead-in for the real thing.

We then progressed to a bombing range in the desert, the target a chunk of concrete located about five miles away. It was in sight of two quadrants at one of which sat the Safety Officer with pyrotechnics and an Aldis lamp for signalling to the aircraft. Two bearings were taken of each 20-lb practice bomb dropped and back at Heliopolis their bursts would be plotted, the errors analysed and discussed with both the pilots concerned. Each session finished with a climax when we dropped a load of 112-lb HE, mere shadows of 1944 block-busters but producing quite impressive explosions. Bombing practices were flown at 10,000ft after a long climb and we felt extremely cold. The Safety Officer also sat swathed in flying kit, in winter shivering in the icy winds that blew off the desert at dawn.

Local bedouin kept an eye out for our bombing exercises and one or two huddled figures always squatted dangerously near to the target so as to retrieve the bombs' brass nose-caps and any other useful scraps as soon as the Safety Officer packed up.

Having completed our annual bombing programme, we would be

detailed for more mundane but enjoyable ferrying duties, often taking us away from Base for days at a time. There were also some fifty desert landing grounds to inspect every year, spread over the Western and Sinai deserts, the latter having been laid out and used by the Turks in WW1. First we had to find these indistinct patches of flat desert and then land to re-paint the empty petrol cans marking their corners before flying on to the next.

It took all day to complete two or three but the job might end with a swim in the Bitter Lakes or be enlivened by a nomad bedouin asking for medical help. The routine free gift of some aspirins worked wonders and was always gratefully received, no matter how inappropriate these pills must sometimes have been.

Our most popular job was to fly 110 miles north to Aboukir Depot, just east of Alexandria. Its small airfield was very dicey, its 60ft date palms growing on two sides demanding a split-arse sideslip at the end of every gliding approach. From this hive of aeronautical engineering we collected spare parts, taking off in the dusk to practise night flying on the way back to Helio. Less than a mile from the Depot was a secluded cove of sand and rock, an old airframe packing-case on top of the low cliff serving as a club hut. Run by the Aboukir Officers' Mess, it housed beer in an ice-chest, available by simply signing a bar book. With packed picnic lunches from Heliopolis, we could spend the whole of a summer day in and out of the crystal-clear lukewarm sea, waiting for our spares to be loaded.

Sometimes we wandered through ramshackle Aboukir village, past its moth-eaten Nelson hotel, towards the eastern bay which swept in a five-mile arc east to Rosetta and its derelict Turkish fortress where in 1799, embedded in its walls, Napoleon's savants had found a famous Stone, now in the British Museum. Inscribed in Greek, Demotic and hieroglyphs, ancient Egypt's writings were at last de-cyphered by François Champollion.

Marine craft rode at their moorings offshore in the bay, ready for any flying-boats calling in from their base in Malta and needing an anchorage. To the north lay the ruins of Canopus, reputed scene of ancient Alexandrian orgies. More prosaically, the site was now given over to barbecues at a beach restaurant noted for its fish and crustacea. Before the new high Aswan dam stopped the annual Nile floods, the shore had teemed with every kind of delectable marine creature fed by the rich alluvial debris. Alas, this has all but disappeared.

A mile to seaward lay an island of low sandhills and scrub, named after Nelson who, by brilliant manoeuvres, sank 13 out of 17 French ships anchored in the bay in 1798, a strategic action which cut off the French forces in Cairo. Napoleon had then slipped back to Josephine in France, leaving his invading army to its isolated fate. Clearly Aboukir was not without its history. Back at Helio we would arrive tanned, exercised, tired and satiated by the pleasant 'swan' beside an unpolluted Med. Could any more delightful day's 'work' ever be imagined?

The squadron was tasked to operate as easily by night as by day and was more or less on 24-hour call, if not on active standby. Sorties were mostly scheduled days ahead and we could usually plan our own spare time; but a 'flap' sometimes blew up without any warning, requiring a flight to anywhere in our extensive 'parish', more or less at the drop of a hat.

Like almost everywhere else in the Service overseas, the vital importance of air navigation failed to be properly appreciated owing to the prevailing excellent visibility. The one serious navigator in No 216 Sqn, Squadron Leader Philip Mackworth, was quietly and unkindly dubbed as 'a bit of an old woman' because he tried hard to improve the squadron's primitive navigation practices when most of his colleagues thought they were good enough.

All through the year, sports teams and athletes were flown from station to station to compete in endless events, these jaunts piling up for us very desirable flying hours in our log-books. Emplaning exercises involved batches of 22 fully-armed troops climbing in and jumping out of our cabins as quickly as possible, without doing themselves or the aircraft any serious harm. We gave them short flips but the troops were often terribly airsick and we wistfully hoped our shared suffering was good for inter-Service morale.

Each junior pilot had to undertake two tedious jobs that came round every month. As Orderly Officer, dressed in boots, breeches, puttees, webbing and with a loaded Colt pistol, he was backed up by a Flight Lieutenant Station Duty Officer and was responsible during 24 hours for the conduct of Service and civilian personnel, the supervision of security and the general administration of the station especially outside its normal working hours.

All flying stations also had a Duty Pilot, forerunner of the air traffic controller. In those distant days, the very idea of being controlled in flight by someone on the ground was quite anathema to all RAF pilots. Control was unnecessary in the sparse air traffic of those free-and-easy days. All flying had to be approved, but authority for this had often to be delegated to the pilots concerned. The Duty Pilot was kept fully informed and was the repository of all flight information and he initiated action in crises. At night, he might have to lay out a flare path in a long T pattern with the help of a squad of erks detailed for the task. The goose-neck flares burnt gallons of paraffin and needed frequent topping up; worse, they had to be man-handled so that the T always pointed into wind. The Duty Pilot controlled night-flying operations by Morse, exchanging signals with aircraft by Aldis lamp. At times he also resorted to the use of a Very pistol and coloured pyrotechnics and in very rare crises could even use a mortar to fire coloured signals above the clouds to help identify the airfield to a lost aircraft – an action I never saw taken.

Little by little we came to evaluate the capability and state of our art. The limiting factor was always the weather, chief among its hazards in Egypt being radiation fog, which could quickly obliterate a destination airfield. At times we were grounded by sandstorms, called *khamsins* in Egypt and *haboobs* in the Sudan – but these could usually be forecast and seldom took us by surprise. The dust and haze often rose above 10,000ft and in such conditions our so-called 'blind flying' instruments were uncomfortably inadequate.

As our passengers had no means of escape in the air, the crew also flew without parachutes and the pilots were secured in their open cockpits only by lap-straps. It was many years before the advent of 'Mae Wests'; a case of sink or swim! We were expected to endure extremes of temperature with all the fortitude we could muster. Head-winds might reduce our ground speed to a pitiful 45 mph, which was not funny on a long haul with rising dust. In the tropics we had to face heavy rainstorms in our open cockpits. On the credit side, we could normally see a long way ahead and I sometimes experienced visibility of 150 miles; though having one's destination in sight for an hour-and-a-half became tedious.

On the international scene, the political murders by Nazis of Dr Dollfuss, Chancellor of independent Austria in July 1934 and of King Alexander II of Jugoslavia at Marseille in October both passed off without impacting much on the prevailing public indifference towards any underlying threat to European peace.

Little by little we grew familiar with our vast and infinitely varied stamping ground; so well in fact that, given reasonable visibility, even after over 50 years I believe I could still find my way around Egypt and up the Nile, the world's longest and most important river, as far as Khartoum without a map. They say he who drinks the water of the Nile always returns to drink again: well, I have! The river, now tamed by the Aswan Dam, still flows majestically along its timeless bed, its great valley winding a green ribbon between barren cliffs as yet mostly untouched by modern man. Undoubtedly, those twin sisters, Isis and Nepthys, still hold their magic court beneath the sun-god Ra.

41

I fear there were times when our youthful exuberance broke the bounds of Victorian propriety that characterised staid Cairo society in contrast to the high life of Alexandria. I would not say we were the forerunners of the 'lager louts' but, like all the 'thirties generation, we were reacting to an instinct to enjoy life while it lasted. Sometimes we seemed to be impelled by a mere impulse to be outrageous.

Occasionally, a visit to a night club, organised on the spur of the moment, had a small group of us gathering at the Auberge des Pyramides near Giza or across the Nile at the Kit Kat, incongruously situated at Embaba, scene of Napoleon's victorious Battle of the Pyramids in 1798. After dinner there was always a floor show and we tended to be intolerant and critical of the down-at-heel wandering Hungarian 'artistes' who had almost reached the end of their road.

One turn which invariably reduced us to scornful laughter involved a man dressed in sinister black from head to foot and an ageing female wearing a daringly low-cut dress. Their act was billed as *'une dance apache'*, the man throwing his partner all over the stage with increasing mock brutality until she lay quivering at his feet: general applause! We grew jaundiced at being taken for these corny artistic rides and one evening set off with our own 'props' to liven things up a bit. Someone had acquired a long but harmless grass snake which he put in a bag and waited until the *'apache'* dance was in full swing. At this point the snake was let loose and started to slide along the floor between the tables. It had travelled no more than a few yards when there was a loud scream from one of the diners, followed by total disintegration of the audience. Some climbed on their chairs, others ran for the exits; the scared waiters pretended not to be there. In the uproar, we bagged the snake up and quietly sloped off to a bar, leaving pandemonium behind.

The idea was tried out again at another night spot, this time with a little pig, let loose among the diners. The effect was electric. If anything, the confusion was even worse than had been caused by the snake. Moreover, it was impossible to retrieve the piglet which was nearly as hysterical as the diners and was running about in all directions, squealing its head off. A tactical retreat was therefore quickly arranged.

For some undisclosed reason – probably just to let off steam – there was another night when George Musson's ancient bull-nose Morris attempted to drive up two flights of marble steps leading into Shepheard's Hotel. It made the first flight with the help of its happy passengers; but it failed to cope with the halfway landing and took a great deal of man-handling to return it to the road. Somehow the incident was brushed off good-naturedly by dear 'WB', alias William B. Delaney, a Director and Chairman of Egyptian Hotels Limited, a charming Cairene who had hied from the Emerald Isle and always did his best for us.

High spirits were never far below the surface nor easy to quench. For instance, there was the cocktail party at Abu Sueir to which we were all invited. Alas, there seemed to be no way of getting there and back, for it was 80 miles away. Then someone suggested 216 Sqn doing a little night-flying practice – but who could be trusted as the pilot to stay on the wagon?

It was our own CO who sportingly took on the job himself and off we went, two up in the cockpit, three crew and 22 passengers in the cabin, wearing flying overalls over our best party suits and with our best hats at the ready. Conditions being perfect, we soon arrived at our former '*alma mater*' in the desert. As we trooped off to the familiar Mess, we were watched no doubt with some envy by the bog rat population of No 4 FTS, who had of course been excluded from the jollification. It was pleasant to renew old acquaintances and to talk familiarly with our once god-like but now human instructors. Recognition by our happily grinning former servants was particularly heart-warming.

Altogether it was a very happy reunion, though needless to say all eyes turned from time to time to see what our CO pilot had in the glass he was holding in his hand. After two hours we bade farewell and climbed back onboard the Victoria, to sit facing each other along its cabin on the two rows of functional folding canvas bucket seats which were, at best, distinctly uncomfortable.

Group Captain McCloughry, then our Station Commander and acting second pilot was a serious-minded New Zealander with a penchant for cigars that often gave away his presence when he was not expected. He was held in proper respect, but we were all in a jovial mood and, to wile away the time flying back across the desert, we took down one of the hats from the cabin rack and flung it up and down the aisle in mock rugby football passes. The sliding windows had been opened for fresh air and a strong draught was blowing inside the cabin. When one player muffed his catch, the 'ball' went flying out into the night. On arrival at Heliopolis, no trace could be found of a new hat McCloughry had bought specially for the party. Its sandy whereabouts remain a mystery to this day. Poor man, he was written off during the war when an aircraft in which he and Lady Tedder, wife of Sir Arthur Tedder, were both passengers crashed during an approach to Heliopolis in a sandstorm.

It took me the best part of a year to save £E50 to buy a clapped-out Chrysler, once built for both comfort and speed. A long leather front bench was clearly designed for 'poodlefaking' but was now a jaded reminder of its glamorous past. Even in top gear, the eight cylinders gave a smooth ride in traffic at 8 mph, but the patches on its inner tubes lifted when hot and journeys of more than 30 miles were fraught with uncertainty. I never saved up enough for a new set of tyres and the car was only good for short runs to and from Gezira Club or for picnics across the Nile to the Giza and Saqqara pyramids, or south to the Toura caves where the pyramids' sandstone had been quarried and where ancient stonemasons had left their personal marks.[2] The lovely El Fayoum oasis was well beyond my reach.

Car insurance was another expensive problem. In those days premiums were high for RAF officers who were all considered to be a very high risk on the road, a reputation we shared in the good company of actors, publicans and members of the Jewish faith! But when Bob Brittain arrived from England to join No 208 Sqn, I embarked on an ambitious journey to show him around and introduce him to some of my friends. He had already founded the RAF Flying Club and was full of bright ideas.

It was late spring and the sun was already too hot for a desert picnic, so I planned to run to a spinney of eucalyptus trees I had spied from the air, not far from the Khankah sand dunes, about 15 miles north-east of Heliopolis. Two girl friends would provide the eats; we would bring ice-cold beer from the Mess. Off we went in the Chrysler, ambling through pleasant country for an hour or so before turning towards the group of tall grey-green trees which were our goal. The copse grew in the extensive grounds of a mental hospital which we went past to reach the shade on the edge of the desert.

A steady cool northerly breeze was singing through this idyllic setting and we ate our lunch and lolled happily with our charming companions until it was time to make a move. Bob said, as good boy scouts, we ought to burn up our litter so as to leave the site as unsullied as we had found it. The ground being deep in fallen eucalyptus leaves, we had to scrape away to reach the sand to make a bare patch safe for a bonfire. It was soon alight, but a piece of burning trash, caught by the wind, fell on a nearby heap of dead leaves which burst into flames with little explosions, spreading our burn-up rapidly downwind. Frantic stamping and beating with anything handy was to no avail and the flames took hold of the tinder-dry, oily leaves. Hurriedly the car was backed out of danger and we returned to the fray, but our beating was hopeless: within minutes, whole trees were going up in flames with a noise like the cracking of whips. So Bob was hurriedly dispatched to alert the asylum, where prolonged ringing on a bell produced an Egyptian at a window telling Bob in Arabic to go away. Try as he would, he couldn't convey alarm to the inmate who shrugged his shoulders and shut the window. He must have been one of the interned 'magnoons'.

By the time Bob rejoined us, the conflagration was too big to handle. Reluctantly we climbed back into the car and drove off, glancing ruefully back from time to time, uneasy at the carnage we had so inadvertently caused. We prayed the wind would continue blowing towards the desert and away from the asylum, a furtive and very forlorn hope. That same evening we had all been invited to cocktails at the Smileys' who lived in a tall Zamalek block of flats on Gezira Island. Under cover of the chatter, we crept up to the roof to scan the horizon towards Khankah but no flames or smoke could be seen. Next morning Bob, detailed for a local air exercise, was able to carry out a quick 'shufti' and reported that half the spinney was now grey ash and the fire had burnt itself out at the edge of the desert. The wind hadn't changed, the asylum was unscathed and we could breathe easily again.

Unfortunately, we were always too dedicated to our flying careers and too embroiled in light-hearted pursuits to find the time to explore the vast riches of our surroundings. Cairo overwhelmed us with its noise and squalid, jostling crowds. The shouting was bad enough, but the open sewers, the flies, the pitiful beggars and the all-pervading poverty assailed our Western susceptibilities. Our predictable reaction was to turn away from the smells and dust, shutting our eyes to the tumult and taking refuge in our own familiar life-style. But beyond the pale of our secure British isolation, untold oriental treasures were only waiting to be discovered.

Once past the pandemonium of Cairo railway station, with its seething mob of shouting porters fighting for the chance to carry enormous loads of baggage, the traveller would be all too aware of pavements strewn with disabled beggars, sitting on haunches or lying prone, some hobbling on home-made crutches or, legless, sliding about on boards fitted with roller-skate castors. Lines of money-changers sat against the walls, their paper wares displayed on diminutive ground-level desks. Here and there, scribes would be reading or writing for clients similarly squatting beside them. Sand-coloured, mangy dogs wandered about; donkeys and camels staggered along under their crushing loads, those from the country drawing carts piled with sugar-cane or bersim, an emerald-green fodder. A funeral would pass by at a trot, the flimsy coffin held shoulder-high, open to the sky, with a cart-load of hired wailing women following behind, just as they had for ages past.

Bakers men, balancing huge baskets of pitta-bread on their heads, would hurry through the crowds, seldom, if ever, stopping; elsewhere, loaded down by massive and ornate brass containers, the water-carriers announced themselves by a distinctive clinking of tiny brass cups to accompany their cries. Meanwhile, dilapidated buses trundled uneasily along, with as many passengers clinging on outside as were packed into the seats inside. Motor horns blew continuously and horse-drawn 'garries', festooned with jingling bells, rolled unsteadily along to the crack of whips and shouts of the drivers. It was sheer bedlam, as if every Cairene had been born stone-deaf.

Nevertheless, the streets and shops of the 'new' Cairo, dating back to the 1880s, had an air of very considerable dignity. Broad tree-lined avenues and spacious midans, or squares, lined with European shops proudly displaying the latest French '*chic*' imparted the ambience of a miniature Paris. Except in the hottest weather, it was pleasant to stroll and to window-gaze. The merchandise was low-priced and yet nearly always subject to oriental haggling for the bargain-hunter.

Handsome office blocks, some housing European banks, lent an air of stability to this bustling Egyptian capital. With the departure of much foreign influence after Nasser's seizure of the Canal and the débacle of Suez in 1956, this affable atmosphere largely evaporated. It must have only been skin-deep but in the 'thirties it all seemed real enough.

Leaving the 'new town' and entering the old city – el-Masr – lying at the foot of the Citadel, the streets became much narrower, noisier and dirtier. Everywhere, sheep and goats now joined the horses, donkeys, camels and dogs. The crush in this human ant-hill became thicker and more fascinating, freed from any western overtones.

The Khan el-Khalili, or 'Mushki', an Aladdin's Cave, lay beckoning the explorer from near the ancient el-Azhar Muslim university. Immense displays of jewellery, gems, gold and silver were everywhere. Tiny boutiques offered exotic perfumes mixed to individual taste. For the connoisseur there were wonderful carpets from every corner of Islam, their purchase at the right price requiring only unlimited time, endless patience, the frequent sipping of '*kahowa mazboot*' (very sweet thick Turkish coffee), a modicum of Arabic and a deep appreciation of traditional oriental workmanship.

A visit to the principal mosques was a 'must'. These great, magnificent buildings, decorated with intricate geometrical and vegetable designs, left my own infidel mind with a sense of cold and impersonal religious detachment. Despite much repetitive dedication to the glory of Allah and his prophet Mohammed, and in contrast to comparably large Christian cathedrals, these mosques resembled places of communal gatherings rather than of religious worship and quiet retreat where one could briefly escape from the stresses of life. This is not to deny that their lofty interiors were impressively very beautiful and dignified.

Forays into the wealth of Egyptology lying on our very doorstep were regrettably far too infrequent. What wasted opportunites we would come to regret in later years! Of course the Pyramids of Giza and Saqqara were much too big to ignore and the Cairo Museum could not be missed; but we really only scratched the surface of a once-hidden wonderland. It has to be admitted with deep shame that few of us ventured up the Nile deliberately to gaze at the magnificence that was Thebes. The flying task of my squadron constantly took us up and down that river; but from the air little could be seen of the fabulous ruins of an ancient culture which had contributed so much to our own civilisation, indeed far more than has ever been acknowledged by our Greek-biased scholars. Mathematics, surveying, mechanics, hydrology, horology, sculpture, architecture, astronomy, painting, weaving, irrigation, agriculture – there was no end to the advances in human knowledge and technology made on such a grand scale by the Ancient Egyptians, forerunners of the Greeks to whom too much has always been attributed, in my humble opinion. Unfortunately, the wonders of Karnak, the Colossii of Memnon, the temples of Queen Hatshepsut, of Dendera and Abu Simbel, all appeared insignificant when seen through sun-tinted flying goggles from an open cockpit at 2,000ft. Oh what Philistines we were!

No honest account of Heliopolis life would be complete without a visit to Madame Karoff's. Strategically situated in the heart of Cairo between Shepheard's, the Continental Hotel and the Opera House, a 'social club' for officers was run by a middle-aged White Russian *émigrée*. There was no entrance fee – 'members' just had to be introduced. It was never quite clear how much medical security this exclusivity conferred on them, but 'complaints' from that quarter were virtually unknown.

Madame Karoff's would have easily passed for a highly respectable apartment in one of the best *sharias* of the new town. By climbing the flight of marble steps up to its first floor entrance, one entered a spacious lounge decked out with sofas, piles of cushions and crude tapestries depicting scenes from ancient Egypt, the oriental aura accentuated by the heavy odour of exotic perfumes. One was greeted eagerly by comely odalisques[3] in diaphanous see-through muslins and gaudy silks.

Drinks were not expensive nor had they been 'doctored'. Bed was an 'optional extra' and many an impromptu party started and ended at Karoff's going no further than liquid refreshment, though there were times when more than beer or sweet turkish coffee were consumed! These houris[4] were mostly Levantine, several fair-haired with pale olive complexions. Unlike the raddled professionals prowling in town, these nymphs had the airs and graces of pert demoiselles. Witty and good natured, they showed no aversion to more than merely playful mauling. Madame Karoff provided exactly the right degree of erotic distraction the average sex-starved young Britons were looking for. Her harem had been well trained in their art and were fastidious when it came to rendering personal services. Depending on prevailing supply and demand, a well-endowed young flame might sometimes find himself on a free all-night session of unlimited duration, subject only to Madame Karoff's prior consent which was never unreasonably withheld from a pleading member of her staff.

The leading light of the establishment was Ziza, a slim but well-endowed young beauty from Beirut who had a fiancé there and had come to Cairo to amass her own dowry, evidently an accepted practice for someone in her shoes! She even handed out studio nude portraits of herself to her favourite admirers.

One evening, 216 Sqn was having a party in town and had called in force on 'Les Girls'. Drinks were flowing and the laughter was reaching high decibels when Madame Karoff herself suddenly appeared and tried unsuccessfully to restore order. It was well-known she was addicted to drugs – possibly cocaine – and her demeanour seemed to suggest she was coming off a 'high' and had become untypically aggressive. So nobody took much notice of her protests. She came back a second time and again demanded less noise and better behaviour all round. As her remonstrations continued to be ignored, she screamed that she would send for the 'manager'. Never having set eyes on anyone fitting that particular job description, we persisted in taking no notice. However, a few moments later, an English face peered into the room and shouted 'Come on, chaps, pack it up! You're making a helluva noise and disturbing the whole bloody neighbourhood!' We were dumbfounded. It wasn't what was said but who was saying it: for the face was none other than that of 'Muzzy', a Captain, seconded to No 208 Sqn for liaison duties. He was one of the more amusing members of our own Mess. Now we knew what kept him out so late at nights. He stood revealed as the elusive manager of Karoff's! *Par excellence* a Rabelaisian raconteur of risqué stories, 'Muzzy' was never afterwards allowed to forget that particular untimely appearance. As we used to say:

'Please don't tell Mother I'm in the Air Force.
She thinks I'm playing the piano in a brothel!'

But I must confess, while all this was going on, we realised we were now totally unable to resist the result of Herr Adolf Hitler's Saar plebiscite of January 1935. The predictable consequence of the inevitable Allied withdrawal from the Rhineland was German re-militarisation. We now desperately needed a matching Anglo-French military policy; but it didn't come. The Maginot Line was certainly no answer.

Our Service in those days was generously endowed with men of unusual and highly colourful character. Some could best be described as the frontiersmen of aviation, rugged independent adventurers, men of action whose scruples might have been a bit flexible but whose basic integrity was unquestionable. They were prepared to suffer the consequences of boldness and to pay for it with their lives. Others, by nature more inclined to conform and able to accept strictly Establishment disciplines, still maintained hard-won reputations for eating fire.

Our squadron had three flights, each fiercely contending for its good reputation. 'C' Flight had a very serious-minded CO who later became an Air Vice-Marshal; the CO of 'B' Flight was a most like-able and brilliant pilot, Squadron Leader Ted Hilton, who was killed in the 1936 King's Cup air race when, flying over Flamborough Head, he was bumped right through his cabin roof. In 'A' Flight we feared our own light-hearted and indulgent Squadron Leader David Earp might end up selling matches in Piccadilly outside the RAF Club. But he was ably supported by Flight Lieutenant Donald Hardman who later became a knighted Air Chief Marshal. They all wore WW1 medals.

We juniors, too young to have been forged in the furnace of war, admired any leader who pressed on against the elements even when he was not battling with warring tribesmen in the outposts of the Empire where the RAF was a proven peace-keeper. Burly, bluff Canadian Raymond Collishaw therefore stood out as a remarkable type. All who had the privilege of serving with 'Collie' admired his transparent humanity, his frankness and his unbounded kindness – he was a very gentle giant. Yet as an ace fighter pilot in WW1, he had notched up the third highest score of enemy aircraft shot down. Now he was our Group Captain and cut a most impressive figure, his tunic covered in 'fruit salad' – rows and rows of medal ribbons including bars to a DSO and DFC and the Croix de Guerre, being one of a dwindling band of exponents of that age of chivalry when aerial combat was an engagement between gladiators. When he arrived in 1935 to command Heliopolis, the largest Air Force station in the Middle East, he was very much in his prime.

Here he presided over two operational squadrons and a busy communications flight, effortlessly dominating the scene and enjoying every breath he drew. His ruddy moon face and close-cropped hair gave him the appearance of having just emerged from a Turkish bath. It wasn't that he was particularly tall – he was just massive. When he stood on parade, his sturdy knees seemed to buckle under the weight of his torso. In more ways than one, he seemed to be larger than life. His sheer bulk stood him in good stead when he entertained in the Mess, for he could easily have drunk everybody under the table without turning a hair, a trial of endurance for which there were no contenders.

It was put about that his daily routine on arriving at 7 am was to write letters, orders and instructions till his pen ran dry. After holding court for any offenders, he would then leave his desk to sally forth on unplanned tours to inspect his sprawling parish, keeping us all on our toes. He was invariably courteous and amiable, even when he caught somebody napping. In one way or another he cleverly inspired everyone to enjoy doing a good job.

Every Friday night at Heliopolis, all officers, whether living in or married and living off the station, were obliged as a duty to dine together in formal mess kit, any new arrival being given a place of honour at Collie's right hand as an introduction to the Mess. This could be a daunting experience for a young officer, considering the difference in rank and age, but it was Collie's way of breaking the ice and getting to know his officers. He was always in great form and, in order to blind the newcomer with science, carefully mugged up the answer to some abstruse problem. Having consulted an authority like the *Encyclopaedia Britannica*, he then sprang his prepared question in the middle of the soup course, well knowing he would himself be answering it, all through the fish, meat and sweet courses, thus leaving the unsuspecting tenderfoot deeply impressed by the time the savoury had arrived. 'How does a sewing maching work?' he might ask. Never receiving an adequate reply, Collie would then expound the well-rehearsed lecture to his spell-bound captive. There was no escape by trying to 'slide further on bullshit than he could on gravel'; but a few dark hints from his mess mates in advance ensured the whole charade turned out to be a joke, even for the newcomer. Perhaps the last laugh was really on Collie?

Not that he ever had any pretensions; his efforts to get everything down in black and white worked very well, as long as he had proper clerical support. Like so many men of action, he could not, single-handed, stop mere paper running amok. This weakness got the better of him in the Desert War against Italy, when, as AOC No 202 Group, he commanded the RAF from an advanced air headquarters located in a converted, underground, ancient Roman storage cistern at Mersa Matruh. Under the duress of such primitive surroundings and lacking normal staff services, he reportedly kept all his records in only two files – one labelled 'IN' and the other 'OUT'. Both files naturally quickly grew far too unwieldly to handle!

From this ancient cellar he directed, as best he could, the fighters and bombers that daily went raiding into Italian Cyrenaica seeking targets of opportunity. For a time, all had gone very well but, alas, there dawned a day of ill-fortune for Collie. Even if he had foreseen it, he could not have forestalled its consequences: when the chips are down, war is war!

On that fateful day, Collie had allotted a fighter to intrude over the enemy-held town of Benghazi. Much to the pilot's delight, as he approached its airfield, he spotted an Italian transport aircraft circling below him. On drawing nearer, he could see its wheels had been lowered for landing – it was now a sitting duck! If he had known its passengers included a Marshal of the Italian Air Force, who was on his way to inspect his troops, the pilot would have been even more chuffed than he was when he opened fire and saw the transport crash short of the airfield. Unfortunately for Collie, the Marshal had been a close buddy of his on the Italian front during the 1914–18 shemozzle. Instead of hushing up their loss, the Italians noised it abroad and the news was quickly picked up by Intelligence and fed back to Collie who, far from being pleased, was utterly heartbroken.

He reacted with characteristic emotion and at once sent an aircraft 100 miles back to Alexandria to fetch a suitable wreath. Then, to general disbelief, another was despatched to Benghazi to drop the tribute from a low level over the scene of the crash. The pilot got safely through and accomplished his unusual operational mission, probably performing the last, if not the only, act of chivalry in what was fast becoming a bitter aerial conflict. It was too bizarre to conceal for long and seriously lacked political discretion in time of war. With the arrival in the Middle East of Air Marshal Tedder in 1941, things had hotted up and Collie's propensity for producing wild schemes, while slapping his knee and saying, 'Got a clue, see!' put him at odds with his staff, who had to argue strenuously to talk him out of many follies. Tedder regarded Collie as a bull in a china shop and decided to get him posted, to make room for 'Mary'

Coningham.[5] So Collie packed his bags and was unceremoniously relegated to a 'safe' post in the north of Scotland.

Discretion may be the better part of valour, but indiscretion can pay off. How else explain Collie's 'plum' posting to Heliopolis? Even promotion has depended on a name being familiar to a Promotion Board, no matter how they had heard of it. All propaganda is good propaganda.

In the case of discretion, it's also worth knowing just when to draw the line. When in 1937 P. D. 'Wings' Day was posted as a Squadron Leader to Aboukir from Abu Sueir, he was so relieved by his move that he threw an unusual celebration party for some twenty friends by setting off with them in a hired RAF flying-boat tender for a day's picnic and romp on Nelson Island, two miles offshore.

When evening came, the party staggered back onboard and happily climbed up on top of the cabin for the ride home. But during the day, a big swell had developed and the shallow craft swayed very insecurely to and fro as it ploughed along. Cresting a large roller, one of the tender's screws came out of the water, churning the air as the launch almost turned turtle.

A mad scramble off the hamper to the deck below saved the day. It would have been a nasty drag to the far shore, with few life rafts and a lot of young females who were much more decorative on land than they could ever be as long-distance swimmers at sea. Thankfully everyone showed instinctive and instantaneous discretion without any prompting and we all lived to tell the tale!

Notes to Chapter III

1 No 216 Squadron's motto was 'CCXVI dona ferens' – '216 bearing gifts'.
2 These caves were used for engine repairs and equipment stores during the Second World War, as part of No 111 Maintenance Unit.
3 An Eastern female slave or concubine (OED).
4 Nymph of Mohammedan Paradise; voluptuously beautiful woman (ibid).
5 Air Vice-Marshal A. ('Maori') Coningham, who commanded the Desert Air Force from July 1941, replacing Collishaw.

IV

Sudan Sortie

WHILE HITLER was ordering conscription and boastfully creating the *Luftwaffe*, Mussolini was beginning to hot things up. For years he had nursed designs to increase 'his share' of Africa by grabbing undeveloped but fertile Abyssinia – the uplands of Ethiopia – by war if need be, thereby consolidating his strategic hold on the Horn of Africa where he already ruled over Eritrea through Asmara and its port Massawa and over most of Somalia with its coastal capital Mogadishu.

By 1934 his plans were well-advanced for a campaign, using poison gas as one of his weapons and making a pincer thrust against Addis Ababa, seat of Haile Selassie, the Emperor and distant successor to the Queen of Sheba. Addis Ababa was an important centre of the most ancient sect of Christianity, the Copts. Founded in Egypt by the earliest Gospeller, the Apostle Mark, their church had spread up the Nile and down the Red Sea until overtaken by Islam in the seventh century AD. Abyssinian Copts had been saved by their impenetrable plateau and were left to their own devices, occasionally raiding their savage neighbours in the Nilotic lowlands for slaves and cattle.

In 1868, a British expedition under General Sir Robert (later Lord) Napier, sent against the tyrant Emperor Menelik, had been thwarted as much by the terrain as by the staunch and elusive Ethiopians who, after their defeat, retired into political insignificance. The Abyssinians' crops suffered cyclical devastation by locusts and their backward highlands had become just about ripe for a takeover bid in the 'thirties by the land-voracious Italians. Wasn't this the Age of the Aeroplane and of Air Power?

It was a stroke of obscene and sectarian fate that modern Italians should follow in the wake of their medieval Venetian forebears who had stolen the body of St Mark, their adopted patron saint, from its former revered Coptic mausoleum in ancient Alexandria, to carry it off to Venice for veneration. Italian ambitions were so half-heartedly resisted by the League of Nations that Il Duce blatantly cocked a snook at every protest emanating from Geneva, aided and abetted by

Adolf Hitler who was also now hell-bent on upsetting the prevailing *status quo* for his own purposes. The paper-thin Hoare-Laval Agreement and the civilised jibes of the then youthful Captain Anthony Eden, expressing British disapproval, were contemptuously ignored by the bully dictator as so much effete posturing.

Thus, the background to our more thoughtful moments was sombre as we watched the Italians preparing for the fray from our grandstand seats in Egypt. Early in 1935, more than the occasional troopship began to pass through the Suez Canal bound for Massawa or Mogadishu. Increasing numbers of fast, sleek Caproni metal-bodied(!) monoplane(! !) transports staged through Almaza, the Royal Egyptian Air Force and civil airfield next to Heliopolis, all heading for East Africa and making even our latest and most admired Mk VI Victorias look like dodos.

The British in Egypt now became alert to the large potential 'fifth column' of expatriate Italians living in Cairo and Alexandria who might be pressed into subversive activity, outnumbering all other expatriates in Egypt by two to one.

To add to our growing discomfiture, the Fascist neighbours in Libya were perceived to be consistently cruel and ruthless to their indigenous natives, dropping dissidents from aircraft over the Libyan sands. It wasn't healthy to be a Senussi nationalist. Sabres also started to be rattled on Libya's southern borders, where Egypt and the Sudan also met in the mountainous area of Gebel Ouweinat, until then merely a name on the Sahara map and seemingly not of the slightest importance. Information to the contrary had, however, come into the hands of our Intelligence. The Italians were up to something and in the light of other suspicious moves, their unwelcome activities on that remote frontier had to be investigated without delay.

From the Sudan, convoys of Defence Force trucks set out from Wadi Halfa westwards for 400 miles across the Nile; but as the troops had to carry all rations, fuel and water with them this ground expedition took a considerable time to arrive. First on the scene were four No 216 Sqn Victorias whose crews had to hump their spares, water, rations and fuel (in ubiquitous four-gallon cans), leap-frogging in short hops across 700 miles of desert south-west from Cairo.

There being no topographic features on any maps, Squadron Leader Philip Mackworth DFC, the CO of C Flight and a leading navigation specialist, sketched a survey of the ground as he flew over it. He still had to plot his courses on an almost bare graticule where the route crossed the great empty Sand Sea. The Victorias took three days and many stages to reach Gebel Ouweinat and, after they at last arrived, a site had still to be chosen for landing and to serve as a temporary camp.

Sure enough, seen from the air, there was much hustle and bustle on the far side of the unmarked frontier, though it was unclear exactly what was afoot. After observing the scene for a couple of days, the Victorias returned to Heliopolis, having at least demonstrated our ability to find and occupy remote desert regions, should any future need arise. In the light of the subsequent 1935 hostilities, it is possible Gebel Ouweinat was used as a staging post for flying Italian reinforcements to Eritrea, crossing the deserts of the Sudan clandestinely, without opposition and unobserved.

Hardly had we drawn breath from the Gebel Ouweinat 'flap' than it was decided to see if No 208 Sqn's Atlases could reinforce the paper-thin ground defences that the Sudan was able to muster on her eastern borders with Abyssinia. For the Atlases to reach those tropical regions, 1,500 miles from Heliopolis, No 216 Sqn was needed to carry their groundcrews and spares. The short-ranged two-seater Atlases, ill-equipped to navigate seriously on their own, had to be convoyed in two-hour hops across desert, tropical savannah and thick bush to reach remote destinations in southern Sudan. We were, of course, unaware at the time that this expedition had in fact been planned during the previous December. Short notice was supposed to keep us flexible: 'flaps' were thought to be good for us. They certainly kept us on our toes.

Thus on 15 March 1935, eight Atlases and two Victorias set off from Heliopolis. The first day, we made for Wadi Halfa with a good following wind, but shortly after refuelling at Aswan, when my 'Vic' had climbed to 3,000ft and we were 30 miles into the desert, an interplane starboard flying wire snapped with a loud bang and our wings tried hard to part company from the fuselage. Happily, the aircraft was still just manageable. Visibility was down to two miles but we were able to pick a flat bit of gravel between rough outcrops and landed safely for repairs. When we tried to report to our leader from the ground we discovered our short-wave transmitter was not working. After 1½ hours, just as we were taking off again, he returned overhead to find out what was going on.

Leaving Wadi Halfa on the second day, several of the Atlases sank up to their axles in soft sand on the desolate landing ground at the Sudan Railway's Station 6, where they needed to refuel. The sand had been so smooth that the Victorias, after dropping smoke candles to show the wind direction, landed first in order to churn up the sand into ruts to give the Atlas pilots a chance of judging their height as they came in to land. The ones that became stuck were then extricated by the groundcrews we were carrying.

We then had a two-day break at Khartoum for briefing and recovery and were entertained by No 47 Sqn, whose Fairey IIIFs could be fitted with floats to cope with the floods of the rainy season down south; one specimen was riding at anchor on the Blue Nile.

On 19 March, after flying south-east up the Blue Nile to Sennar, where a dam supplied water to vast cotton plantations, we continued to Singa where Shell had pre-positioned fuel. Then we groped our way south from Roseires for three hours over the featureless light brown savannah, in visibility at times down to a rather alarming single mile, because of the smoke from the grass fires lit by the natives to encourage new shoots to sprout for grazing when the rains came. Dusk was gathering when at last we found our destination and landed at Nasir with everyone surprisingly still intact.

The boundary hereabouts had been fixed in 1900 by a Sapper Major who had gone up by river from Malakal hoping to meet an Abyssinian delegation coming down from Gambeila. The latter had failed to arrive and as all the country was under water, the Major decided it didn't much matter where he drew the line! However, when the floods subsided, the Nuers came down with their cattle from the hills as usual to the lower pasture. Naturally, the Major's impromptu decision had caused endless disputes along the frontier ever since.

The tiny Nuer village of Nasir was a collection of *tukls* or huts made of reeds and mud, sitting on the raised north bank of the milk chocolate-coloured river Sobat that oozed its way out of the hills of Abyssinia on the far eastern horizon. Passing the ill-defined border into the Sudan's flat grassy plain of black clay 'cotton soil', the Sobat eventually joined the White Nile south of Malakal. It was the only link with the outside world when the annual rains turned the whole area into an impassable morass, there being no all-weather roads.

Nasir was to be our home for a week. Tents were pitched for the erks and NCOs. We eight officers had the luxury of enough space for our camp beds in a rambling house that resembled a large meat safe, its verandahs covered by metal fly-screens. This was the home of Corfield, the District Officer, when he was not away with his half-dozen armed Police *askaris* on his frequent lonely safaris dispensing justice. It was also a roost for bats which came to life at dusk and were chased off by his dogs, gobbling up any that we managed to stun by throwing our pillows up to the ceiling. Almost every day at 4 am, a rainstorm blew into the verandahs and soaked us. We were assured by our host that the filtered brown river water was quite safe to drink.

Father-figure and dedicated DO, Corfield administered an area as large as Lancashire and Yorkshire put together, stretching 100 miles east from the White Nile to Abyssinia. Semi-nomadic pastoral Nuers, Dinkas and Shilluks built their *tukls* on any dry ground they could find. Scratching meagre harvests of maize and millet to add to a diet of milk and fish, they could reputedly go for four days without eating while tending their cattle against predators. According to Corfield, the natives were as truculent as children but they had a fine sense of humour. Despite their nakedness, they had a natural dignity and gave him very little trouble. A small band of convicted murderers wandered around in loose chains, performing public works and always seemingly pleased to help hump our petrol cans when we were refuelling. The villagers fished from dugout canoes, shooting at ripples with arrows attached to long lines or aimlessly prodding the river bed with barbed spears, hoping to stab one of the fish lying on the bottom. We had fresh fish to eat every day.

Our week at Nasir was unforgettable anthropology at close quarters, lovingly expounded by our sensitive host. His native charges, typically very tall and willowy 'Nilotics', wore ivory trinkets and beads but only scanty clothes to supplement the decorations of deep cuts and cicatrice tribal patterns that decorated their faces and bodies. The headman wore a leopard skin over his shoulders, a symbol of authority exactly like those worn by high priests and pharaohs depicted on the walls of ancient Egypt, a long-lost custom that was still alive and well at Nasir in 1935.

The polygamous males tended to hang about in indolent groups, talking in monosyllabic grunts while standing on one leg, for all the world like storks, their spare foot braced against the other knee while they lent on a spear. Styles of coiffure were many and ingenious but straight 'fair' hair was the 'in thing'. By wearing a cow-dung pack, their thick black curly locks could be uncrinkled and bleached to an orange straw-colour when the hard-set pack was chipped off after a week or so. Many were covered from head to foot in white ash as a sign of mourning. True primitives, the men refused to work – it was undignified and reminiscent of the misery suffered at the hands of Abyssinian slave-raiders, a painful tribal memory from a past as recent as 1924.

They had no concept of money and only traded by barter. It was Corfield's difficult official task to introduce a money-oriented economy by the device of imposing taxes which had to be paid in cash and not, as formerly, in kind or by work. All the hard labour was done by the women, who slipped away to bathe on the edge of the river whenever they could, leaving their infants in the care of the 'wrinklies' who, though everybody evidently became decrepit by the time they were 35, still had useful jobs to do. Nasir male society seemed to have evolved a fairly reasonable system for themselves but we wondered if the women felt quite the same way about it, although they always went about smiling and giggling.

The Nuers believed they were closely related to birds and snakes which were consequently carefully protected. Far from being canni-bals, whenever they caught a crocodile it was quickly gutted for fear of finding a bangle or some other indication of human prey, which would have made it uneatable. The Sobat river was alive with croco-diles which were Public Enemy No 1, carrying off a villager almost every month. While the Atlases were co-operating with the Sudan Horse in a 'show of force' on the frontier at Pibor Post and at Jockau Village, we had some time to spare and became instantly popular when a crocodile hunt was mooted.

Riding up the river bank on ponies for a few miles, we found there was no shortage of targets: 20ft specimens lay about on the mud banks basking with their mouths wide open; while attendant white egrets stalked round the gaping jaws, fearlessly picking their terrible teeth clean. Every crocodile we shot at, from almost point-blank range, flopped back into the water, a lost feast for the Nuers. We had to be content with knowing we had probably saved a few human lives.

One night, a marriage barter was held in the village; the respective fathers haggling for hours over the number of cows or goats to be paid for the wife-to-be, depending on her being a virgin or not. Drums had been sounding for days, summoning everybody to the ball by 'bush telegraph' and men had traipsed in for 50 miles to assemble at dusk in an open space to complete their toilet, covering their torsos with butter until they glistened like polished ebony. Likewise, the women anointed themselves from head to foot. Meanwhile, local 'hooch' was being dished out near a huge fire which was the centrepiece of the night's festivities. With no special bidding, they all suddenly began to dance and the drums began to beat louder and louder, though apart from a low murmuring hum from the dancers, there was no music.

At first an outer circle of swaying and stamping girls, their bodies glinting, kept well clear of the men who were leaping up and down in the middle. But gradually the incessant rhythm became more and more demanding and the dancers more and more frenzied and erotic. Enchanted by the velvet night, the horizon aglow with distant burning grass fires, we watched as couples paired off and melted into the shadows cast by the blazing fire on the long grass. As Corfield said, it would have been a very stupid Nuer who could not find a lover in the dark. The participants in this primitive rave-up took quite a time to get switched on: nudity obviously had its natural defences, but for a fascinating hour we had been privileged witnesses of a primeval ritual. Then, feeling rather like a group of guilty voyeurs, we stole back to our fly-proof quarters.

The night before we were due to leave, a cloudburst turned the so-called 'airfield' into a slippery, sticky quagmire and there was no way we could take off. Even the great black maribou storks, that always stood around hunched up like funeral attendants, were unable to fly. When approached, they stumbled clumsily off, weighed down by huge clods of black clay on their feet. The old Service adage about not flying when the birds were walking had come true. It was a long time before the ground was dry enough for taxying, but when on 26 March we left for Juba, three hours away to the south, we felt very reluctant to bid farewell to our generous host and to leave his intriguing savages behind us.

I have often wondered how the Nuers fared without their caring Corfield and now living under the cruel Sharia laws – male and female circumcision, *et al* – imposed by the Muslim fanatics in far-away Khartoum. From all accounts, they have been driven in despair to turn on their Dinka cousins, with Kalashnikovs instead of fish spears and have now become bloodthirsty outlaws, everyone fighting for survival.

We refuelled at Akobo and then flew over almost continuous grass fires, each crowned by its plume of cumulonimbus cloud. Next came trackless swamps and violent rain storms in the afternoon, and we looked down on herds of buffalo, water buck, reed buck, tiang, hartebeeste and gazelle, not to mention hippos, rhinos, giraffes, ostriches, leopards and, of course, the ubiquitous crocodile. Near Bor, on the Nile, we flew low over one of the largest herds of elephant then known in Africa, squelching about in the sudd and at a loss to know which way to turn to escape from our airborne intrusion. Today they have all but vanished.

Juba was an equatorial 'Clapham Junction', a terminus of the Nile steamers and the north end of roads leading to Uganda and the Congo. We were disappointed to find it had a touch of more familiar civilisation, for the natives had already been converted to Christianity: they wore clothes but had also acquired very light fingers and other bad habits in the process. We were accommodated in the comfortable Nile Hotel, each in a separate *tukl*. The Atlases co-operated with the Equatorial brigade of the Sudan Defence Force, flying east to the mountainous region of Torit and Kapoeta and then westwards to Aba on the Congo border. They tried in vain to find mock 'enemy' troops who hid under the trees as soon as they heard an aircraft approaching. Meanwhile, the Victorias flew fuel to Kongor to make a refuelling dump for the Atlases on the return journey. We also returned briefly to Nasir to pick up tents and stores we had left behind to take them to Malakal, to be shipped back down the Nile to Khartoum.

But there came a spare afternoon when four of us hired a Juba taxi and persuaded its reluctant driver to take us a few miles north to where we had previously spotted some elephants, so as to get a closer view of them. In half an hour we found our monsters, almost invisible in very tall grass; but as we slowly approached them, all four wheels of our taxi sank simultaneously into separate elephant footsteps and the engine stalled. We gingerly dismounted and peered across 100 yards to where the herd were lazily grazing. We counted ten and were about to produce cameras when their guardian lookout, a large bull, suddenly opened up his enormous ears and looked in our direction, making menacing noises of disapproval. We lifted the taxi bodily out of its holes, turned it round and hoped the engine would re-start. Thankfully it responded and we quickly headed back the way we had come, this time at a brisk pace: there were no friendly trees around that we could have shinned up in a hurry.

It was uncomfortably hot at Juba and, with no magical Corfield to keep us entertained, we were quite ready to head for home on 4 April, as soon as No 208 Sqn's Army exercises had finished. On the way, flying in bad visibility, we made diversionary visits to Talodi and Dilling, both mere bush clearances in the Barra Mountains 100 miles west of Malakal, where we contacted other units of the Sudan Defence Force. Then we left Khartoum *en route* for Egypt and ran into strong headwinds that reduced our ground speed to a miserable 70 mph which made flying in open formation very tedious. We were therefore more than glad to see Heliopolis again, six days after leaving Juba.

Our four weeks of manoeuvres in the tropics had of course been to assess the possible impact of an Italian war against Abyssinia. In anticipation of the real thing, we had learnt about the mobility of air forces and had managed to enjoy ourselves in the process. Apart from two cases of malaria and two Atlas pilots suffering heat exhaustion due to sitting for hours behind their air-cooled engines, most of us had returned none the worse for wear and everyone had a different story to tell. My contribution as a Second Pilot had enabled me to shoot 500ft of 16mm film, a small surviving part of which is now lodged in the Imperial War Museum.

Sudan Sortie

Within a month of my return to Heliopolis, I completed my schedule of training as Second Pilot and my aerial ciné-photographic reportage from the cockpit had to be relegated to the back burner. But to tell the truth, I could not afford any more ciné film and thought I had better things to do with my money. Ah! If only I could have foreseen TV and all that. . . . If only I had had a tape-recorder. . . . If only there had been video cameras. . . . In any case I should have been less parsimonious, for I was soon to be promoted to Flying Officer and my monthly pay went up by £5: riches indeed! But I took comfort from having complied with the requirements of Squadron Standing Orders and KR and ACIs[1] and was now qualified officially as a Captain. The mantle of responsibility scarcely bothered me. After all, sitting out in front, I would be the first to suffer in a prang and I wasn't aiming to get myself hurt. A letter I wrote home soon afterwards illustrates my reactions more clearly than I can now recall.

No 216 (BT) Squadron
Heliopolis
Egypt
11th June 1935

My dear Mum and Dad,

I'm sorry to have missed writing last week but I was away in Khartoum and didn't have a chance to send you a line. It was actually my first long trip as Captain and I admit I felt a wee bit apprehensive for the welfare of my 17 passengers and crew, but the feeling passed as soon as I became involved.

I first set off from Helio for Aboukir at 4.30 am last Monday to pick up a load of airmen who had been on two weeks' rest-leave by the sea and to return them to Khartoum, 1,300 miles away. We had been in the air for only a few minutes when the Delta below became covered by thick fog which had not been forecast. So I sent a W/T signal to Aboukir asking for their present weather and continued on my way towards them.

After half an hour there had been no reply and the fog down below was as thick as ever. I had no definite idea of my position so decided to turn back to Helio.

The fog was drifting quickly south and I nearly missed seeing the airfield which was already partly fog-bound. With luck, I caught a glimpse of 216's tall hangars and landed just as a bank of fog rolled in. We all got out for a stretch and a smoke, waiting impatiently for the fog to clear at both ends! At last we set off again for Aboukir, but by now it was 6.30, which meant we would be two hours late all day. After leaving

Aboukir we didn't reach our first refuelling stop at Asyut until 11.30 and didn't pass Aswan until 2 pm. By then I was very hungry, having eaten nothing since a boiled egg at 3.30 am. To my disgust I now discovered the Mess had supplied me with only two tough, dry mutton sandwiches as a sort of brunch! The crew passed me up some water in a mug – all they could offer to help my food down. Near Aswan the weather began to deteriorate and sand was rising everywhere. My co-pilot was a sergeant of tender years who had already demonstrated he was unable to steer a steady course. He was no help as a navigator either and began to nod off! So I sent him aft and invited one of my passengers, a pilot friend from No 47 Squadron at Khartoum, to come and sit up in front with me.

We had a mild thrill 40 miles north of Wadi Halfa when one of my petrol tanks ran dry and both engines stopped! We were at 6,000ft over very rough desert, but a bit of quick thinking solved the crisis: I turned on the reserve tank and both engines came back to life! The passengers had been mostly fast asleep, but they were now all sitting up, understandably wide awake and anxiously peering out of the tiny cabin windows!

We arrived at Wadi Halfa at 5 pm, after ten hours' flying and was I tired! It was terribly hot when I turned in – 100°F in my room and still 97°F at 3.30 next morning, when I tried to swallow a fried egg and some greasy bacon with iced coffee for my breakfast.

During the previous evening, I was surprised to meet four crazy Frenchmen who were driving a half-ton covered truck all the way to Paris from Fort Lamy, in French Equatorial Africa. They were also night-stopping at the pleasant Nile Hotel. This was a surprise chance for me to try out my rusty French! But it was too hot for fun and we all turned in early.

The second day was even more testing because, after 200 miles, the weather suddenly became really bad. The sky turned yellow and completely merged with the featureless yellow ground down below. Instinctively I lost height and turned towards the Nile, some miles away to starboard, hoping I would be able to catch a glimpse of its narrow, cultivated green banks through the thick dust.

From 800ft I could only just discern a faint grey-green discolouration that was the Nile; but as I calculated it was 35 minutes overdue, I wasn't sure I hadn't already overshot Atbara, where I simply had to refuel.

I pressed on along the almost invisible Nile for about 25 minutes into a gale of 45 mph that reduced my ground speed to an appalling 60 mph. At last the little depot of the Sudan Railways appeared out of the dust, much to my relief, for I might very easily have missed it altogether.

While on the ground refuelling, Khartoum signalled me to stay put, as they were also under the haboob duststorm. This cleared after two hours and I was able to take off and finally delivered my load of long-suffering and very weary passengers at 1.10 pm. We were all very glad to get out, after such a bumpy nine-hour ride.

I was happy to have the next day off, swimming and lazing at the Khartoum Club which is a very pleasant place, but nothing to compare with Cairo's Gezira Sporting Club.

The return to Helio, starting on Thursday, was just as full of incident. On leaving Atbara to fly north over 200 miles of wild desert, the air was still thick with Tuesday's dust. I couldn't get above it, even at 10,000ft. Losing sight of the ground at 5,000ft, I knew there were some hefty gebels, north of Abu Hamad. Miraculously, 50 miles short of Wadi Halfa, the dust haze suddenly cleared and I was able to see the ground and flew straight in to land. We arrived at Wadi Halfa at 10.30 am and my crew got busy refuelling by hoisting dozens of Shell four-gallon cans up to tanks in the top mainplane, in a vertical human chain. While they were sweating away, the District Commissioner drove out to ask me to look out for the four Frenchmen who had left for Aswan two days before. They hadn't been heard of since being ferried across the Nile. Their route would be more or less on my way north, so I naturally agreed at once.

We scanned the desert very carefully over the 200 miles to Aswan, but saw no trace of the truck or of the missing men. We wondered how anyone could possibly survive in such intense heat – our interplane strut air thermometer read 125°F in the shade when we landed at 1 pm at the desert landing ground three miles north of the town of Aswan. So it was with a heavy heart that I telgraphed back to the D C at Wadi reporting that our search had been in vain.

That night at Aswan was the most uncomfortable I have ever spent. The Cataract Hotel being shut for the summer, I had to put everybody into a native 'hotel' – two and three in a room. There were no fans and only one bath for all 18 of us! The bed sheets seemed to have been made of sailcloth.

At 3 am a thunderstorm blew up, with a high wind, so I had to dig my crew out, find a taxi and drive to the airfield which lay between black cliffs of basalt in a narrow valley three miles away. Our aircraft was tethered to 'screw pickets', 3ft steel corkscrews wound into the ground by crowbar. Luckily it was still facing into the gale and didn't need turning round, but as I walked past the tail, a huge spark leaped out at me from the static chain which was being blown horizontal to the ground. It didn't hurt, but I nearly jumped out of my skin!

The sequel to the four Frenchmen's predicament was later pieced together by searchers on the ground and reported in the *Egyptian*

Gazette. After crossing over the Nile and driving several miles along a very well-marked track, they had ignored the indistinct and seldom used right fork leading north to Aswan and instead followed freshly-made ruts that eventually took them west into the blue. These siren tracks had been cut in the sand the previous year by trucks of the Sudan Defence Force, during the Gebel Ouweinat 'flap'.

They continued in the wrong direction until they ran out of fuel. Even then they didn't realise they were lost and made the fatal mistake of thinking the Nile was within walking distance. Rather than waiting stoically in the shade of their truck, which had a fair chance of being found as a prominent feature on the desert landscape, they left its shelter and stumbled by night over the relentless and unforgiving sand and stony outcrops, burning hot and utterly shadeless by day. They now ran out of water and one by one perished from dehydration in the pitiless desert. The Sudan Camel Corps had set out on their trail from Wadi Halfa and followed their tracks for four days with absolute certainty, eventually coming upon a very empty truck. Footsteps in the sand then led to four corpses, straggled over a few miles of desert where they had fallen, one after the other, looking for an elusive Nile that was in fact far beyond their reach.

Ever since that tragedy, which had felt uncomfortably close, I have thought it prudent to keep an open mind and a cool head when not reasonably sure of my actual whereabouts. Five years later, I was asked to make a contribution to the art of practical air navigation and my then CO, the late Air Commodore L. K. 'Kelly' Barnes MBE suggested I should add a wood-cut showing an ancient mariner using a back-staff as the end page of AP 1234, Volume 1 of the *Manual of Air Navigation*. Its caption read 'Man is not Lost', but unfortunately experience shows that he sometimes can be!

1935 wore on with a medley of tasks including formation flying, intercepting aircraft by day and night, dropping supplies and messages by parachute and trying to fly blind by means of primitive instruments with our head in the cockpit. We also underwent some 'spit and polish' squadron drill to prepare for an inspection of Heliopolis by Sir Philip Sassoon who was then the Under Secretary of State for Air and was making a grand tour of the RAF.

In Baghdad, he witnessed a costly search for Wing Commander Peter Warburton, lost in the Syrian desert. Warburton was eventually found, after Sir Philip's own aircraft had been commandeered to help search, and was, not unexpectedly, asked by the Air Council to state his reasons in writing for getting lost. He said it was really quite simple – he hadn't the foggiest idea about navigation; ignorance of which was endemic in the RAF. The fault lay with the Central Flying School where pilot instructors learnt to fly upside-down and many other things, never how to go from A to B.

Their Airships promptly despatched Flight Lieutenant (later Air Marshal Sir Edward) 'Chillie' Chilton, who was then the navigation specialist for the flying-boat squadrons at Mount Batten, to RAF Wittering to give the Group Captain and the instructional staff of CFS a three-month indoctrination course in air navigation. Ever since then, every QFI has been trained to carry out simple cross-country flights in fair weather and in foul and an important step was taken towards the general education of RAF pilots in air navigation.

In May a severe earthquake devastated the town of Quetta in India, where the RAF and the Indian Army had a big cantonment. Many casualties were suffered and their names were published daily. The story trickled through to Egypt on the Service 'grape vine' that the first Casualty List had reported a certain Leading Aircraftman Peacock 'Killed' and a Leading Aircraftman Pocock 'Missing'. On the following day LAC Pocock's body was dug out of the rubble, but LAC Peacock's was still nowhere to be found. It had been a case of mistaken identity and the next Casualty List carried the following correction:

It is regretted there was an error in yesterday's report concerning LACs Peacock and Pocock. The following amendments are notified: For 'Pea' read 'Po'; and for 'Po' read 'Pea'. The 'cock' still stands.'

In July I was sent for by our Adjutant, Paddy Bandon, and told I was in luck – our acting CO, Squadron Leader Philip Mackworth, had detailed me to accompany him in a supporting aircraft on a six days 'swan'. I would need a swim suit, for we were to take the British High Commissioner, Sir Miles Lampson (later Lord Killearn), and his new wife, Jacqueline, on an official tour of inspection of the Western Desert. In fact it was to be for a short, postponed honeymoon consisting of a week in the five-star Lido hotel at remote Mersa Matruh and a visit to the fabled oasis at Siwa. This was the ancient shrine of the Oracle of Jupiter Ammon to whom Alexander the Great had made a pilgrimage before setting off on his world-shattering military adventures. Siwa lay in the deep south of the Sahara. The VIPs were to be escorted by their ADC, Flight Lieutenant Colin Cadell, flying a Fairey Gordon, and I was required as a back-up and to carry the groundcrews, spares and personal luggage.

Sir Miles had been widowed in 1930 and had, with every good reason, fallen for Jacqueline, a brilliant and charming young school-friend of his daughter Mary. The problem was that Jacqui's father was General Castellani, of the Royal Italian Army, appointed by Mussolini to mastermind medical preparations of the army then poised to attack Abyssinia. The numerous expatriate Italians in Egypt were regarded with suspicion, so the wedding had been a low-key affair. Moreover, the rising political tension resulted in a heavy administrative burden and prevented His Excellency from escaping even for a day from his Embassy on the banks of the Nile. It took a long time for local adverse gossip to subside, since the Cairo Establishment still wore the trappings of a long-past Victorian age.

We set off on 21 July to pick up our VIPs from Aboukir and arrived two hours later at a desert airfield on the edge of a turquoise, sapphire and emerald lagoon that, little did we know, was to be fought over, five years later, by the British, the Italians and Rommel's Afrika Korps. Alongside the airstrip, a guard of honour had been drawn up under 'Bimbashi'(Major) Green, the Commandant of the Royal Egyptian Frontier Force in the Western Desert. After the guard had been inspected by H E, the VIPs were driven off to the Lido Hotel, a four-storey edifice standing with its feet more or less in the lagoon – the only building in sight. I followed on an hour later, having tethered the aircraft, sorted out all the luggage and checked the accommodation for our crews. It was so hot and the lagoon was so enticing that the VIP party of five took a quick dip followed by drinks and cigarettes under beach parasols, before sitting down to the splendid cold lunch that was waiting for us, the hotel's only guests.

The sand was whiter and finer than anything I had ever seen – it could be moulded like snow into little balls and was so dense it left the sea crystal clear. That evening we were taken for an informal jaunt by cars to some archaeological remains alleged to be one of Cleopatra's many baths – she must have been a very keen aquanaut! This one looked uncomfortable and dangerously rocky. Over dinner, plans were discussed for next day's journey to Siwa oasis, which lies in a slight depression below sea-level, some 200 miles due south in the Sahara. To avoid turbulence we took off at 6.30 am and on arrival at Siwa, H E received a most impressive guard of honour consisting of a line of 12 impeccable pure-bred pale desert steeds of the Egyptian Camel Corps who stood looking down their haughty noses at us. Then the local Mudir (Mayor), accompanied by the numerous sheiks of Siwa, all bursting with civic pride, showed us around the oasis in a fleet of cars, the sightseeing being interspersed with frequent wayside receptions.

The Siwans lived in two huge pinnacles of rock, deeply honey-combed with caves, like enormous 'beehives' overlooking the oasis.

Their voluminous, cream-coloured flowing robes were said often to conceal remarkable, un-Arabic fair hair and blue eyes and they spoke a dialect of their own. They were said to be descendants of a Lost Legion, left behind when Rome retreated from its North African granaries. After that withdrawal, Arab nomads with herds of goats had invaded the African littoral, stripping every shred of green, progressively reducing the rainfall and eventually creating a 'sahara', which is the Arabic word for desert.

Throughout the large Siwa oasis, clear fresh water bubbled up into stone-faced Roman wells, 20ft deep and 50ft across, irrigating lush date palms and olive trees that grew the most highly-prized crops in the Mediterranean. Halts were made from time to time in the welcome shade of reed shelters where choice fruits and sweet mint tea were offered. The regal progress came to an end all too soon and by 5.30 pm we were again airborne, heading back for Mersa Matruh and arriving there too late for a swim but still in time for a welcome sun-downer sitting beside the gently-lapping lagoon.

It had been a long and tiring day and after dining in black tie and dinner jacket we were quite glad to 'hit the hay' as soon as our VIPs had withdrawn to their suite. During the night, while we slept unperturbed, a drama unfolded which confronted us at breakfast next morning. Jacqui, Lady Lampson, had given Sir Miles a wedding present of a large gold cigarette box, beautifully engraved and inscribed. We had all admired this glittering object when it was passed around as we sat chatting and slaking our parched throats on the beach. But evidently Sir Miles had wanted a last smoke and the gold box was nowhere to be found.

Panic had ensued and Colin Cadell, the ADC, instantly became involved. Bimbashi Green was summoned from his military encampment and soon had a platoon of Egyptian Frontier troopers working under improvised arc lights to dig up the beach where we had been sitting. They dug all night until the entire beach had been combed and sifted, but to no avail and by dawn the elusive trophy was given up for lost.

During a distinctly glum breakfast, Colin, who had been in the thick of the action all night, wondered if, perchance, all the settees in the lounge had really been thoroughly searched: they hadn't! The gold box, its contents intact, lay just where it had slipped down between the cushions. We would dearly have liked to hear what was said to the Bimbashi and just what his private reactions had been, but we kept a discreet silence.

All that day we slipped in and out of the pellucid water of Mersa's lagoon and in the evening a courtesy call was made on Sheikh Idris, a Senussi refugee who was living modestly with his family and retinue in a bivouac of typical bedouin black tents. He was a short man but possessed great personal charm and sweet mint tea and cakes were laid before us. Little did anyone realise he would be crowned King of Libya in 1944 when the Italians fled; in 1935 neither Libyan oil nor Colonel Gadaffi had been heard of: life for the true Arab was still simple and dignified.

The days passed too quickly while we played and talked in a haze of golden sunshine and superb sea bathing, laced with enough alcohol to prevent any care from ruffling our lotus-eating existence: all we had to do was to respond to our charming VIPs. Alas! On 26 July we headed our three aircraft along the coast, this time towards the east, past El Alamein and Alexandria, leaving behind the now familiar dreamlike setting of white sand, azure sea, crystal clear air and oriental luxury. Home James and don't spare the horses! After two hours we deposited our two VIPs back at Aboukir, from where they were whisked off in a Rolls to resume their ambassadorial life in the shadow of King Fouad in his summer retreat of nearby Montaza Palace.

An hour later we were back at our Heliopolis base, in time for a distinctly prosaic lunch. It had indeed been a honeymoon to remember, especially for this aerial postillion-cum-porter. Numberless battle-scarred veterans of WW2 have since passed that way and must have many another and far less pleasant story to tell of that once deserted and idyllic lagoon.

I wonder if the Lido Hotel still stands, solitary on its glistening shore? I fear Mersa Matruh may have become a very different place from what it was in 1935. Can it have resisted the grotesque attentions of greedy Mediterranean 'developers'? Can the sun and the sky and the sea and the sand have lost the spell they once cast upon a 23-year old Pilot Officer?

Note to Chapter IV

1 King's Regulations and Air Council Instructions.

V

Watching the Italians

WE RETURNED to rising shade temperatures hitting 108°F in Cairo, and high tension also unmistakably growing as more and more Italian troopships passed through the Canal, with light naval corvettes and submarines following in their wake, all heading south for the Red Sea. By now it was estimated Mussolini had positioned at least 63,000 troops facing Abyssinia in Eritrea.

Squadron training took on a new dimension of urgency, with more practice bombing, more navigation and 'recce' exercises and rather futile attempts to fly our twins on one engine. Our CO went into a huddle with the senior Engineer officer and made a passable modification by removing a rear cabin window on each side and mounting a Vickers light machine-gun on a movable tripod which could be swung from side-to-side and so provide a little sting from either port or starboard; always supposing we didn't shoot holes in our own wings and tails! Having no front gun and no armour, we would have been easy meat for a fighter.

Parts of the Home Fleet had joined the Mediterranean Fleet based at Alexandria and Fleet Air Arm squadrons came ashore to Aboukir and Heliopolis, where they were joined by RAF squadrons reinforcing us from the UK. Meanwhile, the British Army in Egypt strengthened its defences as much as possible and attended to anti-aircraft measures. It may sound a little daunting but in 1935 these preparations were undertaken with the keenest enthusiasm. At long last we seemed to be facing up to the facts and everyone's morale rose accordingly and life became increasingly enjoyable. There was, for example, the nine-day stretch in August spent at a practice camp in the desert with our 'Flying Shufti' brothers from No 208 Sqn. The chosen site lay between El Arish and Rafa, at a place where trains going in opposite directions could pass each other on the single-line track to Palestine from El Kantara, 143 kilometres away to the west on the Suez Canal.

At Kilo 143 the desert was flat and hard. Large tents were pitched for three Messes and one for headquarters offices, while we all slept on camp beds under the wings of 20 assorted aircraft. It was too hot and open for mosquitos and the camp was only 400 yards from the steep sandy banks of the shore so the sea demanded attention in all our available spare time. We shared the beach with millions of land-crabs that darted into their burrows at our approach. They were such a novelty that the daily news-sheet, compiled by our journalistic colleague, Malin Sorsbie, and duplicated on a primitive machine in the tented Orderly Room, aptly bore the title *Land-Crab Gazette*. What a pity no single number has survived!

The job of 216 Sqn was to ferry the ground personnel, arms, ammunition and bombs, catering and medical services and all the spares for the two squadrons, maintaining a daily supply of rations and water from Heliopolis, 200 miles away. The camp was completely self-contained and independent of any local support for its 110 officers, NCOs, airmen and Mess servants. While 208 Sqn played mock battles in co-operation with the Army and with RAF Armoured Car units in Palestine, we emplaned troops and reinforced airfields with armed soldiery, giving them short flights that always made them horribly sick.

Halfway through this practice camp set beside the blue Mediterranean we were visited by Group Captain McCloughry who had been left behind commanding Heliopolis. He spent Saturday night in our bivouac and after breakfast on Sunday, went for a swim with Philip Mackworth who was in overall charge at Kilo 143. The rest of us were loafing about reading newspapers and magazines in our open-sided marquee.

The sand had been cool to their bare feet as they walked the quarter-mile to the sloping beach; but by the time they decided to return to the Mess tent the sand had become red hot. Someone watching from our tent begged us to look up from our reading. Away in the distance were the sunny silhouettes of Philip's tall figure and McCloughry's short one, hopping and running and then stopping and jumping from one burnt foot to the other under the blazing sun. When we reckoned our bosses had had enough 'punishment', someone was sent to rescue them with some spare slippers.

The nine days passed all too quickly and we returned to our familiar Heliopolis stamping ground, the invigorating open-air life in Palestine, the daily sea bathing and all our friendly inter-squadron banter fading quickly into pleasant memories. By September the UK delegation at Geneva were mooting the imposition of oil sanctions against Italy, but there was reluctance from the French who feared an Italian incursion along the Riviera; so nothing was done. As if to emphasise its unhelpful international isolation, the United

States now passed a Neutrality Act which was underscored by a certain Mr Ricketts, an American oil magnate, who won a concession to supply oil to Abyssinia and was given the VIP treatment wherever he went in the Middle East.

No 216 Sqn now planned to evacuate embassy staffs from Addis Ababa to Berbera in British Somalia, adopting Aden as our temporary base. Accordingly, two Victorias left on a proving flight to that hot hell-spot, using extra tanks inside the cabin to get enough range to fly round Italian territory. After that, we stood by for further action, but once more nothing materialised. It was also decided to husband our squadron resources by reducing flying programmes to the minimum and to conserve aircraft serviceabilty. 'Swanning' jaunts to Aboukir were definitely out.

Regia Aeronautica traffic through Almaza airport increased and when two sons of Mussolini sailed through the Canal to join their troops, the Italian Cairo embassy laid on free excursions for expat Italians from all over Egypt to Port Said to assemble a massive welcome to speed the Mussolinis on their way. The rent-a-mob chanted: 'Who does Abyssinia belong to? Italy!' An Egyptian in the crowd foolishly shouted: 'And who does the sea belong to? The fishes!' and was nearly lynched on the spot. Tut, tut! No sense of humour.

I now stood in as Squadron Adjutant for an exhilarating three weeks. Gas-masks were issued and, as we had foreseen, as soon as the monsoon rains stopped falling on the Abyssinian highlands, Il Duce declared war on 3 October. To the growing consternation of the British Forces in Egypt, newspapers from home – still determined to turn a blind eye on the deteriorating international scene – insisted that this Italian colonial conflict was merely a sideshow and of no real consequence. In fact, it was of course the death knell of the League of Nations.

Five very old Fairey IIIFs were scraped up from Amman, Helwan, Khartoum and Aboukir, the dregs of Nos 14, 45 and 47 Squadrons and of the Depot. Already clapped out and being replaced, they were given to Squadron Leader (later Air Chief Marshal Sir Gerald) 'Gobbo' Gibbs MC. Two 216 Sqn Victorias then convoyed this ragbag the 2,500 miles from Egypt to Nairobi, where they were to start an indefinite RAF detachment in November 1935. One of the IIIFs had to ditch with engine failure in the impassable 'sudd' of the Bahr el Jebel, where the White Nile becomes a swamp of about the same area as England and Wales. The two-man crew was lucky to be rescued alive four days later by a ground party that had great difficulty in finding them. The remainder flew on via Juba, 'crossed the

Line' at Kisumu and then had to climb to an anoxic 13,000ft to clear the high ridges of the Rift Valley, before dropping down to the Athi Plain where they landed at 5,600ft asl on the 900 yards of 'murram' laid on the green grass of the Game Reserve that comprised Nairobi airfield. They were in sight of Kilimanjaro, Africa's highest peak, the 19,565-ft icy white inverted pudding-basin 120 miles south, while 100 miles north on the Equator, they could also see Mt Kenya's 17,041ft rock fangs peeping over the slowly-rising slopes of the rain forest.

Tents had been pitched for the RAF to keep them from the cold and wet, but their makeshift camp was subject to nightly intrusions by four-legged predators foraging from the Game Reserve which surrounded the airfield. There were no buildings except a flimsy hangar belonging to Wilson Airways and the sprawling wooden bungalow of the Aero Club, consisting mainly of a large bar with a deadly fruit machine that gobbled 5-cent pieces, at 20 to the £. A small committee room with a galley had been generously offered by the Club and gratefully accepted by Squadron Leader Gibbs as a god-sent Mess for the eight RAF officers in his party. But November is one of Kenya's two 'winters' and strong representations had to be made to the colonial secretariat for the Public Works Department, the ubiquitous 'PWD', to produce something more substantial than draughty tents for the Messes of the seven NCOs and our 39 erks.

The officers shivered on camp beds in their tents, swathed in full flying kit at night; but no one else had such warm gear to wear – no leather helmets and no fleece-lined Sidcot suits to sleep in. It was essential to obtain more blankets, if need be from the King's African Rifles (KAR) who were always keen to help. In due course, a set of crude wooden huts like garden sheds were put up and, after a month or so, tents could at last be discarded. For the Royal Air Force, this was the start of a honeymoon relationship with colonial East Africa that was to last, off and on, for the next 28 years until Ke(e)nya was finally handed over to Jomo Kenyatta in December 1963 and became Ken(n)ya. Sadly, the RAF then withdrew from this attractive country to its normally much more mundane and less glamorous locations elsewhere. Like many another honeymoon, a lot of rough edges had to be discovered on both the civilian and Service sides and it took years and years of combined effort to rub off most, if not all of them. There often tended to be a chronic in-built official bureau-cratic lack of comprehension, a parochialism that seemed only too ready to impede the RAF's natural global instincts; but such petty attitudes could usually be overcome by the relentless application of patient diplomacy.

Nairobi in 1935 was very much the wild west town of the movies. Apart from a splendid white stone-faced Government House in the palladian style standing on a hill to the west, the only decent buildings were the Cathedral and the Railway Station, where the capital had once accidentally been founded. The constructors of the line from Mombasa to Uganda, built in the 1900s, ran out of rails on the Athi Plains. This caused a six-month pause, long enough for Indian camp-followers to set up *dukhas* to supply the coolies indentured from India. The Norfolk and Stanley Hotels did their best to keep up appearances and the Nairobi Club offered the more staid Kenya settlers an ambience of cricket, croquet, bridge and billiards. On the other side of town, the straggling Muthaiga Club, with its Grecian architectural pretensions, met the exotic tastes of the more monied and high-born gentry. The rest of Nairobi – bungalows, offices and two hospitals – crowded under rusting corrugated iron roofs, and the unmetalled roads surfaced with red volcanic 'murram' quickly turned into dust-raising furrows and uncomfortable ridges. What saved the city from a total lack of style were its shaded arcades, Indian bazaars and the lovely jacaranda trees blending their mauve with avenues of grey-green eucalyptus – not to mention the graceful Masai, whose copper-coloured, tall Nilotic figures mooched about like living statues. But once into the surrounding suburbs, there were villas with beautiful gardens, green lawns and a profusion of flowering shrubs and trees. Twenty miles west, a skyline of sensuously-curved Ngong Hills invited closer inspection.

Nairobi airfield was four miles outside the town, on an open savannah where herds of zebra, wildebeest, Thompson and Grant gazelle and an occasional water buck grazed contentedly, closely attended by lion, hyena and jackal. Four miles were too far to walk at night with such a high chance of meeting a roving lion so Gobbo borrowed an old truck from the local KAR for ferrying duties after dark; but the cost of beer was beyond the reach of the pockets of our erks whose need for extra pay to match the high cost of living had unfortunately and perhaps even carelessly been overlooked by our paymasters in Cairo and London. The native *askaris* had no such European requirements.

News from the first detachment soon percolated back to Heliopolis where we began to envy our colleagues' tropical adventures. I was therefore delighted to be detailed to convoy another two IIIFs to Nairobi on 9 December 1935 and remain there with my Victoria as a replacement for one that had been written off by Flight Lieutenant Paddy Fagan when trying to land on a tiny airfield on Lamu island in the Indian Ocean. The IIIFs were needed to replace two others that had already failed to cope with the high altitude air-fields and had crashed in the tropical heat. I was going to relieve Maurice Hare, youngest son of a titled General, Old Etonian, ex-bog rat from No 4 FTS and two years my senior in the squadron, who was due home at the end of his overseas tour. Maurice became a test pilot and had a narrow escape in 1937 from a prototype Wellington he inadvertently tested to destruction, finishing a diving trial flight from RAF Martlesham Heath by parachuting into a duck pond!

The 2,400 miles from Heliopolis took 24½ hours' flying and we arrived on 13 December, the whole convoy still happily intact and full of expectation. We must have had reasonably favourable winds for most of the way. Apart from initial breathlessness, my first impression of Kenya was of its amazing greenness and the clarity of its climate. Individual trees could easily be picked out on the slopes of Ol Donyo Sabuk, a large lump of a hill that protruded out of the plain 40 miles away to the east. This incredible visibility was all to our good, for we quickly found the local meteorological information was pretty useless when we left the frequented local air routes. We just had to take chances and hoped to reach our destinations by flying under low clouds and only rarely did a sortie have to be aborted.

Our main task was to reconnoitre the north-eastern borders and to reinforce the small battalions of King's African Rifles in their almost impossible job of preserving the neutrality of the colonial territory by stopping incursions from either of the warring combatants. The threatened frontiers were poorly defined, remote and inaccessible and it was plain there would be plenty of difficulties ahead for us. Aircraft offer opportunities to be exploited by officials and we were always at the beck and call of VIPs and others, cadging air transport. We weren't there to provide lifts for civil servants and Gobbo had his work cut out to fend off unwarranted demands on our meagre resources.

Life in Nairobi in 1935 had to be lived to be believed, for we were lionised by the civilians who were absolutely delighted that some-body actually cared for the integrity of their burgeoning colony. These were the days of the notorious 'Happy Valley' set. The decadents calling the shots were typified by Lord and Lady Carberry, Sir Jock Broughton, Lady Delamere, the Earl of Erroll and the adventuress/aviatrix Beryl Markham who made a serious 'pass' at one of our Flight Lieutenants, later flew the Atlantic solo East to West in September 1936 and was finally lost ferrying an aircraft for the RAF in WW2. The set's Scandinavian crony, Countess Karen von Blixen, had only lately left the scene and to read more about these 'settlers', one must turn to her own *Out of Africa* and to Errol Trzebinski's *The Lives of Beryl Markham*.

As already mentioned, the first RAF arrivals had had a very uncomfortable time in tents. Open to the game reserve, they had nightly visits from hyenas, scavenging for the cookhouse swill, which ran off at the approach of any lion inclined to roam among the tents. Flying Officer Maurice Hare had the alarming experience of being wakened one night by a movement in his tent. Putting out an investigating hand, he found himself stroking the flank of a lion which fortunately then turned away. Little wonder the menu for the RAF 1935 all-ranks' Xmas Dinner sported a lion's head wearing an RAF peaked cap! In fact, big game was a constant nuisance, breaking through the wire fence running round the camp. Small groups of zebra and wildebeest often had to be cleared off the airfield before we ourselves could take off; one gnu in foal actually had a heart attack and dropped dead while being chased away.

Local hospitality knew no bounds and our life in the Aero Club 'Mess' became an alcoholic hazard, for it was the mecca for its members to gather in the evening with wives and friends for mandatory sundowners. Instead of just having to run the gauntlet past the fruit machine in the lounge on our way to breakfast and lunch, it became impossible at weekends to reach our supper without being swept into a round of at least twenty people, all determined to waylay us. The talk was sometimes of flying, but as few of the Club members actually took to the air, we were more often regaled with breathtaking accounts of encounters with big game or stories of the remarkable customs of the Masai, once the all-powerful overlords of all the East African tribes – of which there were said to be no fewer than 16 in Kenya, each with its own dialect. By 1935 the Masai were already in decline, having been deprived of the murder and rapine by which their stock had always been re-vitalised until the advent of Law and Order in 1900.

After we had torn ourselves away from the drinks for a bite of food in our 'Mess', the parties continued into the small hours. On our way to bed, we would often leave four or five club members playing the fruit machine, determined to win the jackpot, which averaged about £50, the container being cleared after every session and totted up by the barman. By the time it had reached £40 it was a fairly safe bet to 'invest' a few shillings, if you could get near enough to play. Sometimes the gamblers lost patience and went home. Then we would try to collect the prize ourselves before breakfast next morning, if it was still there. That was how Freddie Hilton won £75 and bought himself an old 'banger'. One day, on our way to breakfast, three pie-eyed players were still feeding in shillings and at last the five lemons arrived to the happy crash of an avalanche of coins, at the cost of a night's sleep and three bad hangovers.

Hell-fire sessions might develop during any weekend sundowner, taking a cue from the prevailing licentiousness and seemingly induced by heavy drinking at high altitude. At the height of debauchery, the party-goers tended to lose all inhibitions and any-thing could happen – the sky was the limit. On one such night, two young Flying Officers were involved simultaneously with one comely and quite curvaceous wife who blatantly suggested they should all three drive off in her car for a quick tumble. They stopped on a secluded stretch of road in the Game Reserve and she invited them to spin a coin to determine who should have the first turn. The loser, defying lions, walked off down the beam of the headlights and waited until recalled by a flash of the lights, to change places with his friend, who then got out to kick his heels. Afterwards, they all drove back to the party which was still in full swing, to find that Chloe had not been missed by her husband, who was busy with yet another round of drinks. One asks oneself a little incredulously: 'Did it really happen?'

Food in Nairobi market was plentiful and of exceptionally high quality compared with Sudanese and Egyptian fare. Fresh vegeta-bles came down daily from the temperate highlands and up from the tropical areas. Fresh cow's milk, butter, thick cream and excellent cheese were a great treat after the water-buffalo dairy produce we had grown accustomed to in the Middle East. Lamb, beef, chicken and duck were plentiful, supplemented by a variety of game and by such delicacies as kippers and Scotch salmon imported through Mombasa.

Before flying up-country on patrol, it was *de rigueur* to cram our aircraft with crates of 'goodies' from the Nairobi *dukhas*, offloading them on our KAR hosts. They were only too delighted, in exchange, to meet our need for liquid refreshment while we shared the rigours of their remote outposts. The RAF mainly patrolled along the ill-defined borders of Kenya's Northern Frontier District in the Ogaden which stretched north-eastwards over miles of arid waste-land in which the Kenya Government had built a network of landing grounds laboriously cut out of the bush and which entailed flatten-ing hundreds of tall anthills, the skeletons of trees eaten by white ants, the ubiquitous termites. The anthills were stark towers of red concrete-hard mud, mostly inhabited by venomous snakes.

One such clearance in the bush was Ngombo, lying on the plain

2,000ft below Marsabit, a 5,561-ft extinct volcano, itself a delightful green oasis resembling Scotland or North Wales and rising out of the tropical bush, its sides dense forests where elephant, leopard and baboons abounded. Marsabit boasted a green grass airfield and was the headquarters of a District Officer who lived comfortably in the flat-bottomed crater. There was a profusion of flowers such as wild forget-me-nots and I have never seen so many butterflies – it was impossible not to tread on them. Cloud often covered this mountain and made it inaccessible, an unforecast weather predicament only to be discovered on arrival. The need for a cloud-free Ngombo on the arid plain at the foot of Marsabit had been an urgent afterthought.

Further east, Wajir had a 'Beau Geste type' fortress and was the base of the 3rd Battalion KAR. Its landing ground had very soft sand that once had given Canadian Flying Officer Frank Byram a nasty close shave when he tried to get unstuck in the midday heat. The drag of the sand on his wheels was too much and he wrapped his under-powered IIIF round a large tree at the far end of the clearing. Luckily, both he and his air gunner walked away from the wreckage, shaken but only bruised.

North-east, across the rolling bush, another clearance had been hacked out and levelled so that we could land and refuel. It lay 2,000ft beneath Moyale, a sun-baked and castellated fortress perched on the Abyssinian escarpment where Provincial Commissioner Glendaye had his HQ. With our small-scale maps, we hopped, hopefully, over great expanses of featureless bush and black rocky outcrops of the Northern Frontier District to seek obscure outposts like Mandera, at the very apex of the triangle where Kenya meets what were then called Abyssinia and Italian Somaliland and are now Ethiopia and Somaliland.

I was sent off there with Maurice Hare on Boxing Day 1935. A first sortie to such an isolated spot, 400 miles away, was undertaken with some trepidation owing to its reputed invisibility; besides, we had poor maps, no reliable weather forecasts, no radio aids, no astro and no means of communicating from the air with our destination.

We set course for Marsabit, flying round the forest-clad southern shoulder of Mt Kenya. Ngombo had not yet been cleared of bush and we were relieved to find the airfield in Marsabit's extinct volcanic crater was clear of cloud. We refuelled and flew on to the north-east and by and by Moyale could be seen to port, sitting on top of the Abyssinian escarpment. It was the last recognisable landmark we would see for the next 200 miles.

I was glad Maurice had been there once before and knew what to look for. Our maps, compiled by foot-slogging Army surveyors in

1915, were fairly useless and often misleading, for most of the tracks depicted had either moved or disappeared altogether. After three hours, our ETA for Mandera had come and gone, leaving us both anxiously scanning the bush for signs of the little river Daua which might show up against the monotonous bush as a dark green strip of trees and vegetation if the Daua hadn't completely dried up since the last monsoon. At last, 3 hr 35 minutes after leaving Marsabit, the Daua appeared and, in a small clearing, we could just discern two parked IIIFs. Of Mandera village itself there was no sign, as it was cunningly concealed under thick squat thorn trees. However, the great thing was that we had actually arrived and were received with great delight, for we were carrying Xmas mail, which was no less welcome by the three resident English officers for being a day late.

Squadron Leader 'Gobbo' Gibbs was also there to greet us, together with Captain 'Phillipo' Phillips of the Royal Leicesters and his deputy, Lieutenant Freddie 'Kali' (savage) Woolmer of the King's Own. 'Brookie' Brookes of the Kenya Police completed the reception committee. Between them, they commanded a small company of well-trained native troops and police, having trekked up 400 miles from Nairobi into the 'bundu' a few months earlier. Their camp lay a short mile from Abyssinia on the opposite bank of the almost dry Daua river and they had already become accustomed to their tough environment. Like many others, our Army hosts had been voluntarily seconded from their regiments for two years to repair their personal finances: hardship pay and very limited spending opportunities made it easier to save. The case of Brookie was somewhat different – he had been rusticated from a civilised Mombasa police post for daring to make matrimonial suggestions to the daughter of a high-ranking colonial official.

At Mandera we were within earshot of the Italian Army who were busily strengthening their barbed wire defences against possible night attacks by 'Habash' irregulars, notorious for various unpleasant practices. The Italians hammered away until dark. After unloading all the perishable goodies and not forgetting the kippers, of which there is nothing dearer to the heart of any British exile, we saw that our erks were being taken into good care and then walked to the camp, a collection of thatched huts behind barbed wire fences – designed to keep out hyenas. The Officers' Mess comprised a rambling hut made of anthill mud, built without nails, screws, bricks, glass or doors and thatched with dom palm leaves. Inside was a general store and a large oil-fired refrigerator capable of freezing the local river water. It went by the name of Kali Castle and, by day, offered the cover of shade; but at dusk everyone moved outside to relax, eat, drink and sleep under the open sky. Mandera was hot and dry in December and life off duty could always be much improved by cool drinks laced, after sundown, with gin or whisky.

Incredibly, Kali Castle also gave shelter to a huge gramophone from the firm of E. M. Ginn of Grape Street, London WC2. Powered by the smoothest-running Garrard spring motor, it had a grotesque 7ft-long exponential papier-mâché horn, designed to amplify the output of the triangular-cut fibre needles used in its sound-box to reduce groove wear. Kali Woolmer owned this monster and it spoke volumes for his musical enthusiasm as he had had it carried for hundreds of miles through the bush on camelback! Long before the advent of electronic hi-fi, this large hand-made EMG was the unrivalled music machine of the early 'thirties. Steeped in musical appreciation all my life – my very keen brother Jack had even fixed an extension speaker in our loo(!) – I had already heard EMG's more modest table model in a friend's flat in Bloomsbury; but a mud hut in the Ogaden at 4°N and 42°E was the last place to meet this connoisseur's rarity. 'Coco', Woolmer's batman, had been taught to wind it up, cut the triangular-section fibre needles and change the records.

As soon as we had sorted ourselves out, our hosts said there was still just time for a swim if we would like one. We jumped at the idea, scrambled into a waiting truck and, after ten minutes of bouncing along a dusty bush track, came to the brink of a shallow cliff and pulled up overlooking a large pool which was all that was left of the River Daua. Fifty feet away on the far bank was Abyssinia. We had been preceded by a fatigue party of askaris who were now busily filtering water from the river by scooping out troughs in the coarse-grained sand near the edge of the water. The clean water was then poured into long 'fantassies' or oblong water tanks to be taken back to camp strapped on grumbling camels. It took no time to strip off under the dom palms and soon a motley group of black and white men were making for the pool. We were gently restrained by our hosts to let the askaris dash on ahead, rushing into the water up to their waists, shouting and splashing and tearing up and down the pool like madmen. 'What's that all about?' I asked in puzzlement. 'Oh' was the reply, 'you never know – the river's full of crocs when it's in spate. They're supposed to dig themselves down into the river bed when the water table falls but we like to make sure before we go in!' After that, we waded rather gingerly forward, washing off the stains of the day in the soft, cool water and gaining confidence with every step taken by our hosts in front.

Back at the camp and greatly refreshed, we pitched our canvas camp beds on the sand outside the Mess and pulled camp chairs round a rough wooden table. An incandescent lamp was hung from a nearby tree and, as darkness fell, a brushwood fire was kindled, throwing showers of sparks into the now cool night air as a warning to any four-footed marauders lurking in the shadows beyond the lamplight. While an African batman in a white *khansu* passed round deliciously cold drinks, the news and gossip from Nairobi was eagerly exchanged for happenings on the local battle front. Evidently, the Italians were digging themselves in and showing much more anxiety than aggression towards the Habash. It was great to relax on our camp beds, drinks in hand, while appetising smells drifted from the mud hut where *mpishi* was juggling on a wood-burning stove with our latest contributions to supper. The *bwanas* had wrapped themselves in thin cotton kilts of gaily coloured checks, the required men's evening wear at Mandera which had been offered to us by our thoughtful hosts. No need to worry about mos-quitos – it was too dry. The sky overhead deepened to a black velvet, blazing with a myriad stars, while an occasional familiar whooping of a hyena broke the background hush.

We wanted to know how our hosts had coped with life in the wild-erness before the RAF had come on the scene and we were intrigued to learn how they were able to cope, so remote from any workshop, for maintenance of their rather aged, albeit rugged transport. If and when a truck broke down, the driver had been taught to go, parrot-fashion, through a long routine of 'stoppages', just as if he was dealing with a machine-gun. Stoppage No 1 was when the engine failed or wouldn't start: the first remedy was to check the fuel tank. If it contained fuel, Stoppage No 2 called for the petrol feed-pipe to be checked for fracture. Stoppage No 3 required the carburettor to be dismantled and the jet cleaned. The system continued until the fault was found, covering every known contingency. The drivers were trained to strip down the entire engine by 'numbers', though none could read a single word.

Grilled talarpia, a fish from the Daua, was shortly set upon the table, followed by roast gedab – local wild guineafowl – with green vegetables, pineapple and cream fresh from Nairobi. At this point 'Coco' started an enchanting concert on the EMG with Tchaikovsky's *Swan Lake* recorded by the Boston Symphony Orchestra under Arturo Toscanini, followed by a pre-selected pile of 78s. Talk about Desert Island Discs . . . this was only 1935! Romantic music, classical and popular, poured incongruously out of the mud hut into the tropical night. It was magical to lie under the stars, Orion, the Plough and the unfamiliar Southern Cross, listening now to music, now to mysterious stirrings in the African bush. But oblivion soon carried us away: it had been a long day.

Next morning, after an early bite, all three aircraft left for a recce 90 miles westwards up the Daua as far as the police post at Malka Murri and then on round the border to Moyale. Here we made a call on the Provincial Governor, Glendaye. We lunched on cold roast sand grouse and afterwards admired the view into Abyssinia from the battlements of his *boma*. Then we were driven back down to the airfield on the plain below and set course for Marsabit, to stay the night there with the DO in his very remarkable green mountain oasis. Maurice, who had a very ruddy complexion, did his best during the night to live up to his nickname of 'Flying Officer Flare'. Taking a last smoke in bed, he had a final 'drag' and then dropped the still-burning butt over his head, as he thought, on to the earth floor. And so to sleep. The live stub had fallen short and landed on the end of his mattress of cork chips which quietly began to smoulder. When it was glowing from end to end, the canvas bed gave way under his weight and Maurice awoke to find himself being cremated.

But the following morning held some very unpleasant surprises for us. Hardly had we gathered for a quick pre-flight snack and a cup of tea for breakfast than my wireless operator, who had opened up a watch with Nairobi, hastened back with the news that Flying Officer Francis and his air gunner, Corporal Bryant, had both been killed on the previous afternoon in a flying accident while testing the IIIF detailed to replace us at Mandera. We flew back to Nairobi in sombre spirits and on arrival I was surprised to see my fellow Victoria still tethered to its pickets – as, by rights, it should have been on its way to Mandera with a load of goodies from the dukhas, with my boss 'Paddy' Fagan at the helm. But I supposed his sortie must have been delayed by the previous afternoon's accident and I taxied up alongside the parked 'Vic' and switched off. One of our erks climbed onboard, opened the window behind me and asked if I had heard the news?

I assured him that I had – thinking he meant the Francis/Bryant prang; but he still persisted. On being quizzed further, he went on to say that Flight Lieutenant Fagan, leader of No 216 Sqn's detachment, had just bumped himself off inside the adjacent aircraft. Paddy, a qualified flying instructor with 1914/18 ribbons on his tunic, had been inconsolably depressed by being held personally responsible by a Court of Inquiry into the prang at Lamu. Fearing his career had come to an end, he had taken the 12-bore we carried for emergencies and put it in his mouth. Our little Mess had suddenly been stricken down from eight carefree members to six very unhappy ones. The smell of blood from inside Paddy's parked Victoria attracted hyenas from the Game Reserve and they howled around it all night.

After attending three Service funerals next morning, each complete with its firing squad, I took off without delay in Paddy's aircraft which had been hurriedly cleaned up, heading back to Mandera with a new load of supplies and a heavy heart, this time deciding to stage into the bundu through Wajir, a three-hour intermediate hop. Visibility was on its best behaviour and I was able to measure the drift easily to maintain the required track over the ground, passing well to the south of Mt Kenya and heading eastwards across the featureless bush where, many years later, the Adamsons lived with Elsa the lioness and where both were eventually murdered.

It was a clear day so I felt fairly confident of finding the white-washed mud walls of the KAR fortress at 1° North 40° East and only 600ft above sea-level. This was where I would refuel before a final two-hour dash to Mandera, following the Somali frontier near el Wak, from where it ran north-east in a straight line cut through the bush. At Wajir I was able to off-load the mail and a large consignment of kippers, dairy produce, fresh fruit, vegetables and newspapers – recent copies of the *East African Standard* and a selection from the UK – to maintain the health and morale of the tiny KAR garrison. I took a quick look at the twisted remains of Frank Byram's IIIF to see if there was anything to salvage but found that human vultures had already stripped it bare. The day had grown very hot and we gladly retired into the shade of the thick walls of the fort, to be plied with ice-cold soft drinks. Our hosts were, as usual, eager to hear the latest scandals from distant Nairobi before we quickly departed once more into the blinding heat. We taxied over the very soft sand to the far corner of the landing ground and, with both engines going flat out and a much lighter load, cleared the trees on the far side, did a low-level circuit to wave good-bye and set off for el Wak, little more than a crossing of tracks in the bush. As the visibility remained good, we found what we were looking for and picked up the well-defined frontier cut through the bush between Kenya and Somalia which led us up to Mandera dead on ETA in the gathering dusk.

After my first visit, this sortie was a piece of cake. 'Phillipo' Phillips had lit brushwood fires round the airfield to indicate which way the wind was blowing – a helpful ploy – and he was eagerly waiting for us. With co-pilot Sergeant Allsop and my crew of three erks, we were going to spend the next week patrolling the Daua river frontier with Abyssinia. The camp's off-duty, relaxed life style unfolded every evening, starting with a swim and followed by leisurely iced drinks, a first-class dinner and, finally, grand music to lull us to sleep under the stars. What more could we want? Many would have gladly exchanged their urban hassle for a night such as this.

On New Year's day, having seen in 1936 with due ceremony at Kali Castle, eating our hosts' caviar and drinking their champagne, against a background of Beethoven, Brahms, Schubert and Dvorak on the EMG, we all went down before breakfast to cool our heads in the Daua. Hardly had we reached the water than a commotion started in the bush on the Abyssinian bank. Looking towards the noise, we found we were staring down the wrong ends of the barrels of half a dozen rifles levelled at us by red-turbaned Eritrean troops of the Italian Army. Somewhere in the background we could hear a motor vehicle. Then some camels appeared and, finally, a fine-looking pony was led down to the river to be watered.

A rapid and undignified retreat in our birthday suits to the cover of our bank was the order of the day. To our surprise, no shots were fired – the Eritreans presumably saw from the colour of our skins that we were European – but for the next half hour we watched with increasing curiosity while a place was cleared for a table overlooking our bathing pool. Four highly decorated Italian officers presently sat down for an *al fresco* cold meal and a bottle of wine was opened to toast the New Year. The bodyguard crouched defensively on the bank, glaring at us, while a few Blackshirts scrambled down into the river and scooped up water in their topees to drink.

Satisfied we weren't going to be shot at, we resumed our interrupted bathe, now only yards away from the bewildered conscripts. Then we waded ashore, dressed as nonchalantly as possible and left the intruders to get on with their invasion while we went back to camp for breakfast. We had just witnessed the start of the Italian advance from the Ogaden into Abyssinia, no doubt at the impatient insistence of Il Duce.

Our daily routine at Mandera started by rising very early and taking off as soon as there was enough light to see the airfield boundaries. We would then fly ninety miles west along the river, peering down into the bush and noting anything we considered significant, such as concentrations of livestock, encampments of tribesmen or any unusual activities. Looking into the bush from ground-level, it was impossible to see more than a few yards in any direction, but from the air one could spot wandering groups of nomads unless they were hiding under thick acacia trees; even then, their flocks gave away their position.

The marauding Italian Air Force shot and bombed non-combatant tribesmen whenever they came across them in the bush. These poverty-stricken nomads were in a most unenviable predicament, for they were also attacked by the Habash, their natural enemies from the Abyssinian highlands. If they tried to evade trouble by crossing the Daua river southwards, as they had done since time immemorial, searching for grazing before the artificial colonial lines had been drawn on the map, they were picked up by the Kenya border police, and if they persisted in their illicit search for water, grazing and now for safety, their flocks could be confiscated and they themselves imprisoned.

We seldom saw anything suspicious going on, but were ourselves sometimes shadowed by a gleaming, part metal-bodied Caproni 133 monoplane of the Regia Aeronautica, keeping an eye on us! Its sleek modern lines put our bumbling old Victoria to shame and when the Italian pilot became tired of trying to formate on us, hanging in the air on his three variable-pitch propellers at our paltry 105 mph, he would open his throttles and speed happily away at 140 mph. But I doubt if any Caproni 133 would have survived what happened to our trusty old war-horse during the recce on my third day at Mandera.

We had been airborne at 7 am and had reached the tiny British outpost at Ramu, 50 miles up the Daua, where two Kenya police officers were holding the fort alone. Nearby was a very small airfield and I was surprised to see a coded signal had been put out on the ground for me to read. This was basically in the form of a large wooden 'T' painted white and pointing into wind, with white discs placed round it in various positions, each combination of 'T' and discs – of which there were a dozen or so – having a distinctive message decipherable by using the crib carried in our cockpit. My cue showed I was being asked to 'Land for Information', a request I could scarcely ignore in the circumstances, though the airfield looked extremely small and tricky. A smudge fire had been lit in one corner but the wind was obviously only a light easterly, of very little help in reducing landing speed. I would have to make the most of it and so chose the long west-east diagonal which meant touching-down facing the rising sun.

During the last few moments of my approach, gliding at just above stalling speed and now staring straight into the dazzling sun, I was horrified to see a large tree suddenly appear directly ahead; fifty feet tall and almost on the edge of the airfield. The tree had been completely camouflaged by the surrounding grey-green bush and I, inescapably committed to landing, was certainly going to hit it! But instinct comes to the rescue in tight corners. The only thing to do was to minimise the impact, so I kicked on hard left rudder to skid in a flat turn to port and continued for a second or two gliding towards the fast-approaching ground. We clouted the tree at 60 mph, safely out-board from our starboard engine and propeller, but swinging us violently to starboard. I was just able to straighten up before touching down which avoided wiping off our fragile undercarriage and we then taxied to where a car was waiting. The prang could easily have been far worse, but I had a very red face when I climbed back into the cabin to meet my rueful crew. I had torn 17 yards of fabric and broken numerous aluminium former-ribs on the leading edge of the lower starboard wing.

My first question to the two Kenya police officers, waiting at the car, was to ask rather irritably what information they had got. Awkwardly, they said they had nothing to tell me – on the contrary, all they wanted to know was, 'Would I like some breakfast?' The T-and-disc system of ground-to-air communication clearly had its limitations, not to say its serious ambiguities! I decided we would take advantage of their hospitality, before tackling the tedious repairs that lay ahead. Over breakfast, our hosts reported that we regularly attracted small-arms fire from the local Habash irregulars every time we flew over Ramu. We had, of course, heard nothing from the air and had no bullet holes to show them. They had remonstrated with the Greek commander, but he admitted he could not control his men and anyway all aeroplanes looked the same to them!

It was now time to attend to our damage and first we had to check there were no cracks in the main wing spars. Then the rigger produced his box of tricks and handed out five sail-makers' needles. Semi-circular in shape, they enabled thread to be pushed through one side of a tear and to emerge on the other. With all five of us madly sewing away, it still took a very long time to draw all the torn edges of fabric together. After doping the stitched scars, bands of new linen selvage were pasted over the joins and more dope applied on top.

The aluminium former-ribs in the leading edge of the starboard lower wing, which had taken most of the shock, were carefully bent back into shape, those beyond repair being replaced by springy twigs which we cut from thorn trees on the edge of the airfield and whittled into shape before wiring them into position. Once they had been covered with new fabric and doped over, you could hardly tell the difference between our makeshifts and the original ribs. Repairs took four hours to complete, after which we were offered and gratefully accepted lunch.

At 2.30 pm I climbed onboard with Sgt Allsop, started up the engines and prudently taxied for the maximum take-off run, having previously measured it as a measly 360 paces. Leaving the crew behind for their safety, a quick five-minute circuit proved that everything was OK and I landed again, happy to report there were no snags. Taking my crew onboard once more, I then flew pensively back to Mandera, this time with my tail very much between my legs. There followed an exchange of W/T signals with Nairobi and from there with Heliopolis and I had visions of impending disgrace; but all was forgiven. Further inspection of the damage and of our repairs confirmed that Vic 1314 was still completely serviceable and we were allowed to complete our planned missions before returning to Nairobi.

This was all to the good, because Lieutenant Kali Woolmer announced in a moment of financial unease that he wanted to sell his EMG to raise funds to buy a licence to shoot a lion on which he had now set his heart. Transport of the gramophone and horn was going to be a problem for any buyer and severely restricted Woolmer's already thin seller's market. If the huge bell-mouth horn would go through my cabin door, I could buy it; I did and, for £10, became the shy owner of this fantastic contraption and its collection of 78s. Future Nairobi nights would be filled with splendid sounds; its removal to Egypt and eventually to England were problems for another day. This much-travelled hi-fi, now with a modified two-part horn, was sold in 1950 to a Welsh schoolmaster for £30 and must now be quite a valuable antique.

No sooner had I been relieved at Mandera by Flying Officer Freddie Hilton than 4,000 Eritrean troops mutinied, shot their officers and tried to give themselves up as political refugees. They had previously been serving far from home in Libya, had then been shipped to Mogadishu and finally told they were going to fight the British in Kenya, an idea that didn't bother them. But by the time they had marched 200 miles through Somali bush up to the Ogaden, followed by the Italian Blackshirts who rode comfortably in trucks, they found to their dismay they were expected to fight against the Abyssinians who were nearly their own kith and kin. The Eritreans became bitterly disillusioned. They hadn't been paid since arriving in Somaliland and were rationed only every three days.

At Mandera, and later on at Ramu, they could see the British and their askaris actually enjoying life! They decided to desert across the frontier but only 400 managed to make it to Kenya. The Blackshirts disarmed the others, marched them off and left them to starve to death in the bush. The lucky ones posed a serious problem to feed and had to be moved from the area of conflict to prevent the Italians from following them into the Northern Frontier District to take revenge. General Graziani issued pamphlets asking anyone who came across them to cut off their heads to save him the trouble. So they were trucked to a hastily-built concentration camp at Isiolo, on the equatorial north-eastern grassy slopes of Mt Kenya, safe for the time being and held there until they could be absorbed into jobs in Kenya Colony.

VI

Kenya Interlude

THE EARLY days and months of 1936 unfolded in Kenya with unexpected inquisitions. In response to our recent tragedies and to continued failures of our IIIFs to cope with the high-level tropical environment, we became the object of a staff visit by Air Chief Marshal Sir Robert Brooke-Popham, who had been appointed AOC-in-C in Cairo for the emergency and who wanted to know just what we had all been up to. This prospect filled us with some unease and none more so than our strict and efficient CO, Gobbo Gibbs, whose professional leadership in difficult circumstances left absolutely nothing to be desired, as far as we could see.

The AOC-in-C naturally asked to be shown over the bounds of our parish and on one of his earliest sorties went off as a passenger in a Victoria to call on Glendaye, the Provincial Commissioner at Moyale, and to spend a night with him on the Abyssinian border. All went swimmingly until next morning when Sir Robert and his ADC climbed into Glendaye's official car to be driven down to the airfield to fly off to Mandera, his next port of call. The sight of all the 'scrambled egg' on the peak of the Air Chief Marshal's hat so over-awed the native driver that, on reaching the top of the very steep hill leading down from the escarpment, he muffed the precautionary change into low gear and hurtled downhill out of control in neutral. The snag lay ahead at the bottom where the track did a sharp turn round a boulder the size of a house. The car went smack into it, threw the AOC-in-C heavily against his luggage and broke his arm. Fortunately, the aircraft was ready waiting for him to board and he was whipped back to Nairobi within four hours of the accident. This brought an untimely end to his programme, for Sir Robert was admitted to hospital in a state of shock and languished there for a week. During this enforced inactivity he was visited by numerous kindly notables among whom was the wife of the Colonial Secretary, who bluntly told him nobody believed his story of a motor accident. Everyone in Kenya 'knew' he had really been involved in a plane crash and that the pilot was drunk.

The death of King George V that month had cast a respectful

cloud over the usual goings-on at the Aero Club. So when, a few days later, Sir Robert was our guest in the little Mess there, to say goodbye and to speed him on his way by Imperial Airways with his arm in a sling, we didn't have to run the gauntlet with him through the background clamour which normally permeated the entire building.

Over dinner, he recounted his hospital conversations and vowed he would never again believe any rumours coming out of Kenya reflecting on our small but dedicated unit. He went so far as to say he was proud of what the detachment had achieved with our obsolete aircraft.

In late February, heavy rains started to fall more or less continuously, bringing out millions of croaking frogs around our camp and making life more difficult for the 'Ities' advancing half-heartedly into Abyssinia. The threat to Kenya of an invasion from either side was clearly beginning to recede.

At this point we were visited by Sir Alan Pim, an elderly economist from the Colonial Office, who turned up in Nairobi dressed in Edwardian-style knee breeches over spindly legs, his wizened face giving him the appearance of an old-fashioned country grocer rather than of a Government sleuth. He looked a bit too frail for the rigours of the tropics.

Sir Alan had come to re-assess Overseas Allowances for the European elements of the Army serving in Kenya and also, by inference, for the RAF. Nothing could have made him more warmly welcome. The cash allowances for all ranks had been left behind by the rising cost of living in the colony. Naturally, this investigator was the target of intense lobbying and we in our Victorias were particularly well placed to put our own case forward, as we had the task of flying him around so that he could taste life in the 'bundu' at first hand.

I took him on a four-day tour, stopping off at Marsabit, Moyale and Wajir. As usual, we loaded up with fresh produce for all our friends in the 'bush' but with so many crates there was barely room for him to sit with the crew in the cabin. Mt Kenya was spectacular at close quarters and guaranteed suitably to impress my distinguished passenger. It could sometimes be very bumpy, cruising at our normal Kenya anoxic altitude of 10,000ft above sea-level and by bad luck we flew into extreme air turbulence. The cabin passengers were safely strapped in their seats but one down-current was so violent it made all the crates leap off the floor and several landed back on top of Sir Alan whose knobbly knees took some nasty knocks.

This was a pretty poor start and he looked ruefully at me when we took off from Moyale next morning. But when we arrived at Wajir, I was whisked off by the junior KAR officers to the mud-walled fortress for lunch in the Mess where they gleefully described how they intended to impress our elderly 'nark' with their hardship so as to justify the award of higher hardship allowances.

Sir Alan had been discreetly taken away by the CO who had volunteered to entertain the VIP at a luncheon *à deux* in the hottest room of the fortress where they were both treated to the toughest of old goat that could be found. In another room, shaded and cool, I was being offered the choicest venison.

He fared rather better at Mandera where Phillipo had managed to shoot some sand grouse for dinner which was served in the open space outside Kali Castle, after the mandatory evening splash in the Daua river, for which Sir Alan had not been sartorially prepared and had made do in his long-johns.

Champagne, caviare and port were all carefully kept out of sight for another day but it had been impossible to conceal the magic of a night under the stars even without classical music.

Any sympathies I had secretly felt for Sir Alan were later completely dispelled when our carefully conducted air tours of operational areas of the colony for his personal enlightenment produced a new pay award of a miserly two extra shillings a day for all ranks. In the absence of any local NAAFI, such largesse meant our erks could now buy themselves a second daily bottle of locally-brewed Tusker beer. Big deal!

The war moved steadily north, away from the borders of Kenya, and our flying support became less needed by the KAR. At the same time, it became obvious that the probable success of the Italians in seizing Abyssinia would leave them in a strong strategic position on the eastern flanks of the Sudan, Uganda and Kenya, not to mention a potential stranglehold on the Red Sea, a vital artery of the British Empire. So, although life on Nairobi airfield had grown very quiet by March, the Air Ministry, with a view to possible future requirements, decided to make the RAF presence in Kenya a fairly stable one. Our reliefs would serve there on a yearly basis.

I had been kept busy as Mess President, Mess Treasurer and Mess Secretary all rolled into one. The end of the month was always hectic and we began to look forward to having our own premises, due to be built in April.

With Flying Officer Johnnie Johnson, I planned to attack Kilimanjaro which was reputedly only a walk – albeit a long and taxing one – up to its breathless glacial crest. According to legend, it had the distinction of once having been given by Queen Victoria as a birthday or Christmas present to her covetous grandson, Wilhelm II of Germany, who later became the hated Kaiser of 1914/18. To please his vanity, she had the map drawn so that the highest African peak was included in his German East African colony of Tanganyika. Our plans included a sporty local young lady of some twenty years who was keen to make the attempt but she fell ill and the scheme collapsed when Johnnie was posted back to Khartoum.

As I was no rock-climber, the icy rock fangs of Mt Kenya were well beyond my scope, though they succumbed on 22 November that same year to one of my co-pilots, Pilot Officer Jim Irens. He was a rugby full-back and a gentle giant whose hulk was not that of an obvious mountaineer; but he proudly added his own name to six others in a tin at the top. Wyn Harris and Eric Shipton had used its testing 17,000ft as nursery slopes before making their 1935 failed attempt on Mt Everest. There were other diversions available to me.

RAF Kenya
Monday 9 March 1936

My dear Mum and Dad,
I only just managed to catch the Air Mail with my last short note, so here goes for a fuller account of the past week.

Things remain monotonously quiet these days and, apart from a few test flights and routine exercises like practising bombing, dropping supplies by parachute, forced landings and formation flying, there is very little real work for us. There are of course always things to do around the camp and I am always tied up with the Mess accounts at the end of the month, which I find pretty boring.

The weather has improved lately and we've had some lovely sunny days, quite warm considering the altitude. But the rain is still hanging about and sudden storms cause great havoc when as much as an inch of rain falls in two hours!

Jan, a South African friend who has a job in Nairobi with Royal Exchange Insurance and owns a super Auburn safari car, went up country with me last weekend, picking me up from camp after lunch on Saturday. He drove as fast as he could, as the sky looked very threatening, but even so we failed to reach our destination in the dry.

We were heading north to a farm in the hills east of Lake Naivasha in the Rift Valley which is a great geological fault that runs all the way up the Red Sea and the Dead Sea to the Sea of Galilee. The farmer, a friend of Jan's, had asked him to help shoot lions that were killing his sheep and I was very kindly included in the invitation.

First we climbed for about 30 miles to get to the top of the Escarpment, 3,000ft above Nairobi. All the way up we passed

91

'shambas' growing coffee and wattle (used in tanning) or fields of pyrethrum, whose white flowers produce insecticide.

We dropped down to the bottom of the valley, leaving all cultivation behind us and drove for miles through really wild country, past masses of game and many kinds of large birds. An extinct volcano called Longonot towered spectacularly like a sentinel on our left as we sped along.

Before reaching the village of Naivasha, we turned off to the east to leave 'High Street Africa' and started climbing the Escarpment again. The country hereabouts resembles Scotland on a huge scale and at this point the heavens opened and the rain started to pelt down.

We hadn't gone five miles up the steep track before our wheels began spinning ineffectively in deep mud, so I got out to push the car sideways on to drier ground. After a good deal of panting and shoving on my part, the wheels at last found some grass and the car shot away up the hill and out of sight, leaving me to walk alone in the pouring rain to an unknown destination in country alleged to be lion-infested!

After following the car tracks for 15 minutes I turned a corner to find Jan was stuck in the mud again about 50 yards from the crest of the hill. This time rescue was impossible and we both set off on foot to walk and flounder the remaining three miles to his friends' farm, where their bullocks would be available to pull the car out.

I was wet to the skin long before we arrived, but a hot bath in water the colour of coffee, followed by several whiskies and sodas consumed in front of a blazing log fire, soon put us both to rights. 25 lions were reported to be in the neighbourhood and, only a fortnight ago, they had killed 170 sheep in a single night, just for devilment. But the weather was so wet and beastly raw outside, we decided, with faint hearts, not to go out after them! Besides, our host Johansen and his wife, her sister and their two young kids were all so charming, we lamely just turned in after eating a pleasant farmhouse supper with them.

Next morning, two cars drove up across the moors. The rain had stopped and when the sun came out we felt quite warm again. The visitors had come from the next-door farm, eight miles away, and in their car was a lion they had shot during the night near the track we had walked along. I took photos of the trophy – its teeth were as long as my middle finger and the mane was unusually fine.

We left for Nairobi in the afternoon loaded with food for the Mess – mushrooms, cheddar cheese at only one shilling [5p] a pound, a sack of potatoes (200lb for three shillings – 15p) and with a gazelle we had shot for the pot. By and by, another deluge turned our road into a torrent that showed every sign of washing us away. We just had to sit and wait for it to stop.

Sure enough, after a while the torrent subsided and Jan resumed driving, picking his way round huge potholes washed out of the surface. Suddenly what we both at first took to be a hyena got up and lollopped along about 100 yards ahead. But when we caught up with it we saw it was a leopard.

Jan jumped on the brakes, grabbed his rifle and leapt out, but before he could draw a bead on it, the leopard had run into a thicket. Ignoring my cries of caution, Jan continued the pursuit, while I stumbled up behind to give him cover with a 12-bore. But it had quite disappeared and, to my relief, Jan gave up the chase: cornered leopards are said to be highly dangerous and, like buffalo, are apt to hunt the hunter.

We reached camp well after dark but it had been most enjoyable to taste a little of the life of a settler. I only hope Jan will be able to offer a repeat performance. Next time we will take chains for the tyres to cope with mud.

A fortnight after penning this letter I was not at all surprised to be recalled to Heliopolis. The Kenya situation had become too relaxed to justify the continued detachment of two of No 216 Sqn's aircraft, when things were on the boil elsewhere. I was instructed to hand over my various duties by the end of March and fly back with Freddie Hilton who was tour-expired. After many farewells and a final dinner with mess-mates, we signed off and were waved goodbye by tall and indefatigable adjutant-cum-general panjandrum, Flight Lieutenant Jock Lambie. He was one of a rare breed of really helpful accountant officers and had won everybody's respect by not being just a financial nitpicker. One of the first to be detached for duty at Nairobi, he was a burly, efficient and broad-minded officer who had weathered many a local storm on our behalf.

At 04. 55 am on 1 April 1936, with 15 personnel on board, Freddie Hilton and I left the little RAF base on the green Athi Plain and set off for sandy Egypt, little dreaming that, ten years later, I would be back as second-in-command of a very much enlarged 'parish' of the RAF in post-war East Africa and that Freddie would have won a DFC, then had a spell as PoW and, back in 'Civvy Street', would have become Commandant first of Bovingdon and then of Hurn Airports.

It would normally have been a laborious journey down almost the entire length of the Nile via Kisumu, near its Lake Victoria exit at Jinja. But our spirits were high and the aircraft seemed to want to fly itself to Juba and to Malakal, reaching Khartoum for the night. Then on we went next day to Atbara and Wadi Halfa, with a very pleasant night-stop at Luxor before we reached Heliopolis for lunch on 4 April after a leisurely late take-off and a familiar hop of four hours. The 2,400 miles had taken 27 hours in the air and required seven refuelling stops. Winds and weather had been fairly kind but, as so often happens, it had seemed much easier flying back home than going the other way. Something to do with a homing instinct?

Freddie Hilton had been jubilant all the way north; he was being posted to Central Flying School to qualify as a flying instructor. He was saturnine, handsome, well-built and boxed as a welterweight in which class he showed a quite outstanding elegance. Besides all this, he had great hopes of soon getting married. By the outbreak of WW2, he had become the Chief Flying Instructor at the Hullavington FTS. Then he joined Bomber Command and won his DFC. One night he had a most spectacular escape. His aircraft was shot down over the Ruhr and he ordered his crew to bale out. As captain he was the last one to go, but his parachute had scarcely opened when, almost simultaneously, he found himself unscathed standing on the ground. He was promptly captured and, being a Wing Commander, was given a responsible position as the senior British PoW officer in his *Stalagluft* until the fall of Germany.

We had returned to find Heliopolis full of newcomers. Squadrons had arrived in Egypt for the emergency, some having come ashore from Royal Navy carriers. But the 'flap' was now subsiding and gradually our visitors departed. Sadly, many old comrades had gone home since December and getting to know new faces required uncomfortable re-adjustment.

The weather now grew unseasonably hot. The citrus harvest had been gathered in Palestine and grapefruit had become ridiculously cheap at four to' the piastre, the equivalent of a penny today. The Arab fruit-growers were, however, free for the next few months to start violent protests at the relentless Zionist invasion of Palestine, the land of their birth and of their culture for nearly 2,000 years. Widespread riots broke out between both sides and the hapless British officials found themselves in the middle, trying to keep the peace. At the time, their efforts seemed to me to lack resolution.

No 216 Sqn was immediately implicated and stood by to fly reinforcements from Egypt to strengthen the garrisons at Haifa and Jerusalem. At the same time, we flew No 64 Fighter Squadron personnel from Heliopolis to Ismailia for stand-by.

An unusual cargo of 15 RAF wireless operators, complete with their mobile equipment, had to be collected from the Ismailia Signals centre and flown to the hair-raising airfield at Ramleh, which started at the bottom of a steep hill, went up over the top and blindly down the other side. The W/Ops were being sent to man vital communication points and to install their W/T where landlines were being cut by both sides.

After my recent flights over the green uplands of Kenya, the Biblical land flowing with milk and honey looked rather faded to me. But ordinary life in Egypt went on, regardless of weather or world politics. So when a seasonal, but exceedingly hot *khamsin* started to blow the dust up from the Sahara on Saturday 18 April, the annual Round-the-Oasis Motor Rally of desert-driving 'buffs' set off into the Sahara as planned from Mena House at the foot of the Pyramids. This endurance test was arranged as a race under the auspices of the Royal Egyptian Automobile Club, the competitors driving souped-up production models specially modified to withstand not only the pummelling of 500 miles of gravel and soft sand but also the possibly wild variations of temperatures in the desert.

Leaving the Gizeh pyramids, 24 cars headed south-west into the teeth of the severe sandstorm, driving in pairs for mutual support and aiming for the first checkpoint at Baharia oasis, about 200 miles away. From there they would go on south to Farafra oasis in the Western desert. Then the route carried them to Kharga oasis before they turned north to the lovely oasis of El Fayoum, arriving in Cairo after five gruelling days.

Not surprisingly, several competitors had fallen victims to the all-penetrating and choking dust long before they had even reached the first checkpoint and had to be ignominiously towed into the oasis at Baharia for first aid. The failure of the German entry to arrive at Baharia did not at first arouse suspicion since the driver was none other than the very tall, intrepid, ebullient – not to say arrogant – German Minister to Egypt, Baron von Stohrer. He had a reputation for 'doing his own thing' and, sure enough, had last been seen disappearing into the sandstorm in a prototype 'Strength Through Joy' People's Car along a rather southerly route of his own choice and alone, no doubt as a publicity stunt. Incongruously Herr Klein, his navigator and mechanic, was a Jewish employee in the Nazi Embassy motor pool.

The Baron's failure to check in at Baharia even 12 hours after the last competitor had arrived and his continuing absence were reported by the stewards and raised misgivings in the German Embassy, eventually becoming of diplomatic concern not only to the otherwise somewhat apathetic Egyptian Government but also to the British High Commissioner, His Excellency Sir Miles Lampson. As the Baron was still missing on Tuesday, alarm bells began to ring loudly.

No sooner had HE voiced his concern than both the RAF and the

Army began to organise a search and rescue by land and air. That same afternoon I went out in open formation with two other 216 Sqn 'Vics' for five hours to scour the desert in filthy flying conditions – a complete waste of time.

All available aircraft from TransJordan, Palestine and the Canal now joined those already at Helwan and Heliopolis, under control of Middle East HQ in Cairo and, together with a few Royal Egyptian Air Force machines made up a total of 47 aircraft. It was no easy task to employ this motley collection to best advantage. There were seven types, each with its own limitations, even assuming that all could be flown with equal competence. They had wide variations of speed and flight endurance, of navigating ability and particularly of facilities for visual look-out. All these factors affected the allocation of resources to organised flight plans; hence, different sectors of the desert were allotted to each type of aircraft, and squadrons then searched their appointed area by flying across it on parallel tracks, spaced apart according to the prevailing visibility, which continued to be extremely poor.

Each day was dominated by the ghastly *khamsin* which was now howling at an unbearable 109°F. To be reasonably certain of covering the whole area, the spacing between each searcher had to be less than twice the visibility distance from air to ground which, when peering through the thick dust haze, was frequently less than a mile. It was obviously going to take a very long time to comb the large expanse of desert where the Baron might most probably be stranded.

The situation was decidedly unfavourable in the air, for it was often impossible to tell where the desert ended and the sky began. At times the ground could not be seen at all from 3,000ft. Besides, it seemed highly unlikely to the searchers that any human being could survive for long in such dreadful conditions. The lack of any sighting, day after day, became more and more depressing. Dozens of sorties went out into the storm, only to return empty-handed. The aircraft were flown in threes, in open formation at 500ft, from which height it was hoped to be able to see a small broken-down car against the mottled gravel and sand surface of the desert for up to perhaps a mile away.

In 1936 it was scarcely possible to navigate at all in the primitively-equipped aircraft of those days. There were few distinguishing marks on the desert and no radio aids to help. Steering to within 5° either side of a compass course was asking too much of single-engined pilots who were flying in cramped, noisy and exposed cockpits and were expected to be looking carefully at the ground all the time.

In our Victorias we were much better placed for this sort of job than other pilots, though we still had our work cut out. 'George', the automatic pilot, was not yet available for us, so we had to struggle manually at the controls in the turbulent *khamsin*, keeping one eye on our leader while concentrating most attention on the ground. Fortunately, with two pilots we had each other's company and the best possible uninterrupted view from our cockpits.

Nevertheless, the operational co-ordinators could never be sure that gaps had not inadvertently opened up between search sweeps. After each day's flying, we were, therefore, kept busy analysing where we thought we had been and planning the next day's sorties. Like everyone in the squadron since this 'flap' began, I had been getting only four hours' sleep, working on maps and plans and preparing my aircraft till past midnight and then getting up at 4.30 am to start all over again. We all hoped it would soon come to an end.

By 23 April we began to fear we would find only the remains of the Baron and his mechanic, for the weather went on being absolutely appalling. That morning I left at dawn with my flight commander, Squadron Leader Philip Mackworth, formating half a mile behind him on his starboard quarter, with another 'Vic' on his port quarter, also keeping him just in view.

We flew to our starting point in the desert at 500ft in thick sand haze, bumping about in the 50 mph wind. My co-pilot had newly arrived from the UK and had unfortunately never flown a 'twin' before, so I asked him to keep his eyes on the leader while I struggled with the controls and scanned the ground on my right.

Tossing about in the yellow haze, it was easy to lose all sense of proportion and at one point I went down to ground-level to check out a clump of camel thorn I had mistaken for a car. The occasional empty four-gallon petrol tin, discarded years before for some unknown reason in the wilderness, also demanded close inspection. After two hours I was attracted by a couple of trucks parked near a large sand dune; but they turned out to be ground searchers who waved as I flew low past them.

I had fallen a long way behind Mackworth who was fast disappearing in the dust, so I opened up the throttles to catch him. The haze seemed to be clearing a bit and there were occasional shafts of thin sunlight. Suddenly, something vaguely caught my eye in the haze to starboard and instinctively I turned to investigate. Was there anything? There it was again – a pale flash of light a mile or so away! I lost height and turned towards the position as fast as possible. Could it be that what lay ahead was what we were all looking for? There was something small, sitting on top of a low hillock and partly covered by a white sheet! Telling my W/Op to wind in his trailing aerial, I went down to 50ft.

Again I noticed what must have first caught my eye – flashes of light from an improvised heliograph, the pale sun being reflected by a mirror. As I came closer, I could see it was a driving mirror held in the hands of a very tall man. Next to him, a little man was jumping up and down, waving frantically.

Our orders were to report to our leader and to circle over anything we might find until he returned. Mackworth had quite vanished into the yellow sky so I climbed to 500ft and sent him a Morse W/T signal to announce the good news. I can't imagine what the two down below must have been thinking as they watched me flying round and round overhead instead of landing. After ten minutes, which must have seemed an eternity to the impatient men on the ground, Mackworth re-appeared and did a circuit, selecting the least hazardous nearby strip of flattish gravel between outcrops of rock before making a very smooth job of a tricky touchdown.

I went on monitoring events from the air and had a good look at our position on the map. As far as I could make out, we were no more than twelve miles south of Baharia, in an area supposedly searched on Day 1 by our friends of the Royal Egyptian Air Force; but the Baron later reportedly said we were the first moving object he had seen for six days.

As I watched, Philip Mackworth emerged from his aircraft, followed by his passenger, the Heliopolis Medical Officer. As they picked their way across the desert, the two Germans stumbled forward to meet them. Of course I didn't hear Mackworth's greeting, 'Are you von Stohrer?' (Dr Livingstone, I presume?) Nor did I hear von Stohrer reply, 'I'm so glad to see you. I always knew you would come!' But I did see little Herr Klein pour the remains of their drinking water over his head.

Evidently, their steering had been broken by a rock. So, with true Teutonic composure, they methodically boiled their radiator for subsequent drinking, covered the car with a sheet to keep it cool and to attract any searchers and then settled down inside to make what comfort they could in the dust, thus conserving their energy and hydration in the searing heat. It had been their only chance. Luckily, they did not know they were only three miles from the track between Cairo and Baharia, normally within easy walking distance but of course quite beyond reach in a khamsin. They had eaten their last food the previous day and were down to their last litre of water which they reckoned would last for another three days.

I had been joined by our third Victoria, flying round and round watching events. The four men abandoned the car on its hillock and climbed aboard the 'Vic'. Its engines were re-started and Mackworth taxied gingerly back downwind and took off. Then we tucked in behind him as two close escorts to fly back to base.

By the time we reached Heliopolis, a large crowd of journalists and officials from various embassies had gathered on the tarmac to welcome the Baron. He was said to have been highly embarrassed by such a reception on account of a large rent in his shorts. But I was busy landing and when I had stopped alongside Mackworth and switched off on the hangar apron, the Baron had already been swept away to Cairo. Mackworth and I were left to face the photographers and the Press who had been busily playing up the search on an international basis. For a brief day we both become headline news in the UK papers.

On 2 May, three days before the Italians occupied Addis Ababa and virtually beat the Abyssinians, a letter came to me, penned on German Embassy paper:

Dear Mr Richardson,
I have let some time slip by before doing what I had long intended to do – write to you in person to thank you once more for what you have done for me. I felt more shaken than I had expected for the first few days – in fact, quite unable to do my work properly; then came the King's death [King Fouad of Egypt]. But please accept my thanks, though late. I hope, when my wife arrives towards the end of this month, she will also be able to thank you in person.
Yours sincerely,
G. Stohrer.

The search had cost the British taxpayer a pretty penny but we would never, of course, have begrudged any expense for saving lives. In 1936 we weren't to know that, after Spain's civil war had started on 18 July that year, Baron von Stohrer would become General Franco's right-hand man and was still there when we finally went to war with Germany; not that it would have made any difference to our concern for his safety.

I suppose I'm sorry I never met the Baron face-to-face, nor even his Baroness, for that matter! The promised tangible expression of gratitude never materialised; nor did my friends' leg-pulling prophesies of an Iron Cross (2nd Class) from Adolf Hitler! That would have been really something!

To tell the truth, the Baron had been very lucky. I doubt he would have survived had the sun not broken through the dust just in time for him to catch my eye with his driving mirror, itself a most unlikely chance. The RAF probably would not have passed that way again in time to find him alive. With hindsight, he should have carried a signalling lamp or Very pistol to fire distress star shells; even a few blank shots or simple fireworks would have helped the searchers. His disregard of the dangers of driving in the desert in a *khamsin*, all for the sake of publicity for the German Reich, had caused a lot of unnecessary trouble.

Things in the squadron were in a state of flux. Twenty pilots arrived from home without much warning and had to be converted to 'twins' by 216 Sqn as quickly as possible before being returned to form new bomber squadrons in the UK. Paddy Bandon's overseas tour ended in a riot of fun and in the temporary absence of his official relief, I found to my dismay I was sitting in his chair again, acting as Squadron Adjutant and inevitably losing a lot of active flying. This unaccustomed work surprisingly took up to five hours of fairly intensive paper shuffling and telephoning every morning.

I was glad to escape from Egypt in June on the SS *Moreton Bay*, a one-class ship of the Aberdeen and Commonwealth line, reaching Southampton after an uneventful ten-days' carefree voyage via Malta and Gibraltar, a nice lazy start to two months' home leave which I had been accumulating during the past two years of continuous service overseas. How lucky I was not to be able to fly home. There was much to be said for leisurely ocean travel.

VII

Sudan Safari

WHILE I was in England, my father took me to lunch with some of his business friends who shook me to the core by their indifference to my accounts of British military weakness which I had observed at first-hand. It was the same everywhere: nobody wanted to know how poorly our national interests were being defended for lack of modern equipment. Still in a state of mild shock, I left at the end of July to return to my squadron in Cairo by a low-priced Italian Lloyd Triestino liner, the *Marco Polo*, sailing from Venice to Alexandria.

The train journey to Italy turned out to be unexpectedly amusing. I had intended to make a break in Paris for eleven hours, but *en route* I changed my plan in favour of a halt at Lausanne, hoping to be able to catch a brief glimpse of the Alps. From Paris I shared a compartment with the young and extrovert Mr and Mrs Miller of Moulton, Northampton, where his firm made boots and shoes. They were on their way to spend a holiday with her mother and father, the latter being head gardener of a large lunatic asylum in Lausanne. Also in our carriage was a Swiss businessman who had just escaped from war-torn Madrid and he gave us a graphic account of events leading up to the tragic civil strife in Spain.

We talked, and to a great extent, laughed our way across the length of France, scarcely noticing the passage of time, and when we arrived at Lausanne the Millers were met by her middle-aged father who was driving an expensive American limousine.

They absolutely insisted on my going with them to their family villa located in the asylum gardens a few miles out of town. There I was given a guided tour of the gardens and I admired some incredibly large decorative dahlias before sitting down to a reunion dinner *en famille*, after which the three males visited the cellars. Here we joined two very old gardeners who were already sampling the estate's 1935 sparkling *vins mousseux*, using a small tumbler which they repeatedly filled, tossed back and passed round. The trick was to swallow the wine before it stopped fizzing.

After an hour of this, I was in no fit state to find my own way back to the railway station, nor was my host fit to drive me there. So I was put on a passing bus and the conductor was asked to put me off at the correct stop! I'm not sure how I managed to discover my platform – the innumerable international destinations on display filled me with alarm. Even after having found the correct *quai*, I had repeatedly to resist climbing into the wrong train; mine was due sometime around midnight but they kept coming and going and one train looked like another in the dim light of the station.

Eventually, I clambered onboard the Venice express and squeezed apologetically into an already packed wooden-seated compartment whose occupants viewed my intrusion with thinly veiled hostility. It was so crowded that, once seated, it would have been impossible for me to fall over. I dropped off into a coma which took me all the way through the Simplon tunnel, past the Italian Customs who tried in vain to wake me up, and on and on as far as Milan before I came to.

It was a Saturday and hordes of Italian holidaymakers boarded the already overflowing carriages. We bumped along in rising heat, rising smells and rising noise to Venice where we finally all belched out of the train. Thanks to Mussolini's single concession to international convenience, my train actually arrived on schedule and I was going to have time to spare for a quick look round that unique and beautiful city.

By chance, a fellow traveller on my train was also heading for SS *Marco Polo*. A Swiss, she turned out to be Secretary of the Cairo YWCA employment bureau; her husband worked in Cairo as an Egyptologist. We joined forces, took our luggage to the ship and, *Baedeker* in hand, returned to 'do' as much of Venice as possible, the sailing having been postponed for two hours at the request of Sidky Pasha, an ex-premier of Egypt. But in the heat of the day, all my energy suddenly evaporated while we were only halfway round an art gallery, so I decided to return to the comfort of the sleek Lloyd Triestino ship.

The voyage down the Adriatic, along the Greek coast and past all those enchanting islands lying under the brazen August sky, was utterly delightful; but our platonic encounter ended abruptly at Cairo where our paths diverged and we went our separate ways, never to meet again.

The chair of Squadron Adjutant was still empty and I was slotted into it again. Palestine was straining our resources and we had to retain some of the pilots we were converting to 'twins' instead of returning them to the UK. Plans were also afoot for 216 Sqn to fly to India and to West Africa in 1937. Personally, I now had to start swotting for the November specialisation exam in which I had been allowed to compete to secure a permanent commission. My studies involved some very unfamiliar subjects – there would be a three-hour paper in advanced mathematics, two three-hour science papers and three hours of practical and applied geometry and mathematical drawing, whatever that was!

I attacked this daunting task by literally sweating in the heat of my room for three hours every night, having played squash or swum at Gezira in the afternoons to keep a clear head. I often emerged from my books dazed and spouting formulae. The unusually prolonged summer of 1936 didn't help, the shade temperature reaching 96°F even in November. I can't recall the actual trauma of the exams which were spread over three days. Four of my friends in Egypt were also competing; altogether, there were 81 of the RAF Class of '33 trying for 16 permanent commissions. When the exams were over, it took three nights of sleep before I felt entirely normal. Thank goodness, once out of the way, the ordeal became just a nasty memory. It was wonderful to have some spare time again.

Plans for a squadron detachment to the north-west frontier of India in mid-January were beginning to take shape and I was chuffed to be nominated as No 2 i/c. We were going to send three Valentias as supporting transports carrying the groundcrews and spares for 12 Vincents of No 45 Bomber Squadron from Helwan who were practising a move to reinforce Risalpur from Egypt via Baghdad and Karachi. We expected to be away for six weeks, which was an intriguing prospect.

My three-month stint as Squadron Adjutant came to an end on 10 November with the posting of a full-time replacement for Paddy Bandon, who was now a student at RAF Staff College, Andover. Ten days later, I was sent to rescue a seriously ill medical officer from faraway No 47 Sqn, Khartoum. He had damaged a leg while playing football; it had turned septic and he needed urgent surgery in a less tropical climate.

The journey from Heliopolis took the normal two days but, on arrival, I was asked to make the return flight in one day if possible, because of the patient's deteriorating condition. So I got up at 3.45 am and we were airborne at 5.55 am, by which ungodly hour it was just light enough to see across the airfield.

Wadi Halfa was reached non-stop in five hours by chancing a direct route of 430 miles over the desert *via* Merowe which we normally avoided as being too remote for safety. I had been faced with strong headwinds cutting down my groundspeed to under 80 mph and it became obvious at that rate I couldn't hope to reach Asyut to refuel before nightfall, as previously planned, and there were no night-flying facilities available there.

I therefore signalled for fuel and oil to be waiting for me at Luxor instead, three hours after leaving Wadi Halfa. I noticed that the ancient temples of Luxor looked very intriguing in the setting sun as I took off after refuelling and I arrived over Heliopolis at 8.25 pm and received a 'green' on the Duty Pilot's Aldis lamp. To avoid troubling Base for a flare path, I had signalled I would land by wing-tip magnesium flare, two of which were duly connected up at Luxor. When ignited by pressing a cockpit switch, a single flare would shed enough light downwards for the last 400ft of glide to land alongside the fire engine sitting on the near edge of the airfield, its headlights pointing into wind. There were two flares for luck. Five minutes later I was on the ground.

Hungry and tired, my face and lips chapped by the cold at 10,000ft where I had been trying to escape the headwinds, I certainly didn't expect to find a small crowd on the tarmac to greet me. I was even more surprised to be congratulated by Group Captain Raymond Collishaw and by my squadron CO, Wing Commander Bill Mackey. My new flight commander, Squadron Leader Sidney 'Bill' Storrar and several friends were also waiting there. I wasn't the first in No 216 Sqn to have completed that journey in a day, so why all the fuss? I never found out but it had been a long 19-hour day before I could once more hit the hay.

Apart from the total hour-and-a-half spent on the ground refuelling as fast as we could from four-gallon cans at Wadi Halfa and at Luxor, three hours of night-flying had brought that day's flying time up to a total of 14 hours.

Sergeant Ramshaw, my 'second dickie', as we called our co-pilots, was a trainee fresh from UK. He flew very well but had as yet no confidence in his own navigation and airmanship, so it was difficult for me to relax. We had been unlucky with the winds which had reduced our groundspeed to an overall average of less than 85 mph. On the other hand, visibility had been exceptionally clear, which really was a great help. It had been a tough physical effort for passengers and crew alike, but we were well rewarded by a wan smile from our prone casualty as his stretcher was carefully eased through the bomb-aimer's window and finally transferred to a waiting ambulance to take him off to the Citadel hospital. Happily his leg was saved and he was invalided home. I am very bad at catching names and, to this day, I don't know who he was!

In December we were traumatised by the abdication of Edward VIII, of which we had had little or no warning; but we were back at work after Christmas trying out corner-cutting on the long haul between Wadi Halfa and Asyut by going via Dunqul oasis. Then we were off and away with our friends of No 45 Sqn in their 12 Vincents heading for India. The plans had been altered and now we were going only as far as Baghdad. There, No 45 Sqn would be taken on by our twin-brothers in No 70 (BT) Sqn, stationed at Hinaidi in Iraq.

The winter weather was bitterly cold and rainy and the hills of Palestine and Transjordan were covered by snow. Baghdad was a great disappointment. It was very dirty and had a nasty smell all of its own. A shared taxi trip south, to see the fabled Arch of Ctesiphon, proved to be well worth the time and expense and we spent another afternoon exploring the very noisy copper and silver *souks* of Baghdad in a successful search for attractive and useful mementos.

A few hours of heavy rain reduced the airfield at Hinaidi to a morass and delayed our departure by a day. After four fairly wild parties preceding Twelfth Night, in and around Baghdad with our RAF hosts, we turned our three Valentias back towards Heliopolis, landing for fuel at the austere military outpost of Rutbah Wells after I had been obliged to make a brief, unplanned landing at the then still unfinished RAF airfield of Habbaniyah to allow me to 'shed a large tear for Nelson' upon the bitterly cold Syrian desert. We then flew on to Amman for lunch and to refuel again.

Perhaps to cut a dash, Squadron Leader Bill Storrar then took us off in V-formation, flying westwards below the lowering clouds towards the Dead Sea, with me close on his starboard quarter and George Musson equally close on his port quarter. As we flew along, the clouds became lower and lower and the country around us more and more rugged. A wadi appeared ahead descending steeply in the right general direction; into it we all dived, hard on the heels of our leader. Its cliff walls grew closer and closer and the cloud not only showed no signs of breaking up but its base disconcertingly went lower and lower, descending into the wadi with us.

Both the wing aircraft had tucked in very close behind Storrar to avoid the rock walls on either side, while trying not to lose sight of his tail in the cloud base through which we were all now flying. But the wadi grew alarmingly narrower, every second increasing the chance of our colliding with each other or over-running Storrar.

Unable to look both ways at once, George and I glued our eyes on his tail, only a few feet ahead. We were now directly behind his engines and being wildly buffeted by his slipstream so we had to work furiously at our controls to keep station. Meanwhile our co-pilots were anxiously watching the converging cliffs lest we had to break away for safety and climb steeply into the cloud.

Discussing the situation in the Heliopolis Mess afterwards, George and I agreed we had both felt very unsure of survival. Luckily, the wadi had eventually opened out, the cloud base had stopped descending with us and we could both breathe again, no longer scraping along, helter skelter over the rocks. At long last we had reached the Dead Sea and Storrar had been able to set a steady course for Base, taking us over the Sinai desert and the Red Sea hills which were cloudless.

R. G. Musson was an outstanding cricketer and an amusing and highly dedicated officer. He became a star navigation specialist and for 30 minutes held the world long-distance flight record, navigating a Vickers Wellesley of the RAF Long Distance Flight non-stop for over 6,000 miles from Ismailia to Australia in 1937 until his tanks ran dry. A second Wellesley of the Flight, piloted by Squadron Leader Dick Kellett and guided by another pilot navigation specialist, Flight Lieutenant 'Nick' R. T. Gething, was able to reach Darwin before their fuel ran out.

George finally 'bought it' when in command of No 172 Leigh Light Wellington squadron at Chivenor in 1945. He inexplicably flew into telegraph wires in low cloud on the cliffs above Clovelly, a few minutes after taking off at night to attack U-boats in the Atlantic, having carefully warned all the crews who preceded him to fly out well beyond Hartland Point before turning towards the Scillies. His death was a very bad loss to the Service.

The anti-climax of our curtailed cruise to India was soon overtaken by other exciting news. I was now detailed by my Flight Commander to fly one of the two Valentias that were to cross central Africa in late April, in support of five Vincents of No 47 Sqn from Khartoum which were to pioneer the reinforcement route between West Africa and Egypt.

We would also be celebrating the coronation of King George VI and Queen Elizabeth in May with flying displays at Lagos and Accra. Meanwhile, 216 Sqn had to perform in the annual air show at Helio on 16 April. In one item three Valentias crammed with 90 armed airmen landed to 'rescue' the beleaguered garrison of a plywood 'fort' set up in front of the crowds. Our much less ambitious displays in West Africa were planned to have us formating with the five Vincents, culminating in a ground-level 'beat up' as a grand finale.

Before all that, I was to take the newly-arrived Senior Air Staff Officer, Air Commodore André A. Walser MC DFC, on a personal four-week tour of the Sudan, Uganda and East Africa, starting on 1 February. He intended to choose his itinerary from day-to-day as we went along. It sounded challenging!

The projected RAF West African cruise to Lagos and Accra across equatorial Africa was, however, going to expose its crews to the dreaded yellow fever and all participants had to be inoculated. Anti-malaria mepacrine had perhaps also not yet been invented; but there was an anti-yellow fever prophylactic serum, using a very attenuated 'live' strain.

The health authorities in Cairo had good reason to fear any hint of yellow fever, for this dangerous and often fatal scourge is transmitted by the anopheles mosquito which was already prevalent in Egypt. Consequently, the late January arrival by Imperial Airways of a civilian medical specialist carrying undeclared doses of the live serum from the Burroughs Wellcome laboratories, had to be kept under very close wraps.

The doctor worked his way with a syringe round everyone in No 216 Sqn nominated for the West African cruise before he departed for Khartoum to deal with No 47 Sqn. He left with a warning of side-effects which might be delayed for a week or two. My arm had received its jab, but there had been no reaction at all by 1 February when I left Heliopolis with the Air Commodore on his grand tour of East Africa.

With night stops in Khartoum and Juba, the trip to Kenya took its normal four days and I invited SASO to sit up in front with me to see the usual assortment of buck, giraffe, elephant, buffalo and rhinoceros roaming the grassland and swamps of the White Nile from Malakal all the way to the Uganda border. We arrived in Nairobi for a late tea and I retired to bed for two days with a high temperature – a slight touch of yellow fever! Four days later I had quite recovered and we set off for my old stamping grounds in the Northern Frontier District, flying over Thika and round the jungle shoulder of Mt Kenya to Marsabit and Ngombo, before stopping for a night at Moyale with the Provincial Commissioner, Glendaye, in his battlemented toe-hold on the Abyssinian plateau. Then we flew back to Nairobi via Isiolo, where we stopped to inspect the Eritrean deserters.

Next day we took off for Dar es Salaam, going the long way, west of the impresssive white Kibo – Mt Kilimanjaro (19,565ft) – and its smaller brother Mawensi (17,562ft) then skirting round Meru at 14,978ft to over-fly Arusha, the seat of the Provincial Governor. Then on we went, south-east, down to the coast of the Indian Ocean. The circuitous flight to Dar took four hours.

All the Ismailis in Dar es Salaam were preparing for a visit by their spiritual leader, the Aga Khan, and the streets outside my New Africa Hotel were festooned with gay banners and triumphal arches to welcome the great man. The 'Brilliant Star of the East and West' was coming to be weighed in gold for the benefit of the charities maintained by his sect.

After the cool Kenyan plateau, the climate of Dar was very hot and oppressive and we dripped uncomfortably the whole time. The Air Commodore was put up for the night at Government House and I was lucky to be free because, when my Wireless Operator contacted Heliopolis by W/T in the evening to receive any messages for the Air Commodore, there was a personal signal for me.

I had come sixth in the November competitive exam and could expect a place on my chosen specialist course, air navigation. Footloose and fancy free, I was able to take my crew out for a private celebration. George Musson had beaten me to third place and George Bush had come ninth – not a bad score for three Abu Sueir bog rats, I thought!

Next day we flew for 40 minutes across the ocean to Zanzibar where a call was paid on the Resident, the so-called 'adviser' to the ageing Sultan. Most unusual, massive, brass, door furniture in the ancient Arab town itself caught our eyes as we drove to look at the port, itself filled with dhows from Arabia and beyond, this being formerly the centre of the East African entrepot slave trade. Now there were no slaves and the air was heavy with the scent of cloves, the island's principal remaining export.

We then flew on to Chake Chake on Pemba, a tiny satellite clove island, an hour north of Zanzibar. Here the District Commissioner met us and plied us with *mdafu* (coconut juice) from a pile of green coconuts which were trepanned on the spot by a native wielding a panga, to slake our thirst in the midday sun. Shades of Robinson Crusoe!

Another 80 minutes' flying north, over the shark-infested Indian Ocean – without benefit of an inflatable dinghy or 'Mae Wests' (which were then unknown) – brought us to Mombasa Island which in 1937 boasted a tricky little airfield set among tall palm trees. We stayed in the Mombasa Club that night and enjoyed a sea-water swim in its shark-proof swimming pool, followed by several long *mdafus* which were greatly improved when iced and laced with gin! A dinner party and a visit to the open-air cinema, organised by the Provincial Commissioner, completed an interesting day. Like Dar, Mombasa was unbearably hot and sticky.

Next day we made a late start and called in at Voi, an hour away, before continuing for two hours in rain up through the rising hills to Nairobi where I was glad to be given a couple of days out of the cockpit, apart from a short proving flight following scheduled maintenance which my erks had been carrying out. On 15 February we took off for Entebbe, the administrative capital of Uganda, over-flying Kisumu at 10,000ft and looking down at Jinja, where the White Nile flows out of Lake Victoria.

Large aeroplanes were still something of a novelty and we were met on Entebbe's grass airfield by several of the Colonial Governor's staff, eager to have a guided tour of my Valentia. Then I was whisked off with our bags to catch up with the Air Commodore at Government House where we had both been invited to spend a night in luxury. My crew were being well cared for by other British officials.

The building was a handsome and spacious stone edifice built in the Palladian style with tall porticos and high airy ceilings. It stood in parkland reminiscent of England but seemingly set beside a blue sea, surrounded by lovely green lawns with, most unexpectedly, a sizeable open-air swimming pool built for a planned visit by the Prince of Wales which had never materialised.

Sir Philip Mitchell had been installed less than two years, having previously held high office in Tanganyika. His strong views for advancing the natives through further education conflicted with the self-interests of the Asian artisans. He was also impeded by a sloth-ful Colonial Office, but was determined to go ahead. The table-talk was consequently lively and lunch was graced by Margery, his homely and amiable Lady.

We were asked how we would care to spend the afternoon after the customary snurge. Would we play tennis or prefer to visit Lutembe, a local celebrity crocodile to whom the former Bugandan tyrant, Kabaka Mutesa, had fed political dissidents? This diet had now been reduced to sun-dried fish, administered by a keeper at a little cove on Lake Victoria five miles away. Lutembe sounded distinctly inter-esting to us and cars were ordered for after tea. A short drive through lush green country brought us to a sandy lakeside beach on what could easily have been taken for the shores of the Mediterranean, except that reeds were growing out of the 'sea'. Hanging from a line strung across the beach were chunks of rotting fish; but of Lutembe there was no sign.

Presently the Ugandan keeper appeared and was asked to summon Lutembe. Thereupon, he started running up and down the shore, calling loudly to an empty horizon and begging Lord Lutembe to come. Nothing happened although the prancing and adulation continued and, as the sun began to set, I wondered if our legs had been pulled. Then, straining our eyes over the water, we dimly made out what seemed to be a log breaking the surface some hundred yards out. The Ugandan became very excited and the 'log' advanced very slowly, gradually making its way up a swathe that had been cut through the reeds. Lutembe came to rest on the shore with an audible sigh. Very slowly, enticed by lumps of fish proffered by his keeper, he crawled awkwardly up the beach until all but two or three feet of tail of his eighteen-foot length was on dry land. Encrusted with green moss, his head gnarled with age, Lutembe measured about four feet across his middle but had obviously seen much better days! We declined an invitation to approach closer to those enormous jaws but I was able to get a few quick snapshots in the rapidly fading light of the equatorial dusk.

Lutembe lasted well into the 'fifties and featured as one of Uganda's tourist attractions, his pictures decorating first-class compartments of the Kenya and Uganda railway which climbs so dramatically all the way up to Nairobi and up and then down into the Rift Valley before finally climbing over the 9,000ft Mau escarpement, to descend at last to Lake Victoria, 4,000ft above the coast at Mombasa.

Next day we turned towards Khartoum, landing at Juba for fuel and a pleasant lunch at the White Nile Hotel. Three and a half hours later we reached flat and dreary Malakal, to be guests of the Provincial Administrator. It was extremely hot, humid and desperately uncomfortable inside what could only be described as his large 'meat safe'. My crew fared even worse in the rest house. With great relief we left next morning and climbed into the cooler air at 7,000ft for four easy hours' flying down the White Nile, past the great dam that irrigated the long-staple cotton fields of the Gezira, and so down into another oven at Khartoum.

But the Air Commodore was a glutton for punishment and now decided he wanted to go back the very next day south-west as far as the then railhead at El Obeid and on into the bundu at El Fasher, flying towards central Africa for five hours. We flew through rain and contended with poor visibility all the way, arriving at El Fasher for a late lunch with the Governor of Darfur province, Mr Ingleson and his wife, who was accompanied by 'el Lewa' Renouf, the Colonel of the Sudan Defence Force (SDF) in Darfur; in fact, all 20 English inhabitants had turned out. 3,000ft above sea-level, El Fasher was pleasantly cool and the night's sleep was not distressful, as it had been in Khartoum and Malakal.

Next day my starboard engine showed signs of misbehaviour which was finally diagnosed after intensive investigation as being only plug trouble. But our departure had to await a second night spent with the hospitable Sudan Defence Force. El Fasher had been the last stronghold of Ali el Din from whom a mixed Anglo-Egyptian army had wrested the whole of Darfur in 1917. His enormous copper war drum, measuring 6ft across, stood outside the SDF guard room and was only struck to mark the hours. It could be heard for miles around. The crescent crowning the minaret of the town mosque had been cast from aluminium salvaged from a Victoria Mk V of my squadron, crashed a few years earlier by 'Firpo' Chichester, and was a warning for all to behold.

Five and a half hours' flying *via* El Obeid brought us back to Khartoum where I was accorded another day's respite, lazing and swimming at the Khartoum Club, while SASO conferred with the Army and Air Force commanders.

Then it was back on the trail, this time up the Blue Nile to Sennar where I awaited the arrival of the Air Commodore who was riding pillion in a Vincent of No 47 Sqn on one of his diversions to look at Wad Medani. We continued up as far as Roseires before cutting south to the Abyssinian border post of Gebel Kurmuk, to pitch camp beds under the ample wings of our tethered aircraft. A cold katabatic gale suddenly blew down from the mountains in the night and we had to cling on hard to save our bedding from being blown away in the dust.

From Kurmuk we flew in a four-hour hop to Kassala, with its strange bald mountain rising out of the plain and where the natives traded highly-prized edible gum which they collected from indigenous trees. The next hop of three hours brought us to another very hot spot – Port Sudan – where we spent two uncomfortably sticky nights in the Sudan Railway's Red Sea Hotel and hired a glass-bottomed boat to marvel at the wonders of the offshore coral reef. I was sorry there wasn't enough time to visit the ghost port of Suakin.

After that, we turned towards home with a vengeance, flying north along the west shores of the Red Sea to spend a last night at the Shell oil wells at Hurghada, six and a half hours' flying away. This was beyond my range even with full tanks and the only intermediate petrol available was on a desert landing ground at Hassa Lagoon, on the edge of the sea about three hours away.

I had never been there before and discovered to my horror that, of all the maps of Africa I had taken on board for the excursion, there was a small but vital part of the present route missing – the sheet that contained the petrol dump at Hassa Lagoon. Visibility was fortunately good, so I followed the coast for an hour until I ran off my map. Then, with my co-pilot as concerned as I to find the fuel, we kept our eyes skinned as we combed the desert to port for signs of a landing ground.

All along the way on our port side, the barren crests of the Red Sea hills rose out of the desert coastline in jagged fangs like a moonscape. After two hours of scanning, a dump of petrol cans came into view, piled up on the side of a flat patch of sand in the centre of which was a faint circle of once whitewashed petrol cans – it was Hassa Lagoon!

We landed and just helped ourselves, filling the tanks for the next leg, and I simply signed a printed receipt to hand to the Accountant Officer at Heliopolis. It had been carried there by Shell on camels and left unattended, the nearest village being 50 miles away across the lifeless mountains. Hurghada hove in sight after three hours and we were cordially entertained by the handful of Shell company staff living in this remote corner of Egypt on the shores of the Gulf of Suez opposite Mt Sinai and the Gulf of Aqaba. Despite the slurping oil pumps, we found some much-needed sleep after the hard going of many previous nights of great discomfort.

Next day we were graciously allowed to decline to tarry with our hosts a minute longer than necessary after a very early breakfast: wild horses could not have delayed our departure. Three hours later I was standing on a familiar tarmac with a 10,000-mile safari safely behind me. It had been a fascinating 28 days' slog and my flying logbook showed a healthy 93hr leap forward. I could now visualise the vastness of the Sudan, 1,000 miles long and 1,000 miles wide, embracing enormous variations on the theme of Man and his Environment.

Perhaps more to the point, my globe-trotting SASO, like the proverbial airman's wife, had at last been satisfied and seemed glad to get home. I had lost 7lb in weight in the process; but in my travels had completely missed hearing the glad news of HM Treasury's launch of a £400M Defence Loan – a late, very small step in the right direction. Someone in Whitehall must have heard the bell!

VIII
West African Cruise

WHILE I had been away, the squadron had acquired a new CO, Wing Commander G. C. Joe Gardiner DSO DFC, a quiet-mannered married officer who had had the misfortune of having been castrated by tribeswomen into whose hands he had fallen after a forced landing some years before, somewhere in Syria. He was a much admired leader.

Growing anxiety on the European front was being steadily stoked up by Hitler, making outrageous demands and stirring up unrest from German minorities in Austria, the Polish Corridor of Danzig (Gdansk) and the Sudetenland of Czechoslovakia. The Spanish civil war was destabilising the peace, serving as a testing ground for all the new weaponry of the Nazis, the Fascists, the Falangists and the Communists. The latter were supported by the International Brigade, recruited from many heroic but rather starry-eyed do-gooders, dedicated in the name of democracy to establishing a left-wing proletariat dictatorship for the poor Spaniards! There was little to choose between either side when it came to personal liberty and nothing we British could do anyway.

We were kept busy, practising for the annual air display to be staged on 16 April at Heliopolis, but the most exciting event in our lives at the time was the fitting of an automatic pilot to our Valentias. 'George'[1] could maintain a steady level course in the bumpiest air conditions, far better than any human hands and feet. We were delighted by this latest technological development and eagerly looked forward to the prospect of giving 'George' a chance to prove himself on the long-haul expedition across the tropics to West Africa and back for which we now began active preparations. We were to travel in style and even our notepaper bore the printed heading: 'Middle East Command – West African Cruise'.

Air tests of the two Valentias earmarked for the journey being entirely satisfactory, I flew to Khartoum on 21 April, in company with Squadron Leader Bill Storrar who had Air Commodore André Walser, the commander of the cruise, as his passenger. On arrival at Khartoum we were met by a stinking hot 108°F, a veritable furnace which the huge ceiling fans in the bedrooms of the Grand Hotel failed to alleviate. Even the sheets felt hot to the touch.

We spent an exhausting day with No 47 Sqn, dividing up the spare parts for their five Vincents, compiling various alternative loads for our Valentias and trying to make two and two add up to less than four. If anything was inadvertently left behind, it would be just too bad! Later, we attended a guest night in our tropical mess kit comprising half-wellingtons, close-fitting white overalls (i.e. stirrup trousers), a white bum-freezer jacket, blue silk cummerbund, a starched-front dress shirt with a separate starched wing collar, starched cuffs, gold studs and cuff links and a double-ended black, silk bow tie. I sat nattering to my old friend and suave host, Kenneth Rampling, who several years later sired a lovely daughter, Charlotte, the international fashion model and actress. But in spite of much banter, the stifling heat made the dinner a trial of endurance and we began to wonder how our friends would cope, sitting behind the hot engines of their Vincents for the take-off at dawn.

We flew from Khartoum to what was then the railhead at El Obeid, where we refuelled and went on to El Fasher, arriving, very hungry, at 2.30 pm, nine hours after picking at an early and hence unappetising breakfast. El Fasher, being 3,000ft higher than Khartoum, felt cool enough to play a few games of squash, for which we had to ride to and from the court on borrowed ponies. The hospitable Sudan Defence Force then gave us all a most agreeable evening.

The next day was much more dramatic. Our destination was El Geneina, an insignificant outpost on the frontier of French Equatorial Africa (now Chad), where we expected to have to rough it, considering that we were a party of nine officers and 26 NCOs, all our erks having been appointed acting sergeants for the duration of the cruise to avoid accommodation difficulties in native Army installations.

We left El Fasher at 8 am and headed west in deteriorating visibility and rising dust, skirting round the Gebel Marra with its one spectacular bald rock core rising to 10,000ft, all that remains of an extinct volcano. This peak turned out to be the last recognisable feature we were going to see for quite a time.

Flying in formation makes it difficult to keep an accurate navigation log because airspeed and course have to be continuously changed in order to 'keep station'. All the same, we were better able to keep a check on the leader's progress than any of the solo pilots in their Vincents who had to follow, more or less blindly. Jim Irens and I soon formed the impression that Bill Storrar was flying at least

10° too far north and, unless he changed direction, we were going to miss El Geneina by perhaps 30 miles at the end of two hours. Visibility was poor and the ground offered no help, covered by monotonous bush as far as the eye could see.

Due to our constant manoeuvring, our own observations of drift and heading were fairly unreliable, so it seemed impertinent for me to question the leader's course by sending him a W/T signal. We were also too far apart to 'zog' a visual signal discreetly to him by waving an arm over the side of our cockpit in Morse code movements. Anyway, I figured he would signal me if he wanted help; so on and on we went, over the endless scrub of Darfur. Not surprisingly, the calculated time of arrival came and went with no sign of El Geneina, the grey and brown semi-desert and bush extending uninterrupted into the haze. We now grew anxious for our friends in their Vincents, uncomfortably throttled back so as not to over-run the leader. They were faster than us but had less range and must have been getting short of fuel.

If the Valentias had to land in the bush, we might get away with only a few scratches. We carried a comprehensive first-aid survival kit, with morphia and all that, not to mention a 12-bore for shooting for the pot. We also had a good supply of water. By comparison, our companions would fare very poorly.

Knowing there was no alternative diversion airfield, we had been monitoring our leader with growing concern; it had to be El Geneina or else. . . . Tension was, therefore, rising steadily in our cockpit as the minutes slipped away without the slightest sign of habitation. The dreaded question began to form in our heads: lost? Meanwhile, Bill Storrar pressed on without changing course, though he must have known the Vincents' fuel tanks were running low and that their fate depended on his finding El Geneina pretty soon.

Quite unexpectedly, we crossed an unmapped track cutting through the bush from port astern to starboard bow, running from south-east to north-west. We guessed the track must certainly lead to El Geneina, but which way should we turn – to port or to starboard? The sensation of being lost was not to be so easily dispelled! Fortunately, Bill Storrar had been developing the same sense of error as we had in our cockpit during the past hour. Wheeling the whole convoy through 135° to port, he began flying back south-east, following this Heaven-sent but unrecognisable track. It was only after another twenty minutes of nail-biting that a distant discontinuity of colour loomed ahead out of the haze. Eureka! A small sandy bush clearing emerged and, judging by the dismal remains of the Imperial Airways *Daedalus* airliner which could be seen where it had crashed after overshooting the boundary was clearly an airfield. Storrar went in to land first, while all I had to do was to wait for the Vincents to land, one by one – they had only a few minutes' fuel left. Sighs of relief in my cockpit were only in order when, as if in a bizarre game of aerial musical chairs, I touched down, 'Tail-end Charlie', with as nonchalant a three-pointer as I could manage. Instead of only two hours, the flight had taken three and we had been straying far into the wilderness of French Equatorial Africa.

Three years before, in 1934, Francis Chichester had made air navigation history by using a single position line to find Lord Howe Island in the middle of the Tasman Sea. Like us, he had no diversion, so he pre-computed the sun's altitude for his ETA[2] at the island and deliberately flew grossly to one side of the direct track so as to know which way to go when his marine sextant gave him his clue to turn. The bubble sextant had not yet been developed for astro over the land and our life-saving bush track had not even been on the map. To all intents and purposes we had been lost!

All three European inhabitants of El Geneina – the District Commissioner, the Shell representative and the local Medical Officer – were waiting for us on the airfield and took us off to quench our thirst and have a bite in the welcoming shade of the government rest house. As a diversion, after taking a much-needed siesta, we went with the MO to visit his little hospital, where we were shown the dismal sights of natives in the last stages of syphilis which he said was rampant locally. We were shocked to hear that officials in the French colony whom we were about to visit often kept harems of three or four black girls as a normal way of life. In the circumstances this sounded very dicey, if it was true. Evidently, the previous MO had harboured such an obsession for amputation that he had had to be removed by the District Commissioner before the entire population of El Geneina had become one-legged.

Our indefatigable Air Commodore then organised a sports day. At his request, all fifty of the male population of El Geneina were called out, bringing their spears and throwing sticks, the latter looking like long boomerangs. He offered a piastre to anyone who could hit a mark at about 30 paces with his stick or throw his spear into a tree trunk at 100 paces. The marksmanship was quite impressive and the games a great success; but when a handicap race was proposed open to everybody, it was only the very small boys who responded; all the older males considered it far beneath their dignity to be seen to run at all!

El Geneina had no pretensions to creature comfort but we made the most of the austere offerings of the rest-house and slept fairly well under the mosquito nets of our camp beds slung from hooks in the ceiling. After a quick bite of boiled eggs and tinned ham, we were eagerly on our way early next morning for what we had good reason to believe was going to be an interesting if long and demanding day. Our route through French Equatorial Africa went *via* Abecher, one hour from El Geneina, where we had to refuel for the next stage of five hours to Fort Lamy, the capital (now called N'Djamema).

The French authorities had invited us to lunch and to stay overnight and it was a point of honour for us to arrive punctually. This meant aiming to have a few minutes to spare up our sleeves towards the end of the 550-mile flight so as to arrive dead on ETA. We were also gaining an hour on the clock by going east to west.

My previous experience was that few French spoke English. Unfortunately, the reverse was also true. Apart from the Air Commodore and myself, hardly any of our party had more than schoolboys' offerings and my own degree-standard was distinctly rusty. The prospect of socialising for the entire length of a blistering day in central Africa was intimidating, no matter how *cordiale* the *entente* might be.

We took off at 6.30 am and set course westwards across the now familiar, dreary, flat bush, to land 80 minutes later at another bush clearing, far away from anything slightly resembling a town large enough to boast a name. At Abecher airfield there was nobody to meet us and no sign of the fuel we needed for our seven thirsty aircraft. However, at 8.30 we were glad to see the dust of a safari car approaching at speed through the bush and at its wheel was the local French District Officer, still dressed in pyjamas and wearing a good three days' growth of beard. 'Designer stubble' had not yet been invented.

Monsieur Dubois seemed able at one and the same time to express both surprise at our arrival and apology for his tardiness. He soon had the fuel compound unlocked to help ourselves from the dump of four-gallon cans of aviation petrol pre-positioned there for us by ubiquitous Shell. This pre-taste of ramshackle organisation warned us of what lay ahead for the next 24 hours.

We landed at Fort Lamy on the dot of 1.30 pm and found a Guard of Honour of Sénégalese troops drawn up on the airfield apron. As he stepped down from the cabin, our Air Commodore was welcomed with a flourish by the French Governor-General. After inspecting the Guard, to the background musical strains from a native brass band, the 'Marseillaise' and 'God Save the King' were played just recognisably and the troops marched past the saluting base, the boot-polished tops of their bare black feet shining brightly in the sunlight. To our amazement and quiet amusement, the Guard were then marched up and down the airfield to more music, barefoot under the blazing sun, till we feared they would drop. The Guard of Honour had been standing on the red-hot sand in loose-thonged sandals, cut from old motor tyres; but when they moved away, their footgear fell off and was left disconsolately lying in two empty rows where they had been standing.

We were distributed for the night among officials and their wives who had come out to greet us. Jim Irens and I were introduced to a charming young couple who proceeded to drive us to our quarters, a large mud hut located in the middle of the native area of a rather grotty town. Our room contained two beds and several large spiders but no chairs, no tables, no bath, no sanitation and a strong cocktail of indescribably bad smells. An adjoining cubicle with a concrete floor had a central drain and a four-gallon petrol can suspended overhead on gimbals. It was filled with water which, being just underneath a corrugated iron roof, nearly reached boiling point by midday. Its contents could be tipped out by pulling on an attached rope. This was at least ingenious but it produced a dowsing of such hot water that it was quite impossible to dry after the 'shower'.

In haste to return to our hosts, we failed to register on these finer points of our abode until much later in the day when we also discovered we had to cope in the light of a solitary low-powered electric lightbulb for our struggle into Mess kit: dress ties had to be fixed by feel! We dropped our bags on the floor and went off with our hosts for aperitifs at a civilian club. We were on the verge of starvation, it being ten hours since we had snatched some breakfast at El Geneina and cocktails were not our favourite poison on a hot afternoon; but they helped the faltering conversation when nobody seemed able to utter much English.

A little verbal contact having been achieved, we were at last trundled off to the Palace, an oven-hot barn of a place, to be entertained to a nine-course lunch. I was sitting between two French officers and found the going appallingly difficult. It wasn't that I hadn't already found some of their British 'pongo' counterparts couldn't also be a bit boring at times, but it seemed the meal would never end. At 5 pm we were taken back to our mud hut where we tried unsuccessfully to snatch a little shut-eye. Ahead of us lay a call at the French Army club, followed by another banquet at the Palace which was due to start at 9 pm.

The interlude at the Army Club provided enough whisky to clear our dazed wits and the subsequent banquet, laid on in the gardens of the Palace, was greatly improved by the presence of the ladies.

Something like sixty diners sat down under the stars at a long table elegantly set with white linen, gleaming flat ware and glinting wine glasses, the whole brightly lit by electric standard lamps and surrounded by beds of tropical flowers in full bloom. This second gastronomic marathon of the day was made endurable by the air becoming a trifle cooler. I also had a charming French wife on either side. (Are not all Frenchwomen charming?) Now at last, inspired by the alcohol, I was getting into my stride in stumbling French, having lost all sense of shyness and no longer ashamed of my linguistic incompetence.

With the best will in the world, the next three hours were bound to be gruelling. It was surprising to see men leaving the table to walk off into the garden to relieve themselves every now and then; it was more astonishing when the waiters, following suit, did not even bother to be so discreet. They calmly turned their backs on us and urinated into the nearest flower bed. The banquet finished with speeches and toasts in champagne. Dizzy with fatigue, Jim and I hit the hay in our hovel at the end of a very enervating 22hr day.

Fortunately, the cruise was making a late-ish start at 9 am and we had been invited to breakfast with our host and his wife at 7.30 am. They had obviously been briefed that the normal British breakfast consisted of fried eggs, bacon and almost neat whisky! Manfully we tried to cope with chunks of half-cooked greasy fat bacon and tumblers of scotch, slightly diluted by tepid water which we somehow managed to swallow without throwing up. Talk about keeping a stiff upper lip: '*Vive la France! Vive l'Angleterre!*' The outside temperature was already climbing above 110°F as we thanked our French hosts for their overwhelming hospitality, hoping we sounded sincere. Then, trying not to show undue haste, Jim and I climbed into a waiting staff car and sped off to the airfield to join our colleagues. Everyone was nursing a hang-over but singing in his heart.

In truth, we just could not get airborne quickly enough and only had to make a short 200-mile hop in the health-restoring coolness at 7,000ft, before we would be in another world, well-ordered and familiar. With unspeakable relief, we crossed the south end of what remained of the formerly extensive Lake Chad and, in less than two hours, had landed at the neat little town of Maiduguri, seat of the Muslim Shehu of Bornu in north-east Nigeria where he ruled under the beneficent eyes of the Colonial Office.

The landing ground was V-shaped with two all-weather runways and clear approaches, but because of yellow fever regulations it had been built out in the blue, seven miles from town. The connecting

119

road was extremely bumpy and we came to loathe the shaking we had to endure every time we used it.

Hundreds of the Fulani had walked and ridden for many miles to greet us and could be plainly seen from the air, among them finely dressed courtiers representing the Shehu. Even at a glance, the Nigerians appeared more prosperous and dignified than their kith and kin across the border who seemed neglected by comparison, despite the fact that our recent French hosts had adopted much of the native life-style themselves.

As luck would have it, for the next four nights Jim and I were accommodated together with the Air Commodore and Bill Storrar, living in the lap of luxury with Mr J. Patterson, the British Resident, who possessed a lively wit and whose spacious and spotlessly clean Residency resembled a baronial hall but was equipped with large ceiling fans rotating in every room. Air conditioning was, of course, as yet unknown throughout the length and breadth of Africa, so it helped a lot to have the air indoors stirred up by electric fans or by *punkas* waving overhead.

We met these ingenious Indian devices in the rather primitive Messes of the Royal West African Frontier Force in Nigeria. An array of heavy drapes hanging from beams was swung to and fro with the minimum of effort by a servant who was often reclining out of sight in an adjoining alcove. He pulled rhythmically with a foot on a rope that passed through a hole in the wall and was connected to the *punka* in the next room. Gravity simply pulled the whole contraption noiselessly back the other way like a pendulum, but the cooling effect on those sitting underneath was very soothing.

The contrast of life at Maiduguri with that at Fort Lamy beggared description and the Resident was most solicitous for our comfort. When our demand for cold water overtook the daily rate of production, he was in a quandary: every drop had to be carried to the house on the heads of women from a water-hole in a dried-up river bed a mile away. After filtering and boiling, it had to be cooled, bottled and finally chilled.

Did we mind, he enquired diplomatically, if he gave us bottled mineral water instead, or perhaps even iced lager, to slake our insatiable thirst, until the supply of chilled, fresh drinking water could catch up with our consumption? We were permanently dehydrated in the steady 115°F which, unlike the summer heat we had learnt to live with elsewhere, scarcely fell at night, let alone by the 40° drop we always enjoyed in Egypt. Overcome by heat on arrival, we lazed around listlessly and responded only out of politeness to Patterson's kind invitation to stroll with him after tea to visit a camp of freed slaves, escapees from the neighbouring Camerouns and now living in a safe sanctuary nearby.

'Mom o'Liberty', their tall leader, exuded a natural dignity but at a hint of some 'baksheesh' in the form of small cash prizes, he immediately organised races and a display of spear-throwing by his fellow refugees. The sports over, they spontaneously started up Afroethnic musical stomping for our benefit by a group of mixed sexes who were obviously only too happy to be free to dance.

The following morning was spent on aircraft maintenance but Jim and I were then dragooned into taking a pre-lunch 'constitutional' with the Air Commodore, who didn't very much like his own company and correctly guessed we both needed some exercise. So off we went, the Air Commodore striding ahead at a brisk pace, none of us casting much of a shadow under the blistering sun which was now shining almost dead overhead. As we went plodding along, following in the tracks of the Air Commodore over the hot sand, Jim nudged me and whispered in my ear, 'Mad dogs and Englishmen . . .' so I whipped out my camera with an eye for a possible future laugh and surreptitiously snapped the figure that was so energeticly receding in front of us and casting no shadow at all! Unfortunately for our host, we three needed more cooled H_2O when we returned to the Residency.

After a second hot night of restless sleep, we spent an hour in the air practising close formation flying in a gaggle of seven aircraft as preparation for our forthcoming air displays at Lagos and Accra. Then a succession of armed squads of RWAFF troops were assembled on the airfield so as to jump in and out of the two Valentias to practise emplaning, while we anxiously looked on, expecting a large black foot to miss the small metal strip provided as a step and, instead, go right through the flimsy silver-doped canvas lower mainplane. As a reward for all their efforts, we then gave them a flip round the airfield, 22 at a time, the first of 514 passengers to have a baptism of flight in my Valentia during the cruise. Their reactions of gleeful incomprehension were mixed with fearful amazement whenever we flew through a cloud, for they had imagined clouds were actually solid! For our part we learnt their name for aircraft which, translated, was 'Canoes of the Sky'. These emplaning exercises were repeated at every stop we made in West Africa and were always performed most enthusiastically by the troops.

That afternoon we were treated to a spectacular display of horsemanship organised in our honour on the spacious maidan in front of the palace of the Shehu who was in his declining years and sat under a huge parasol of State, surmounted by a golden lion, with his favourite 'toy boy' beside him. He was attended by a nobility of Mais and Fulanis who had shortly to appoint his successor before our return in May. The RAF had been given ringside seats on a shaded balcony of the palace.

Scores of horsemen arrived in sections by tribes and advanced across the maidan towards the Shehu to make their obeisance with spear-waving and much shouting. Chanting filled the air, accompanied by drums and a continuous flow of warbling from reed instruments, the players using their large flexible cheeks like the bellows of bagpipes, breathing in while at the same time blowing out. It was a trick I hadn't seen before!

The mounts were decked out in gaily-woven saddle cloths with loose-fitting trousers and trappings of armour. The riders wore flowing white robes and tattered shreds of Crusader chain-mail brought from the Levant by ancient trans-Saharan trade routes to Chad and into Bornu, to be handed down by their ancestors. This ceremony continued for over an hour and concluded with a stately parade by the Shehu's grooms, leading unmounted stud horses decorated in bright accoutrements. The Fulani horsemen then assembled on the far side of the maidan and, with wild shrieks, suddenly galloped all together at full speed towards the Shehu, shouting and brandishing swords and spears as they charged. Just as suddenly, when only yards short of the spectators, they reined in and turned away with final warlike gestures, while we were enveloped in the clouds of dust they had raised. It was colourful and exciting to watch this scene enacted from the distant, feudal past.

Next morning we took off at dawn for a three-hour recce of the western shores of Lake Chad. On board, we carried the Resident and eight of his officials who wanted to see for themselves if the Anglo-French attempts to stem the southward advance of the Sahara were having any discernible effect. A type of coarse running grass commonly found in coastal sand dunes was being planted to try to stabilise the encroaching desert. This aerial survey was not encouraging to our passengers, for everywhere fields and trees could be seen being buried alive under the wind-blown sand. On the other hand, they were delighted to see and take note of much more cultivation and farming activity in one part of their province than they had expected. It would mean a very welcome windfall for the Bornu tax collectors!

That evening was our last at Maiduguri and our generous host threw a farewell party for all the RAF. It was attended by his staff and their wives and when it was in full swing, a French and an English official arrived, unannounced and quite unexpectedly. They had both been away for weeks on a joint Anglo-French study of the encroaching Sahara, on a very long safari and had been badly delayed by one of their trucks breaking down out in the wilderness. Travel-stained, tired and dishevelled, they were hailed with delight and general relief, especially by their wives who had both been anxiously waiting for their safe return.

Our next move of only three hours away to the west was to Kano whose red brick walls served as a fortress for the Emir. Garbed in flowing white robes, wearing a white turban and tribal scarf that covered his chin but revealed a handsome bearded face, he was waiting with members of his Council to meet us on the airfield. He seemed delighted to be promised flights around his domain accompanied by his entourage. The Air Commodore and Bill Storrar were whisked away by the Regimental Colonel and the rest of us were taken to the RWAFF Officers' and NCOs' Messes for the next six days.

Kano was also very hot and enervating and we found little common ground for nattering with our Army hosts who seemed to be enslaved by the unlimited equine facilities for playing polo. It was an obsessional topic of conversation, but for us polo was a closed book. There appeared to be a more fundamental difference of perception between us of what was going on. We also noted with unease a tendency to arrogance on their part. An incident of which I was an unwilling and indignant witness was the physical chastisement of a Nigerian barber who had apparently kept two RWAFF captains waiting for their appointments. They were the worse for drink and I had never before seen an assault on an African by fellow British officers. The behaviour of these two senior 'pongos' quite appalled me.

Our hosts also practised a vice which was quite new to us. The sun set late by local clock time and drinks were not served until 7 pm, when they began to flow without pause for hours on end and without the solace of any 'blotting paper'. It would be 10.30 pm and sometimes even later before food appeared, by which time everyone was absolutely screeching. As the meal seldom finished before midnight, this uncouth routine made the penance of our early morning rising more than usually harsh.

Some of the RWAFF subalterns seemed keen to fly with us; but the idea of troop reinforcement by air had never occurred to them. When not exercising with their troops, we continued practising combined flying manoeuvres, trying out various patterns of air formations for the coming displays at Accra and Lagos. Our finale was going to be a 'beat up': led by the Vincents, it was decided that the seven of us would approach the spectators at 4,000ft and then dive as steeply as possible to ground-level in line astern. The stately Valentias could only manage about 140 mph before their wings started to flap even when empty, but it was fun to behave skittishly for a change.

One evening, as we sat cooling off in the dim light of oil lamps in the Mess garden, relaxing with our first long whiskies and sodas of the day, the ground suddenly became alive with scorpions, creeping out of holes under our feet. Probably sensing the approach of rain, these three-inch-long insects with their venomous curled-back barbed tails put paid to any peace and quiet until, after the next half an hour of hopping about in the chase, we had accounted for more than a score and could once more settle back into our chairs.

By the time we came to leave Kano for our next halt at Kaduna, the skies had started to fill with storm clouds in the afternoons. Southwards the bush and scrub gave way to greener country, with noticeably more trees and vegetation than in the north. Scarcely had we landed at Kaduna and tethered the aircraft to screw-pickets than the first tornado broke on us, with high wind, heavy rain and violent thunder. It was a warning that the settled conditions of the Harmattan, a season of hot, dry northerly winds, were breaking up.

The following day the two Valentias flew north-west to Sokoto, three hours away, where we were met by the Sultan, the traditional spiritual leader of Muslims in West Africa. After lunch, we demonstrated emplaning the local soldiery and in the evening were warmly entertained by the small British community who – guess what – all drank like fish!

On returning to Kaduna, we flew more troops around their stamping ground but afterwards had to face a midday drinking session with the RWAFF in which the ritual of 'one for the road' went on until 3.30 pm! We recovered from this tribulation just in time to attend a regimental guest night in the Mess dressed in full Mess kit. It was lucky we were rapidly acquiring hollow legs.

On 10 May we set course for Lagos. For the second time since leaving the Sudan, we now ruefully shook the dust from our feet, for this was our own colonial dust. But once in the air, we had plenty to think about – flying was a life apart. Above the broken clouds, the air temperature was only 60°F and we felt distinctly cold, but we were soon forced down underneath a sheet of continuous low cloud so as to keep in sight of the ground.

With our trailing aerial wound in, we scraped over the tops of the dense tropical forest, passing through wisps of steam rising from the tangled canopy of enormous trees and thick undergrowth. Every now and then the sun, reflected from a patch of swamp below, glared balefully up at us through the dense leaves. It was no place for the forced landing we had been trained to anticipate. Anyone unlucky enough to have to come down into that jungle would simply disappear. Presently, we crossed the Niger which was now meandering and dividing into wide branches. After four hours, out of some brightness ahead, a long creek of the sea loomed into view, and there also was Lagos, spread across a green coastal bar with great rollers of the South Atlantic crashing in tumult on a steep sandy shore.

Bill Storrar and I were the guests of the wife of a middle-aged Government official whose CMG appeared in next day's Coronation Honours list. Their house was a picture of loveliness, with tree-spangled gardens sweeping down to a private lagoon and to our great relief we were once more in civilised society, with no more waiting for meals to all hours. Moreover, the cuisine was absolutely first class.

Unfortunately for everyone concerned, heavy rain interrupted all the Coronation Day celebrations in Lagos on 12 May, but we performed a last-minute flypast in our arrow formation over Government House at 5 pm and another similar flight over the postponed ceremony of the Trooping of the Colour on the dot of 8.15 am next day. In the afternoon we took on a hefty Nigerian AFC XI and lost 3:4 – not bad, considering we were playing in our tennis shoes. Whenever we could cadge a lift to the beach, we went surfing in the tremendous Atlantic swell and soon discovered playing squash in the comparative cool of the evening was still too sticky to enjoy.

On 14 May, as scheduled, we flew to Accra, capital of the Gold Coast (Ghana), an easy two-hour stooge westwards, keeping a few miles offshore along the coast past French Dahomey. There we were met by the Colonial Secretary and by officers of the Gold Coast Regiment who were to be our hosts for a week. Ours were the first military aircraft they had seen for four years. Unlike the swampy background of Lagos, grassy slopes ran down to the sea at Accra and the climate seemed much drier. It was hard to realise that yellow fever had only recently been raging there.

Next morning we gave our set-piece display over a mass of some 60,000 enthralled spectators who had trekked for miles to watch. After our final 'beat up', the Valentias finished off the show by emplaning and flying around with loads of armed soldiery, much to everyone's delight. During the ensuing week we continued flying scores of troops and officials from Accra, while the Vincents visited Kumasi in the interior of Ashanti and went west along the coast to survey Takoradi. When WW2 came, three years later, Takoradi became a vital back-door port to the Middle East for air reinforcements from the UK and the USA.[3]

125

At Accra we were well into the middle of the expedition and were programmed for a welcome pause, our first complete day off duty in four weeks. The prospect of a long laze with nothing to do gladdened our hearts; but instead, we had to contend with a very kindly-meant invitation from the local British community to a 'peanut chop' from which there was no polite escape. It turned out to be a buffet lunch with an enormously varied selection of salads, sliced banana, mango, grated coconut and rice as the background for a very hot curry laced with peanut oil and spices of every description. Before we could attack this great spread, we were plied for two hours with endless pink gins until we grew rather more than ravenous. It was a crude way of spending a hot afternoon and inevitably ruined the rest of our free day.

Fortunately, surfing was still accessible in the Atlantic close by and as I tumbled about in the breakers I had time to ponder and decided that West Africa could not really compete with East Africa for either scenery or climate. Our stay at Accra ended with a game of soccer against a schoolboy XI in which we were trounced by lean and barefoot boys who ran rings round us; hulking rugby forward Jim Irens being singled out for special attention. He was mobbed after the game with requests for the autograph of 'Mr Aeroplane'.

Returning to Lagos, we repeated our display of formation flying and troop emplaning on 22 May, finishing with a 'beat-up' of the multitude gathered on the race course. Another day of flying with more troops and officials brought our visit to an end. The Vincents had already established their ability to fend for themselves on short cross-country flights and now went off to 'show the Flag' over neighbouring towns. We planned to rejoin them again at Kaduna where there were more troops needing to be trained and emplaned.

On 25 May, Bill Storrar decided that he and I should take off in formation in pouring rain and fly in close company back to Kaduna. In the absence of any weather forecast for the route, he was perhaps asking for trouble if conditions continued to be as unfavorable as they were at Lagos. It would be many years before the RAF would be equipped for an all-weather role. Within a few minutes of leaving Lagos we were skimming the treetops in the base of thick cloud into which Storrar kept disappearing. There was only one thing for me to do for safety – turn away from him and climb up through the cloud. We emerged into the clear at 7,000ft, surrounded by towering tropical cumulonimbus cloud but with no sight or sound of the leader. Undaunted, Jim and I pressed on regardless on what we had calculated to be a four-hour flight.

After an hour and a half, with only occasional glimpses of forest and swamp below, my attention was drawn by our Wireless Operator who pushed open the little communicating hatch behind me and handed up a pencilled signal which I have kept ever since. It read:

'To (Valentia) K3663. From (Valentia) K3611. Have turned 240 degrees. Am returning Lagos above clouds. Position 25 miles east of Oshogbo. Where are you?'

There is no record of my reply, but any position I reported could only have been by guess and by God. A quick glance at the map failed to show me Oshogbo and it was impossible to say just where I had got to. I had been planning to let down through the cloud a few minutes short of our ETA and hopefully feel my way into Kaduna for the last ten miles or so. There was no valid reason to question authority and I assumed I was being invited to return to Lagos. The cloud below was dense and the ground invisible, so I turned back on a reciprocal course. I guessed if we flew back well beyond the coast, the clouds would probably not be sitting right on the deck, and I could expect to find enough clear space to fly below them.

Sure enough, we broke cloud at 800ft over the sea and again turned right about towards land, gingerly approaching the rain-swept coast. Ten minutes later, Lagos came into sight and by the time we arrived, we could see Storrar's Valentia already sitting in a parking bay. It had been an abortive three-and-a-half hours' flying and he now decided to stay for another night and fly to Kaduna the following day, hoping for better weather. As it turned out, his luck was in.

At Kaduna we spent our last morning emplaning troops. Thereafter, all seven aircraft of the expedition headed for home, carefully avoiding Fort Lamy and spending single nights at Kano, Maiduguri, Abecher, El Geneina, El Fasher and Khartoum, where we left the Vincent groundcrews and bade farewell to our fellow pioneers.

After a last very hot night at Wadi Halfa, we flew into Heliopolis for a late lunch on 2 June. The main route had measured 7,700 miles there and back and the viability of this new trans-African military air route had been satisfactorily proved. The only unserviceability in the total 200 hours' flying by the two Valentias occurred three hours out of Fort Lamy when No 2 cylinder of my starboard engine started to play up; but my erk fitter had put it right while we refuelled at Abecher. We thought the world of our dependable Bristol Pegasus engines and Vickers airframes. They had no vices and, within their own limitations, stood up to the torrid tropical conditions with a kind of Olde Worlde dignity. To my oft-felt regret, the

West African Cruise was my swan-song in beloved No 216 (BT) Sqn. Never again would I sit at those familiar controls; never again fly such delightful old, head-in-air mastodons. I was now 'overseas tour-expired'.

June was a time of farewells to many good friends whom I would, alas, never see again and a parting from others whose paths would not cross mine for years to come. Jim Irens would join the small illustrious band of victors of Mt Kenya later that year, but would, sadly, eventually be lost during WW2 flying an Anson (of all things!) over the Persian Gulf.

After four years living in and around Cairo I had been privileged to have been befriended by many warm-hearted British civilian expatriates who had laboured all their lives lovingly and with dedication on behalf of their host country, Egypt. First and foremost, I recall the charming and hospitable Mr and Mrs Little and the young Gubbins couple. The husbands worked in the Egyptian Survey department and tolerated my endless questions.

Professor Archibald Cresswell was ex-RFC, a universally respected archaeologist and an Arabist expert at the American University of Cairo. He helped design the Aga Khan's mausoleum at Aswan and was a most fascinating raconteur, even though he was exceedingly deaf and was knighted at the advanced age of 90! The Garden City welcome from Dr and Mrs Llewellyn Phillips, doyen and matron respectively of Cairo's Kasr el Aini hospital, knew no bounds. Their elder daughter, Barbara, was women's vice-president of LSE's Students' Union in 1933. It's a small world!

Mr and Mrs Matthias of Marconis had always made me feel part of the family in their prettily laid-out suburb of Maadi, as had the Watts who, after many searing years in charge of the original British-built Aswan dam at the First Cataract on the Nile, had been relocated at the delightful Nile barrage, north of Cairo. The company of 'WB' Delaney, Chairman of Egyptian Hotels Ltd, was an endless delight, for he was a notable raconteur of local anecdotes.

On a more serious note, Dr Harold E. Hurst CMG MA DSc was a mine of unique information, having walked most of the 4,210 miles up the Nile from the Mediterranean to its source, south of Lake Victoria where, as the Kagera, it rises in the hills near Lake Tanganyika. His book *The Nile* remains a masterly treatise on that great waterway.

Finally, there is my enduring indebtedness to that stalwart Egyptophile, Richard H. Greaves, formerly head of the Mines department, a naturalist and authority on the native and migratory birds of Egypt. His study in Zamalek was filled with stuffed speci-

128

mens and his pleasant villa contained two live charmers, one of whom literally stole away to become my wife.[4]

Internationally, the future was menacing, but no one cared to peer too far ahead. Italy had bombed Guernica in April, sending shock waves of hysterical fear across the world, although nobody seemed much put out by the even greater carnage between the conflicting armies. In May, Mr Chamberlain had formed a coalition with Labour. Then, in July, Japan unexpectedly attacked China. Yet, between my Service friends, our *adieux* were untinged by misgiving; for our tomorrows still shone with bright expectation. I only wished I could have had the last four years of shenanigans all over again. Were they really coming to an end?

Notes to Chapter VIII

1 'Automatic pilot of aircraft' (OED).
2 Estimated time of arrival.
3 The West African Reinforcement Route (Takoradi to Cairo) was a major source of the supply of aircraft for the Desert Air Force and for the Far East theatre of operations.
4 Air Vice-Marshal Wilf Oulton has recalled that Dickie's "years of service in Egypt did not absorb all his energies and he caused astonishment and consternation in Cairo 'high society' by snatching from under the noses of his many rivals the debutante of the year and marrying her despite considerable opposition" (*Journal* of the Royal Institute of Navigation, May 1996).

IX

Specialist Navigator

ON 26 June I sailed wistfully away from Egypt on the SS *Marco Polo*, leaving Alexandria for Venice. I had been granted permission to make my own way home and to recover whatever the cost would have been for a Government 1st Class trip by P & O. Post-buses and Shanks's ponies took me leisurely through the Dolomites to Innsbruck and trains carried me to Andermatt in Switzerland and to Paris for the International Exhibition at the Palais de Chaillot, opposite the Eiffel Tower. This was notable for two outstanding examples of architecture which stood glaring at each other across the concourse. If buildings could speak, these were screaming defiance. The German pavilion, with its blatant *décor* of swastikas, faced another containing the USSR exhibits, itself topped by a bold sculpture of the proletariat striding victoriously towards the light, or was it to communist slavery? With abandon, I lashed out my last few pennies on an hour's flight by Imperial Airways from Le Bourget to London and landed in fine style at Croydon. Actually, I was clean broke.

In August I reported to Manston as a new boy at the School of Air Navigation. With the pace of promotion increasing, I might be a Flight Lieutenant by December, which would mean a welcome extra £100 p. a. I vaguely wondered if, at that rate, I might even reach Squadron Leader by 1944: what wealth! What responsibility! Never for a moment could I have imagined I would by then have already been an acting Group Captain for a year. It really is rather amazing what a war will do.

The School of Air Navigation had moved in 1936 from the flying-boat base at Calshot, where the cost of using flying-boats for its training programme was quite prohibitive. At Manston, on the Isle of Thanet, No 48 Sqn could combine the training of its own pilots for their maritime reconnaissance role with providing taxi-drivers in Avro Ansons Mk I for the flying exercises needed by the School. In 1938 enough Ansons and spare pilots became available to give the School its own fleet, freeing No 48 Sqn to concentrate on its maritime job and to move to its war station at Thorney Island. The

School and its successors enjoyed this hard-won flying independence until its purely air navigation identity was lost by being absorbed in a move to RAF Manby from Shawbury in 1956.

Although the Anson Mk I was still largely made of wood and canvas, it was a monoplane with two engines and an undercarriage retractable by tediously cranking a handle – a great step forward! Easy to fly, it cruised at 120 knots and had a good all-round view from its glass-house cabin and bomb-aimer's window, from where the angle of drift could be measured with the bombsight. The navigator's table behind the pilot on the port side had an airspeed indicator, an altimeter and a magnetic compass for monitoring the course flown. A W/T operator sat behind.

The Anson's ability to fly at 19,000ft was invaluable when a view of the stars was needed on cloudy nights, but lack of oxygen and heating were severely limiting, human factors. Its Mk II successor was metal-bodied and, being heavier, had a lower ceiling. There was still no oxygen or cabin heating and the crew wrapped up well. As a weapon for the maritime war, the Anson Mk II was just as bad a joke as the Mk I.

Pupils were detailed to fly in pairs, alternating duties as first and second navigator, the latter's first job on take-off being to wind up the wheels – 150 turns of a crank-handle were five minutes of very hard puffing. But comparisons with dear old Valentias were breathtaking! For me the biggest flying changes concerned weather and air traffic density. Unlike the normally very clear, empty skies of Africa, here was a land of clouds, rain and fog, with plenty of aircraft flying around. Other aeroplanes had been only rarely encountered in African skies, and although we had had plenty of sandstorms, smog had been quite unknown.

This last horror was very common in industrial Europe and with south-easterly winds it always drifted across the UK from industrial Northern France, Belgium and the Ruhr. One summer day, flying over Sheffield in yellow sulphurous fumes at 5,000ft, I could only just make out the chimney stacks of John Brown's steel mills spewing filth into the air: the town itself was invisible. To make matters really exciting, weather is notoriously variable from one place to another, especially over the British Isles, where a drop in air temperature of a mere 1°F often made the difference between the possible and the impossible for landing. Such forecasting finesse remained for years well beyond the skill of the duty Met officers on our stations. But despite the urgent promptings of obviously dire necessity to deal with weather limitations, 'Their Airships' lacked the vision and the funds to sponsor adequate national research and simply relied on the meagre resources of the RAE at Farnborough.

In 1937 a squadron of Heyford 'heavy' bombers, flying from Aldergrove in Northern Ireland to their base in England, ran into icing conditions and all but one crashed. Incredibly, our Masters did nothing more than wring their hands for more than a year, leaving it to AOC-in-C Bomber Command to put together a national network of available radio aids, which was really making the best of a bad job and only a makeshift solution. 'Blind Approach' for the RAF was still a long way off and our acquisition of the ability to fly in all weathers had to wait for the arrival of that important revolution in air/ground communication, radio-telephony (R/T) and for foreign-invented radio aids in the late 'thirties and for refinements of British radar in the War.

The School, acutely aware of what is known in military speak as the Weather Factor, was now commanded by Wing Commander P. D. Robertson AM of quite outstanding character. He had sailed before the mast in the testing days of his youth and had lost an eye and half his face trying unsuccessfully to rescue a pilot from his burning crashed aircraft, for which bravery he wore the Albert Medal. Gaunt and austere, he concealed a heart of gold, but 'Robbie' was noted for his often justifiably caustic views on the merits of some holders of high rank. He was a master of the science of navigation and led a dedicated staff who were willing to follow him through Hell and high water. Determined to attain the highest standard of excellence, his influence could not be overstated. He inspired universal admiration and 'aficionados' respected him as the true Father of RAF Air Navigation.

With a dozen pilots, one being my chum Bob Brittain from No 208 Sqn (he of the spinney fire at the Khanka lunatic asylum which I described earlier), I embarked on a three-month 'short' navigation course which was followed by six months on the advanced course to qualify myself for a career commission, which all but three members of the Course already possessed, having entered from Cranwell or from Oxbridge, the latter with very valuable ante-dates. (In 1933, graduates from London University had had no such enticements.)

Our senior student was tough Geoffrey Paddon who later won fame and a DSO as one of the heroic PoW escapees from Colditz. The Course senior instructor was Flight Lieutenant Wilf Oulton who, after a brilliant war against U-boats in 1943 when he won the DSO and DFC, as an Air Vice-Marshal commanded Operation 'Grapple', the British thermonuclear bomb tests at Christmas Island in the Pacific in 1957.

Like all RAF stations in the 'thirties, Manston possessed very few officers' married quarters. Most of the married staff and all the married students had to find their own digs off the camp. Luckily, in the country as a whole and for many years to come, there was still an ample supply of furnished flats and houses to hire, especially in seaside resorts like those fringing the Isle of Thanet. The *esprit de corps* on such a station could obviously not depend to any large extent on the centripetal influence of its Officers' Mess and it fell to the living-out officers to keep the Service flag flying socially.[1] To me, the pace of life was perceptibly more intense than it had been at Heliopolis due to our being so much nearer the hub of affairs: it was all happening in Europe.

My eyes were opened when, despite having thumbed my way for four years around some of the wilder parts of the Middle East and a fairish part of untrodden Africa, the three-month preliminary air navigation Course revealed that I scarcely knew anything about the theory of air navigation and also very little about its proper application! I had just been very lucky.

Between the wars, the RAF trained all its permanent General Duties officers for one or other of its so-called specialist duties – armament, engineering, photography, signals, air navigation and flying instruction. Apart from medical, dental and a few other professional activities, no specialist officers were directly recruited if they could be trained from within existing resources. After years of neglect, when I joined the Service in 1933 it had only 14 fully qualified navigation officers listed, a serious deficiency for which it was going to pay very dearly in WW2. The RAF had failed to understand that all flying involved an element of air navigation: ridiculously, navigation had become regarded as a special activity, when in fact it was an essential part of every purposeful flight.

To 'Bradshaw' along railways, and to land in order to ask the way was just not good enough; but such uncouth practices stemmed from the old RFC days and had been accepted, if not actually encouraged, as displays of airmanship and initiative on the part of pilots rather than crass incompetence. The air observer had worn the distinctive badge of a single wing sprouting from an O, sometimes jokingly described in coarser terms by his pilot brethren, whose double-winged badge emphasised their superior pecking order! Air observers had been phased out after 1918 and thereafter all air navigation had been undertaken by pilots – there was nobody else to do it.

When at last a timid expansion of the RAF was actually authorised by a reluctant Government, a shortage of the physical material for pilots was foreseen. So the extinct air observer, possessor of an adequate supply of the 'little grey cells' but whose knee-jerk reaction did not have to be so pronounced as a pilot's, was revived in late 1937 though it took another year to recruit and train them before they could reach our squadrons.

For lack of qualified RAF air navigation instructors, retired mercantile marine officers were recruited for the task, though some had never flown, let alone navigated an aeroplane! Nor were there enough really suitable aircraft for the task of practical flying training. It was therefore no surprise that the first trickles of air observers were poorly received when they arrived for duty in the Front Line.

These problems were unknown to us in 1937 when we assembled at Manston to begin our own laborious climb through the higher mathematics and sciences that underpin the mysteries of air navigation. We had been joined by Captain James McEvoy of the Eire Air Force and by swarthy Captain Jawad, an Iraqi Air Force officer who had also been seconded to the course but whose sole interest lay with the girls on Margate beach. Some members of the course had been pilots in flying-boat squadrons and were well versed in coping with our elementary navigation exercises of long flights over the sea to find distant lightships in the North Sea and the Channel. We must have been very welcome diversions for their lonely keepers.

Our web-footed comrades had another advantage, having already encountered the marine sextant as a tool of their trade! In acknowledging their privileged membership of the 'Flying-boat Union', we also gradually came to believe in ourselves as members of an equally *élite* 'Navigators Union'. After much discussion and combined effort in the coming years, this unorganised body of opinion was destined to influence and ultimately transform the future RAF, as we shall see.

Those pre-war Manston days, while we grew acutely aware of the gathering storm, still revive memories of autumn mushroom-picking, winter walks along the cliffs to Reculver and fireside teas with hot buttered toast and lardy cake. There were Sunday morning noggins in the Cherry Brandy at Sarre and unique fluffy omelettes at the George and Dragon in Fordwich. Sherry and beer parties were thrown every week by the married friends and, in place of the non-existent TV, there were mandatory twice-weekly visits to the local movies. But many a cold night was spent scanning the sky to identify the stars. The 'long' six-month air navigation course followed in January 1938 and we had to make great efforts to keep up with our tutorials while coping with the intensive flying schedule in fair weather and foul. The course was featured in an early 1938 issue of *The Aeroplane* magazine and the publicity was indicative of a slight ground-swell of opinion that a lot of leeway perhaps needed to be made up in our technical field. In the summer, the sand dunes and empty Sandwich Bay shore offered a pleasant retreat, often shared with Jack and Doreen Davis who had both met at Cambridge. Jack had had the distinction as an undergraduate of scaling the highest pinnacle of his college one night to crown it with a chamber pot, much to the surprise of the dons in the morning. He went through 1942 as CO of Coastal Command's No 269 Hudson Sqn and in peace became AOC-in-C Flying Training Command, being appointed HM's Governor of Jersey in retirement.

The comforts of Manston compensated for some extremely 'hairy' night flights, navigating through continuous ice-forming cloud over Scotland, with the threat of fog back at base and only poor radio aids to help. Manston had no homing device except for a coded flashing light beacon sitting on the airfield – if it could be seen.

We worked hard and, in the best tradition, played hard. Every day we heard on the radio and read in our papers how the Nazi menace was growing. In March 1938, Austria was annexed by Hitler in defiance of the Treaty of Versailles and 250 miles of Czechoslovakian defences were thereby outflanked without a shot being fired. In the same month, the Italians bombed Barcelona, killing 1,300 civilians and injuring another 2,000. This made people think hard about any future conflict which now seemed to be on the cards: what about London? Actually, everyone kept missing the point that Spanish casualties were nine times greater 'in the field' than these civilian figures. In other words, what about doing something to protect our own fighting Services from the air?

We had travelled to Greenwich in the course of our studies to meet the astronomers at the Royal Observatory; we spent an afternoon in the Admiralty Compass Observatory at Slough and attended the National Physical Laboratory at Teddington to study gyroscope technology. At the Barking factory of Henry Hughes, where the new Mk VIII bubble sextants were being made for us, we were shown round by their technical 'rep' who, in 1941, came to share my office as a Flight Lieutenant in the Air Ministry. He was a highly esteemed colleague and after sharing many good yarns became my much-lamented friend – none other than the one and only Sir Francis Chichester.

Finally, we had a hilarious week with the Sappers at Chatham learning survey by mapping the Great Fields with a plane-table. We made invaluable contacts with the Royal Engineers and their brilliant Major J. C. T. 'Chris' Willis, who was ADI(Maps) in the Air Ministry during the war and in the 'fifties became the Director-General of Ordnance Survey. He did more with his inspired map production service to help us win the air war and to guide us in the early pre-NATO days, when we set about standardising maps and charts for the Allied air forces, than has ever been properly recognised. It so happened that he and RAF navigation specialists shared a strong mutual admiration. His brother Anthony became the inspired editor of *Tee Emm* and invented the (in)famous Pilot Officer Prune; but that is a story belonging to 1941.

As a result of the months of cramming that climaxed in July 1938, I had to concede first place to my closest friend, Thomas L. Moseley from Tamworth, who had entered from Cranwell and was a much better mathematician than I. He was always the life and soul of any party. Together with all our course, we were annotated 'N' in the Air Force List and both of us felt flattered by being retained as new instructors at the expanding School.

For my end of term leave, I made a dash for New York and New Hampshire, to stay for a month with two Columbia University professors, my sister Eve and her husband Dr Arthur Burns, who had himself been seriously wounded as a Sapper in 1918. They were now both American citizens and provided a privileged introduction to their exciting and now burgeoning country and to a multitude of stimulating academic and artist friends.

I sailed outwards at speed on the brand-new Blue-ribboned SS *Normandie* on her second ever westbound trans-Atlantic crossing and, to save myself £5 on the round trip, returned on the Hamburg American liner, the *New York*, which was a very bad mistake. The beautiful French ship had been most impressive, even at the 'blunt end'. After being fascinated by seeing all the condoms, some coloured red, white and blue, among the flotsam of the Hudson River where we docked, I found New York itself was truly exhilarating, especially when viewed from the top of the highest skyscraper – the new Rockefeller Center.

I returned to New York from Boston by ferry, just in time to see Tennessee Williams' moving play *Tobacco Road* on Broadway, before rushing to catch my liner with only minutes to spare; but the voyage across the Atlantic in August with a shipload of beer-swilling Nazis was quite another experience. The men wore *lederhosen* and donned their Brownshirt uniforms the moment we cast off from the West Side pier.

At the entrance to the tourist-class dining saloon stood a large open wooden tub into which any sea-sick diners just threw up – it always seemed to be half full and was quite the most disgusting thing I had ever seen. Of course it became a self-perpetuating requirement for a great many of my fellow-diners! Each evening everybody watched episodes from the endless Nazi propaganda film of the recent Berlin Olympics, depicted as a walk-over by the 'Master Race' by that notorious sycophant of Hitler's, Leni Reifenstahl. I was more than thankful, after six unpleasant days onboard, to dis-embark into a tender at Spithead and make my way back to Manston for duties on the staff.

Six years to the day after I had walked into the RAF Depot at Uxbridge, my short service commission expired and was replaced by a permanent one. Should anything now happen to me on active Service, any dependants I acquired had become partly the concern of HM Treasury! But no ante-date was conceded to remove the very significant eighteen months' handicap I bore with my contemporary Service graduates from Oxbridge. I always felt that decision a bit mean.

To my present retrospective disbelief and astonishment, it was still pre-Munich when I reached Manston; but the time-scale of events had begun to quicken almost daily and I had already succeeded in shaking off those leisurely and delightfully undemanding days of lotus-eating in Egypt. We were now living in highly menacing and very different circumstances. It was a clear case of all hands to the pumps.

It is never a good idea for any organisation to 'eat its own young', though in our case maybe there was no other option open to the School. Someone, somewhere had 'de-digitated' and decided to re-arm seriously and the race for survival was on. In air navigation we were carrying a heavy handicap of lost time and nursing a bagful of false hopes pinned on improving astro. Unfortunately, there was simply nothing better to offer and although great strides were being taken to simplify its use, as seen from today astro was almost a non-starter. If only we had seriously considered the practical effects on a bubble sextant of a pilot weaving about, trying not to be shot down, our first years of night-bombing failures could have been anticipated and alternative electronic devices developed much more quickly.

'Mose' and I were now each appointed to run separate 'Short N' courses and to modernise the syllabus for the doubling of the School's output. After two such courses, we handed over to the brightest pair from the latest batch of 'Spec Ns', while we ourselves were asked to run the next Specialist Course and to revise its syl-labus. This latter task involved writing memoranda and monographs on various aspects of air navigation, scribblings which were shortly to have quite unforeseen consequences for me.

We had each qualified on Ansons which were a doddle to fly and, in addition to running our courses and flying our students on exercises, we both participated in air trials of a new drift sight and an air log to evaluate their suitability for the Service and their general performance. I had no illusions about my luck to have been coupled up with 'Mose'; working as a team together reinforced my high opinion of him. He was a quite remarkable officer with a brilliant brain, an outstanding presence and natural charm. Always bubbling over with fun, he towered intellectually over his colleagues, among whom I was to be numbered for the next three years. His tragic death as the CO of No 228 Sqn, when accompanying the Duke of Kent on a Welfare staff visit to Iceland in one of his Sunderland flying-boats, in which all onboard except the tail gunner perished near the summit of a 1,300ft mountain in north-east Scotland on 25 August 1942, was never satisfactorily explained, as will be mentioned later. I had always thought Mose deserved to reach the top one day: *c'est la vie!*

Meanwhile in 1938, pressure in central Europe from some 30 German divisions pointing at Prague continued unabated; so in September the Royal Navy was temporarily mobilised. But it made no apparent difference to Chamberlain's humiliating shuttling to and from Germany with the French Premier, Daladier; nor to their reception by Hitler at Bad Godesburg and Munich. Chamberlain's return from Munich in September, pathetically waving a scrap of paper, provided a little valuable time for us to try to catch up with the vast German re-armament. Naturally, it also let Hitler off the hook and he continued expanding as fast as he could.

Munich had seemed a ghastly anti-climax for us in the RAF. We were hopelessly out-numbered, ill-equipped and lacked any effective war plan; but for weeks we had girded ourselves for the fray, far from confident but gritting our teeth for the outcome. The clash never came and to our dismay the public seemed convinced the trouble had somehow gone away for good! Wishful thinking died hard, but we in the Service now knew we had only a brief respite before the panic returned.

Hitler was arguably in no position at the time of Munich to deal with an advance by some 60-plus available French divisions with their huge collection of obsolete aircraft positioned on Germany's western flank. As it was, neither the French nor the British politicians had the stomach for a fight.

The French trusted in their infamous Maginot Line which offered no protection against any out-flanking attack through Belgium but gave them a false sense of security. To make us really depressed, the School at Manston had an official visit from a French General who bluntly told us of the powerful opposition from the political left wing in France to any armed initiative. He stated that the French trade unions were threatening to call a general strike at any minute. The prospect of any future combined ops with the French seemed very bleak.

The outcome of a serious conflict before Munich had been unimaginable but the whole RAF could read the message loud and clear: war had only been deferred and we ourselves were very, very far from being ready. So we found it only faintly encouraging in late 1938 to see a lone Hawker Hurricane occasionally flash across our sky and we had to wait much longer for the first Spitfire to appear. Round the corner from Manston on the South Downs and also across the Thames Estuary on the East Coast, strange wooden towers were being built: the RDF^2 system was under way but we could only guess at its full purpose.

Munich had really caught the School with its pants down and if 'Robbie' could help it, this wouldn't happen again for lack of realistic planning. Foremost in the equation, we needed to know just what our wartime role would be and where we might be located. We would certainly be in everybody's way if training tried to continue at Manston, regardless of any hostilities on the Continent or at sea.

To the casual observer, our activities might have seemed like business as usual. The new specialist students who now reported for training were as dedicated as ever and went through their paces without difficulty. At the end of six months, they went off to strengthen the navigation sinews and were in great demand everywhere in the RAF. Mose and I started another Specialist Course and could not have picked a better dozen students if we had had access to the Air Force List for choice. They were absolutely first class.

But events in 1939 waited on no man. The features on the world scene spelled out a relentless march towards the brink. Thus, while in February Britain had recognised Franco, this was capped by Germany annexing Bohemia and Moravia and all the rest of Czechoslovakia – so much for the Munich Agreement! April saw the collapse of the Spanish civil war, but Italy immediately seized Albania; while Hitler renounced the Anglo-German Naval Agreement and his non-aggression pact with Poland. So Britain replied by ordering national conscription.

In May, Britain came to a formal non-aggression agreement with one potential enemy, Turkey. Not to be outdone, Germany and Italy announced a formal pact – the vaunted Rome-Berlin Axis. To draw a desperate line somewhere in Europe, even if it could in no way be upheld in practice, we reaffirmed Britain's pledge of Poland's territorial integrity in July – a final throwing down of the gauntlet, so to speak. Hitler rejoined in August with a seemingly unbelievable pact with Stalin. Now things really started to hot up: Holland mobilised on 28 August and on 31 August our Navy was again mobilised. The very next day Poland was invaded and the fat was really in the fire.

This was the exciting back-drop to the School's last few months at Manston. Not to be distracted from our aim, Moseley and I pressed on with our gifted students whose enthusiasm knew no bounds. Little did we know what Fate had in store, but we all accepted our lot with a cynical and indifferent fatalism. Bomber Commmand was in the charge of Air Chief Marshal Sir Edgar Ludlow-Hewitt who, at the instigation of his navigation staff, thought it propitious for as many commanders of his squadrons and flights as possible to be indoctrinated into the latest processes of air navigation, time permitting.

A series of highly concentrated astro courses were at once organised at Manston for dozens of navigationally-illiterate Wing Commanders and Squadron Leaders, in fortnightly batches. To reach clear night skies often meant flying Ansons at 19,000ft in the perishing cold without oxygen. This task was repeated again and again until the programme had been completed and was a considerable feat of endurance on the part of the instructor concerned, Flight Lieutenant Jenkins. It was at least better than doing nothing; but it was really only clutching at straws. Sadly, Jenkins 'bought it' in his next post at the Aircraft and Armament Experimental Establishment (A&AEE).

The decision to evacuate to St Athan in South Wales, so as to leave Manston free as a forward base for the battle, was announced only when it was thought to be not only prudent but also no longer avoidable – in other words, at the very last minute! Everyone was now reading the tea leaves and widespread relief was felt when we were at last told to prepare to move. Schedules were compiled of essential equipment to be packed in numbered boxes, the larger items being crated. Blackboards and easels were listed, not forgetting the chalk and dusters. These arrangements began in mid-August, but every effort was made to keep instruction programmes free from disruption. Our brilliant Specialist Course still had six weeks to run.

Having put all the gear into packing-cases, including bulky spares for the Ansons, we were now split into two parties: one to fly to our new base and the other to trail behind by train with all the crated equipment and two hundred or so airmen and NCOs. I was detailed for the 'train' party. Four days before the balloon went up, the goods wagons were already packed and waiting in a Ramsgate siding for someone to blow the whistle. We were much better organised now than we had been in 1938.

I shall never forget the last few days at Manston. We were so relieved the waiting was over that even our more staid seniors were prancing about like foals. Our Chief Instructor, Reg Cooper, the most circumspect of Squadron Leaders, let his hair down at a party in his married quarters which ended with his lounge being festooned with loops of lavatory paper and decorated with 'pots, chamber, officers, for the use of'. None of us had the vaguest idea if or when we would ever meet again to celebrate. In fact it wasn't to happen until at least VE Day, 8 May 1945; but we knew in our bones there would be many grievous gaps among us if and when we did.

Sunday 3 September 1939 was calm and sunny. No need to wait for Mr Chamberlain's announcement: we knew quite well what was coming. The 'air' party flew off and the 'train' party boarded trucks for the short run down to Ramsgate. Arriving at the station yard, we paraded by flights and 'Stood Easy', while the Adjutant went off to find the stationmaster to sort out our appointed coaches. He had hardly taken a step before an air raid siren began to wail. There was just nowhere to shelter even if we had wanted to; but neither was there any sound of aircraft so we continued to stand in parade order, not feeling particularly anxious nor exposed to danger but enjoying the bright morning sun.

However, we hadn't counted on the valiant stationmaster who appeared in all his finery, running towards us at the double. Waving his arms and pointing upwards, he shouted to us to take cover; but his fears were quietly brushed aside and, instead, we invited him to show us to our carriages without more ado and to make sure our waiting locomotive had full steam up.

The train then set off, puffing slowly through the quiet, deserted corners of the southern counties, all bathed in golden sunshine and looking the picture of peace. I recognised one familiar straight section of the line that runs due east and west between Tonbridge and Redhill and had often been used to check our compasses from the air. On and on we crawled, for ever westwards, travelling for the most part on unfrequented rustic tracks.

St Athan was finally reached in pitch darkness and we crashed down on any available flat space – billiard table-tops or equally hard floors in the overcrowded Messes. The School had beaten a retreat to the comparative safety of South Wales; while the wives and families had all been left behind in the Front Line, with only themselves to provide mutual moral support. Typical, but this was War, dammit! There was much more to come.

Notes to Chapter IX

1 Air Vice-Marshal Wilf Oulton has recalled that Dickie 'and his charming bride were a very popular young couple in the social life of Manston' (*Journal* of the Royal Institute of Navigation, May 1996).
2 Radar Direction Finding – 'the Air Force name for what the Press and the public, when they were permitted to know, called 'radar' (John Terraine, *The Right of the Line*; Hodder & Stoughton, 1985).

X
AP1234(1)

FOR A day or two there was general mayhem at St Athan, but the School was soon back at work in makeshift classrooms. Flying exercises were rearranged to comply with air defence restrictions, limiting their scope and cramping our style. The Bristol Channel, Irish Sea and St George's Channel were substituted for the larger, wilder North Sea. It was novel to fly about in Ansons with fixed forward-mounted guns operated from the pilot's seat in the hope of a chance meeting with a 'hostile' in the course of a navigation exercise. But as we had little effective air gunnery practice, our weapons were more of a morale booster than anything else.

Married officers snatched brief moments off duty to scour the neighbouring Vale of Glamorgan for temporary lodgings and then made overnight dashes back to Kent to rescue deserted wives and family cars. The Service still failed to recognise that married aircrew needed cars if they were allowed to live off the camp – a concession which had become socially and politically unavoidable. By 1939 the RAF could not have functioned without personal cars, for the Messes could not have accommodated all the aircrew without having to be extended. But the aircrew received no financial help nor any tax concessions for buying or running their cars and the Treasury were getting away with murder.

Like many RAF wives, mine had concluded after Munich that my own future was not worth much of a bet. So she decided to try for a keepsake and this was now due to arrive at any minute. Two other broody wives were also sheltering under our roof at Birchington so a cutting-out operation by three members of staff from St Athan was on the cards.

Trevor Watts, who fattened bullocks at Llanmihangel, had unhesitatingly offered me a large room for my own prospective family and the Welsh welcome from his big-hearted wife Mary more than warmed the cold dampness of their huge old stone farmhouse. A nursing home in Cardiff was organised to give maternity back-up when needed in late October.

Mose and I completed the curriculum on schedule for our exceptional Spec N Course and the graduates were posted away to spread the gospel; but within months, three of them had 'bought it' in the Battle of Britain and their valuable influence was lost. On the other hand, Flight Lieutenant John Miller, seconded from the RCAF, went from strength to strength and after the war became Deputy Commander of Canadian Defense. Many other graduates from this Course also subsequently had brilliant RAF careers.

The 1939/40 winter was cold, 6ft snow drifts adding to transport difficulties in the black-out. On free Saturday afternoons we went to watch exciting Welsh rugby at Cardiff Arms Park and joined in the singing. But driving back in the dim glow of masked headlights was distinctly hairy when loose horses were often encountered in the narrow farm lanes.

Our next course was unsettled by events on the Continent. The progress of the British Expeditionary Force was not making headlines and our Advanced Air Striking Force was inadequately equipped. No one had confidence in Fairey Battles, and Blenheims were only a little more offensive; consequently heavy RAF losses seemed to be inevitable.

Following the U-boat sinking of SS *Athenia* on 3 September, the air of political restraint during the next six months of conflict was distinctly surreal. Instead of dropping bombs, Bomber Command was kept busy scattering futile leaflets over Germany. Daylight attacks became very costly, because of a complete lack of long-range fighter support. Our bombers were safer at night but the operational ceiling of the under-powered Whitley was too low to avoid 'flak' and the Wellington wasn't much better. The unpalatable fact that our bombers were ill-equipped for night navigation against defended targets had not been foreseen by our Masters. Lessons had to be learnt the hard way in that dangerous task.

The Royal Navy kept its heavy ships in safe anchorages in the North, as far away as possible from the prying eyes of the Luftwaffe and ready to deal with the much-feared German naval raiders. Low-performance Ansons and cumbersome, slow flying-boats from Coastal Command, the only effective 'eyes' of the Royal Navy, were easy game to flak and only managed to survive the daily surveillance of enemy naval bases, starting from day one, by large helpings of luck and using every scrap of available cloud cover. They had a most unenviable remit.

1940 turned into a fine summer – 'Hitler's weather' – which greatly favoured sudden *blitzkriegs*. Observed from our South Wales hide-out, Hitler's attacks on Poland, the over-running of Holland and

Belgium, the replacement of Neville Chamberlain by Winston Churchill in May, the Dunkirk rescue and the fall of Norway and France were deplorable but, to us, rather distant dramas. Only when a Dutch squadron and later a French one dropped in unannounced out of the sky and stayed on to join us in the future battles did we have a direct contact with the war. The sun continued to shine day after day from cloudless skies over Glamorgan and, to our dismay, a tanker was sunk by a U-boat in the Bristol Channel within sight of our airfield. But even then we could do nothing to retaliate.

Specialist navigation courses were now temporarily suspended and my colleague Mose was posted north to be Chief Instructor at No 2 School of General Reconnaissance at Squire's Gate near Lytham St Annes, No 1 S of GR having been over-run in Guernsey. Robbie, now a Group Captain, sent for me to say that a recent attempt by Wing Commander F. L. Hopps AFC to rewrite the basic textbook on air navigation had fizzled out. As the monographs I'd scribbled for my course showed a gift for simplifying abstruse theories he asked if he could nominate me for the task. Unfortunately, it would mean a back-room job for a time; having once written the Manual of Air Navigation for the RNAS, he was well aware of the implications.

This seemed to me to be an easy challenge considering that the current manual was so inadequate. Badly outdated even by the languid pre-war rate of changes in instruments, the old textbook did not reflect advances in aircraft performance nor the 'new look' into the practice of air navigation now being taken by our few enlightened pace-makers. Astro had lately become an everyday element of our trade but while its theory had been very fully expounded in Air Publication 1456 by the pen of Squadron Leader L. K. Barnes MBE, his treatise was way above the heads of most aircrew. The 'Navigators' Union' were now convinced that practising air navigators needed to learn the new astro techniques only by rule of thumb and could safely skip the study of the underlying mathematics.

The title of the existing Manual – *Air Pilotage* – betrayed its early origins and indicated its inadequacy. When all else failed, the pilot/navigator had been expected to use his wits and flying skills to extricate himself from every navigational disaster. Air pilotage wasn't a science but simply a matter of instinct, reinforced by bitter experience and by the accepted wisdom of past survivors. Its name was an insult to the logical air navigator, its text as dry as dust and the illustrations poorly presented. A loose-leaf affair in orange cardboard covers, seemingly tied together by bootlaces, it was very unfriendly to the reader. Nobody familiar with current RAF air navigation doctrine could fail to improve on such an uninspiring treatise.

I wondered if, in the panic of war, it might even be possible to break the old mould completely. Keen young men, fresh from all walks of life, were having to be turned as fast as possible into RAF pilots and air navigators: an easy-to-read book, illustrated in multi-colours, seemed most likely to hit the nail on the head. I began to visualise a handsomely bound, attractive light blue hardback, looking as unlike any official publication as possible. With the now relaxed financial constraints, a personal copy could perhaps be issued to every RAF pilot and air navigator for him to keep and dip into whenever he felt like consulting it. He might even want to take the thing to bed with him to study, if only I could hit the right approach!

The new book was needed by yesterday; but operating notes had still to be drafted for new or emerging instruments, many of them still in the pipeline. Moreover, innumerable user-helpful pro-formae were waiting to be worked out and designed to cope with the new technology. 'Yesterday' would definitely not even be 'tomorrow'! I didn't anticipate these hurdles in mid-1940 nor realise the text would take so long to compose, let alone steer through the mysteries of publication, before it would see the light of day.

Nor, when I said 'Yes' to my austere but greatly respected Group Captain, did I foresee that Air Publication 1234 (1941) was going to hang round my neck like a millstone for the next 17 years of my career in the General Duties branch of the Service. Nobody ever warned me it would be potentially fatal for my career as an RAF executive pilot to become type-cast as 'Mr Air Navigation'.

William Shakespeare has Brutus say in *Julius Caesar*:-

> *There is a tide in the affairs of men*
> *Which taken at the flood leads on to fortune;*
> *Omitted, all the voyage of their life*
> *Is bound in shallows and in miseries.*

Was this my tide, I wondered? First, I had to consider what was already available in the field but I soon discovered there was very little to help. Unknown to me at this time, Francis Chichester was writing a series of eight popular pocket handbooks, capitalising on his outstanding feats of solo pilot air navigation. But in the event his *Observer* booklets fell rather short of the professional stance we needed in the RAF.

The recognised authority on the subject was the excellent *Complete Air Navigator* by D. C. T. Bennett, himself a former RAF pilot who had later flown *Mercury*, the Supermarine single-seat floatplane carrying transatlantic airmail. *Mercury* had been so over-laden with fuel for its non-stop journey to New York from Southampton that it had to be lifted into the air piggy-back on top of *Maia*, the special Short flying-boat. Don Bennett's 1935 book had been acclaimed as the world's best manual for civil aviation use; but by 1940 it had already only a passing relevance to the indoctrination of RAF aircrew. Bennett was recalled to the Service in 1940 and was eventually given command of the Pathfinder Force in 1942, initially as a Group Captain.

Neither of these authors had the advantage of the very latest RAF-informed air navigation ideas nor of our planned instrument development. Neither had had to ponder the problems raised by an enormous training plan, nor to foresee the limitations imposed by war on the practice of air navigation. My captive readership was to be vast: 125,000 HMSO copies in the UK, countless reprints in the Dominions and translations for the Czech, Polish and Norwegian air forces. Even the Chinese had one! But who was to guess the Germans would also make a translation by 1943?

Not surprisingly, the USA, land of 'Riding the (radio) Range', had little to offer on navigating in an air war. Without radio ranges, they would at least need daylight to see where they were going in Europe. Capt Weems USN apart, I couldn't put my hand on a single innovative publication from North America. Elsewhere, the Japanese were reputedly promising; but their approach was tire-somely mathematical and translations were unavailable.

I spent a day with the navigators at HMS *Dryad* in Southwick Park overlooking Portsmouth. Welcomed by the staff whose brains I went to pick, I was very gratified that they were so keen to help. After all, our bubble sextant had turned marine astro on its head by measuring altitudes against an artificial vertical; and to solve the 'PZX' triangle[1] quickly, so as to get usable data for its airmen, the heretical RAF accepted the slight inaccuracies of a very 'short' method. Clearly, navigating from aircraft carriers differed radically from the land-oriented RAF activities.

I discovered that all existing textbooks were quite content to describe the acquisition and functions of the 'bones' of the process of air navigation but none tried to fill them out with 'flesh'. To change the metaphor, there was a plethora of DIY air navigation kits on offer, but no construction notes. The student learned how to measure the track, calculate the course to steer, measure and allow for wind velocity, calculate groundspeed, determine time of arrival, use a compass and many other instruments and maps, but the poor uninitiated airman would search in vain for instruction on how all the bits and pieces fitted together in practice. Ideas for integrating these activities were never even suggested in print. The basic science of air navigation was quite adequately explained, as far as it was then understood, but the fledgling practitioner received no guidance as to its application.

In practice, air navigation had consequently always been something of a hit-and-miss affair and success was so personalised that our Top Brass regarded it as a Black Art, an attitude that was now having a devastating spin-off. Situations in the air never being cut and dried, nobody had ever dared to postulate procedures. The urgent flying training of the multitudes for war now demanded that a serious attempt be made at synthesis. This would be quite unique and maybe it would be challenged as eccentric, but I guessed that a worked-out example of at least one possible system of practical air navigation for our bomber aircraft might make a good subject for a final chapter.

I was unaware I was sowing a germinal seed which has grown during the past 50 years into a flourishing international industry concerned with the essential man/machine relationship in navigation systems. 'System' is the buzz word. Nowadays there is even more need to understand and devise integrated systems, given the extent of computerization and automation. Neither the air navigator nor his most sophisticated machines are without their limitations.

Fortunately, I was by no means on my own, for I had the active help and advice of a dedicated young colleague, Flight Lieutenant Gerry Robinson, the School's expert on aircraft compasses. I also had the moral support of the nebulous Navigators' Union, anxious for me to put the business of air navigation in the RAF once and for all where it belonged. It was a subject that cried aloud for proper recognition and even for a revolution.

I was now a Squadron Leader, had been allotted Miss Evans, a full-time civilian shorthand typist, and had painfully begun dictation. One sunny afternoon, lost in my thoughts somewhere in an early draft of Chapter 1, I scarcely noticed the shrieking of a *Stuka*[2] diving upon us, until a stick of bombs straddled the wooden hut where we were at work. There had been no warning and I looked up with surprise, only to see no Miss Evans: she was already under the table as the bombs went off, by which time all danger had passed.

St Athan was filled with excited clamour as we all hurried to our slit trenches, lest there was to be a return match. The pilot's aim had been very poor, for my little wooden hut nestled alongside the biggest hangar in the RAF – larger than the whole of Selfridges. This monster building was unscathed but the wooden huts of Sick Quarters – 200 yards further on – had taken the brunt.

The Air Council Member for Training and the AOC-in-C Flying Training Command were already considering what to do with the School. One compelling option was to take advantage of the offer of Canadian airspace and ship it, lock stock and barrrel, to join the basic training schools for RAF aircrew already starting up over there.

They apparently did not realise that the life-blood of the transferred advanced Navigation School depended on a rapid feed-back of problems and technical developments in front-line squadrons and that a close liaison with air operations would become more and more necessary as the war unfolded. The die being cast, the School, led by its redoubtable Group Captain Robertson, sailed away to Port Albert, Ontario, Canada where it was re-named No 31 Air Navigation School and, cut off from all operational 'gen', began to languish. Poor Robbie, with his severely burnt face, began to suffer from the bitter cold.

By 1943, the restrictions of UK air defence being somewhat relaxed, this unsatisfactory location was redressed; but by then the Operational Commands had perversely surrounded themselves by unscalable walls of secrecy, erected during the war. Re-sited at Cranage and re-named the Central Navigation School, the staff ironically now found it doubly hard to assert their need to know, to analyse and to assess all the facts of an air navigator's operational tasks.

I was in a similar predicament – I needed to know just what was going on, not only in the squadrons but also in technical developments which had begun to take off in all directions. If it could possibly be helped, the war was not going to be lost for lack of British inventions and I had to be aware of what was coming just round the corner if the book was to have any up-to-date pretensions when it appeared. St Athan was too remote from the scene of action. Sweeping aside a superstition that I might regret interfering with any official decisions as to my postings, for the first time in my life I now asked to be sent to London. *Blitz* or no *blitz*, I had to be near the people who mattered.

Before the M4 Motorway and new Severn Bridge had been built, it was a long haul with my wife, infant daughter and all the family gear in a Ford 10, from Glamorgan to my parents at Norbiton, a suburb of Kingston-on-Thames. I decided to break the journey a few miles short of the *blitz* and drew up in the evening in the attractive old Thames-side square of Shepperton, dominated by its church and the Anchor inn.

Going inside to enquire, it took me some time to catch the eye of Mine Hostess who was much too busy attending to her cronies at the bar to notice the arrival of a mere Squadron Leader in a rather crumpled RAF uniform. Her customers also seemed reluctant to be interrupted in their prattle.

Yes, she had a double room free for the night. But on my return from the car, carrying a cot and its sleeping contents, the landlady at once changed her tune. No! I couldn't stay. I must find another place. The Anchor never took children. By 1940, anyone in uniform felt welcome everywhere and, indeed, people seemed only too glad to have a bit of the Light Blue around. I was amazed at such inhospitality; but the lady was as adamant as her stony face so I left in a huff and continued my journey to Norbiton.

Next afternoon, and at night, I watched grimly as towering smoke and a baleful glow in the sky, 16 miles away, marked where the *Luftwaffe* was torching London's docks. How many travel-stained airmen, I wondered, would be rebuffed by that unkind bitch at the Anchor? It has changed hands many times since 1940, but whenever I've passed its door I've remembered my reception.

In London, I had been given a navigation niche in the Training department of the Air Ministry, ostensibly for writing though I soon became lumbered by other duties. From my fourth-floor office in Adastral House, on the south-east corner of Kingsway, I looked straight across a very familiar white-tiled 'well' into an office I had once occupied in 1931 as joint secretary of the LSE Sudents' Union. In nine years, I felt I had come a very long way, from one side of that well to the other!

The conflict over London by day was now at full tilt. The outcome seemed far from certain to most informed RAF onlookers, though it fortunately ended as the victorious Battle of Britain. Driving along those once-familiar roads to Kingsway from Norbiton, I knew there was ample scope for making diversions round bombed areas encountered *en route,* though new obstacles appeared between one journey and the next.

One late summer evening, homeward bound by Ford, I crossed Barnes Common and was approaching the traffic lights at Upper Richmond Road when I noticed people looking upwards and starting to run and when I leant out of my window, I could see a dogfight going on, high overhead.

Ignoring red lights, I dashed on up Roehampton Lane but a very close and almighty bang persuaded me to pull up and hurriedly abandon the car. The bombers had started to dump their loads and as I couldn't squeeze under the car for cover, I ran across the lane and lay alongside a low brick wall, feeling rather sheepish and still uncomfortably exposed. When the din of battle and explosions had moved away, I went back to the car and pressed on. On reaching the Kingston by-pass I found the road had been replaced by a large crater, so I U-turned and drove over Kingston Hill.

Near the top I passed two houses well and truly ablaze and noticed the road had been well peppered with incendiaries. My heart sank as I turned into our road and saw the house opposite my parents' was in flames. A burnt-out incendiary lay on our front path but all three generations of the family were safe and sound, crowded into an Anderson shelter inside the garage. There was mutual relief all round but no sign of panic or dismay.

It was the battery of heavy ack-ack guns operating about half a mile away in Richmond Park that really got me down at Norbiton. They threw up a terrific and noisy barrage every night, making it almost impossible to sleep. After several weeks of this racket, my writing began to dry up. Something had to be done so I called up a friend who was serving at Coastal Command Headquarters in Northwood and learned that his nearest AA battery was about three miles away at Bushey Heath. He also reported that Northwood had been mainly evacuated by its population of City executives whose firms had dispersed for safety to the provinces.

There were plenty of properties for hire and three days later I moved into a beautifully furnished four-bedroom house at £4 a week. With a rent like that, even a Squadron Leader's pay could stretch to a living-in maid. Of course the occasional bomb fell on Northwood to keep us on our toes, but with no AA gunfire to ruin my sleep I soon began to write productively again. Later, when the book had reached a more advanced stage, I discovered the best way to grapple with its demand for space was to commandeer my own dining-room and spread the text and diagrams all over the floor. You may gather I had a very long-suffering wife.

My immediate plans were to go and taste real life with operational squadrons. So I took off in one of the Moths kept at Hendon for Air Ministry flying staff and flew up to Wyton near Cambridge where Wing Commander Paul Wood DFC, a Spec N contemporary of mine, was CO of a Wellington bomber squadron. Flying back to Hendon was always a bit dicey, as the only approach towards the south-west passed low over the embanked main railway line and sometimes coincided with an LNER express hurtling along a few feet below.

Next, I went off to Yorkshire to make contacts at the very busy bomber station at Driffield. While there, a company of stage stars

151

gave an ENSA[3] show in the station cinema. Afterwards, the artistes came to the Mess for a bite and a drink in the ante-room and one of their number, John Gielgud no less, responded to popular request and delivered an impromtu and extremely moving, intimate rendering of Henry V's speech before Agincourt. He was very appropriately splendid.

These winter visits gave me a faint insight into what Bomber Command was facing. In 1940 it was not yet known that, despite all their training, courage and determination, the air navigators, like all their brothers elsewhere, were so ill-equipped for their difficult operational task as to be lamentably ineffective. Just how inaccurate the early bombing sorties had been did not come to light until 1941 when Professor Lindemann (Lord Cherwell) reported to the War Cabinet. Analysing intelligence data from photographic reconnaissance and other top secret sources disclosed that in the first two years of war no fewer than 19 out of every 20 bombs had fallen more than five miles from their targets. There had been a ghastly waste of well-trained and highly intelligent men, not to mention the loss of costly aircraft.

This indictment gave a most welcome impetus to long-overdue developments of aids for our air navigators, especially of the electronic inventions which had previously been exclusively concentrated on air defence. Fighter pilots had of necessity been relieved of all but the simplest navigation and freed to develop tactics to maximise their advantages of location, manoeuvrability and weaponry. Providentially, by 1939 air-to-ground radio communication had been perfected and RDF was functioning in the nick of time. Thus from the start, Fighter Command pilots were accurately directed within allotted UK combat areas by ground controllers. The results had made air history.

My next priority was to ascertain what the 'boffins' had in store for us all; but as they largely worked on projects at the behest of the Air Staff, my quest for information had to begin with those officers who framed our Operational Requirements. OR3 being the Branch where the needs of air navigation were put into words. The Richmond Terrace habitat of OR3 was headed by Wing Commander David J. Waghorn AFC, of whom Francis Chichester wrote that he had 'the exceptional and most valuable combination of originality in devising methods of navigation and a keen practical sense of what is required and feasible in the air.' David was a charming, handsome, fearless and highly efficient officer and nothing was ever too much trouble for him.

He had previously achieved an excellent development of the integrating bubble sextant at the Aircraft and Armament Experimental Establishment, Boscombe Down, in conjuction with Professor Plaskett, the Cambridge astronomer. David spent his life battling for commonsense in the initial production of aircraft, so they could actually perform useful military tasks. The weakness of all manufacturers lay in their inherent short-sighted obsession with high performance, regardless of operational effectiveness.

Subsequent essential changes were both enormously costly and very time-consuming. Thus every new type of bomber had to be modified in such vital details as ensuring the navigator's station was large enough and had, for example, the requisite instrumentation and easy access to the drift sight and the astrodome, an optically-true perspex window in the roof. The types that came from the great American aircraft industry had to be even more severely modified to convert them into effective weapons of war. It may seem surprising how never-ending this tiresome struggle turned out to be.

Himself a senior navigation specialist, David welcomed me to his holy of holies in Whitehall and carefully monitored the information I was collecting about the shape of things to come. His was a most important yard-arm for me to clear and only after several discussions did I feel confident to proceed.

His brother in the RAF, H. R. D. Waghorn, had achieved great fame before the war by winning the Schneider Trophy in 1929 in one of Mitchell's sleek Supermarine seaplanes (forerunners of the Spitfire). The two Waghorn brothers were both highly respected aviators but both eventually shared a tragic fate. David came to grief when, one afternoon late in the war and now an Air Commodore flying an advanced mark of Spitfire, he took off from Boscombe Down in a display of *joie de vivre*, doing a climbing slow roll. There was much too much *joie* and not enough *vivre* and the 'Spit' flew into the deck.

His brother had been even more unlucky. When testing a large and rather ungainly twin at Farnborough, with a boffin passenger, he also embarked on a slow roll. He managed to turn the plane on to its back but could not get it right-side-up again. After numerous fruitless attempts, he reluctantly gave up, advised his passenger to bale out and then followed suit. His parachute deposited him safely on the sloping roof of a hangar, but when its air spilled out, the parachute collapsed and he started to slide down the roof. Unluckily there was nothing like a ventilator nor even a cowl to tangle with the shroud or cords of the parachute and he fell 50ft on to very hard tarmac.

The book now completely possessed me and its progress was marked by encounters with the likes of David Waghorn for whom I could only feel great admiration.

In a perverse way, WW2 seemed to me at this point rather 'fairer' than WW1 had been. The Great War had scarcely touched the major contestants' homelands; but millions of civilians in uniform had been slaughtered, conveniently out of sight on the fields of battle. Whether we liked it or not, we were now all in a total war, with everyone justly having a taste of hell. In fact, the whole country developed a remarkable siege mentality which was, among its other less debatable qualities, a great leveller. Those of us who could not, or would not by choice, escape to safe havens abroad – and who now indulged in feelings of noble endurance – discovered bonds of kinship that permeated the population and broke the reserve that normally inhibited social exchanges between the classes.

A queue was always a sign of something to buy: people would join one without even knowing what was on offer at its head. A pet shop in Northwood with a queue was a 'must' for every owner of a dog or cat; but one lady, who had no pets of her own, regularly tagged on – because, she said, they were always such nice people to talk to!

After the daylight battles had been won, London found itself in the throes of a nightly *blitz*, its citizens sleeping in troglodytic shelters or packed like sardines along the draughty platforms of the Underground. Surface rail services often broke under the relentless attack, but the buses struggled gamely on. One morning, arriving at Adastral House, I saw the remains of a red double-decker bus plastered over the upper windows of Bush House. On another night, the Strand had taken a bad pounding and by morning the entire road was ankle-deep in glass.

Bicycles, motorbikes and cars still circulated, but as petrol was rationed drivers clubbed together to share journeys. About half the Adastral civilians chose to stay put in the building and slept in its sub-sub basement; while the RAF element struggled to and from hirings in the suburbs. Everyone took turns as Fire Wardens, a small band of worthies detailed for a night on the roof in tin hats, with buckets of sand, water and stirrup pumps. The view of Town on a bad night was pretty horrendous.

Luckily for our morale, we did not know that on Guy Fawkes' Day 1940 Lord Beaverbrook, who was in charge of aircraft production, actually recommended transferring Coastal Command to the Navy! The Admiralty declined this preposterous idea, although for political reasons they changed their mind in 1941 and tried hard to implement it.

Sometimes I needed the solitude of an empty office for my work, when everyone had either left for home or else descended into the sub-sub basement for the night. Oblivious of the *blitz* outside the blacked-out windows, I could concentrate on my drawing board to produce a diagram or some illustration needed for the text.

Once, when not on a fire-watching stint and mindless of the racket outside, I was alone and engrossed in my fourth floor office late at night, when a dark shadow caught my eye. Looking round, I found myself staring from about three feet into the eyes of a large black rat which had emerged on the central heating pipe that led to the radiator. About eight inches long, it stood transfixed and gazing at me as if I were the intruder. Then it ran off along the pipe into the next office. I put away my drawing tools and went down to the sub-sub basement to seek human company.

Windy? No! Creepy? Yes! It was a last straw. That rat was the first of many I encountered in the course of 25 years in the Service. I can only say they don't improve on acquaintance.

Notes to Chapter X

1 In a spherical triangle, P was the nearer Pole, Z the navigator's assumed position and X the sub-stellar point.
2 Junkers Ju 87 dive-bomber. 'Stuka' is short for *Sturzkampfflugzeug* – dive-bomber.
3 Entertainments National Service Association.

XI

AP1234(2)

NOT BEING a case-hardened journalist I found working in a London office far from compatible with writing a book. Any inspiration I had needed to be quietly wooed and did not respond to being turned on and off like a tap. Daylight raids over London were commonplace when I had first arrived but it wasn't the air raids that I found so distracting.

After the first few days of traipsing to and from the sub-sub-basement shelter, with all the other inmates, at every alarm or all clear, the entire Light Blue contingent in the 'Air Box' adopted a sensible fatalistic view and stayed stolidly at their desks. The sirens were sounding on and off so frequently, no one could recall whether there was an alert or an all clear, so it really didn't matter and work went on regardless.

Most of the distractions came from the extraneous tasks that found their way into my office. For a few weeks I had been a small cog in an Assistant Directorate headed by friendly, laid-back Wing Commander Gareth G. Barrett. But the growing load of training justified its upgrading to a Deputy Directorate and 'GeeGee' was posted off to Oban to command No 210 Catalina flying-boat squadron. He was replaced by the one and only L. 'Kelly' Barnes, a very dynamic Group Captain who had earned the reputation of *enfant térrible* as well as recognition as probably the most erudite air navigation specialist then in the RAF and even in the world. He was a most light-hearted leader and at once renamed the Air Ministry the 'House of Shame'.

Kelly, the name by which he was universally known, had once been summoned to the Air Council to be told of their Airships' grave displeasure. He had actually struck a senior officer when, as captain of a flying-boat cruising in the Far East, he had been so provoked by his VIP passenger persistently interfering with the navigation that he socked him on the chin, an action that many fellow officers had often felt sorely tempted to perform. Within days of this serious admonition, Kelly had been awarded the MBE for his outstanding contribution to the advancement of air navigation by writing AP1456, Volume 2 of the RAF Manual!

During the winter we were joined by Flt Lt Frank (later Sir Francis) Chichester, who was then nursing a duodenal ulcer by constantly sipping milk and munching digestive biscuits. He and I formed a lifelong friendship and together cooked up a lot of schemes to ease the beginners' task of learning air navigation. Among these ideas, we devised a series of eleven large black posters showing well-known star groups that served as simple guides for identifying the 22 stars needed for worldwide use with the new Astronomical Navigation Tables (AP1618) that were the pride and joy of the RAF. Our posters were for display in classrooms and navigation offices but reappeared in a private booklet called *The Heavenly Bodies* by Edwin Link, the American inventor of our flight simulators and (later) of deep-diving submersibles. He produced a simulator for astro training in 1943 and improved our strictly functional posters by superimposing female forms over the stars, to imprint them more vividly on air navigators' sexist visual memories.

Frank and I had our say in helping to re-shape the layout and contents of the *Air Almanac*, AP1602, that remarkable joint brainchild of Kelly and the late Dr D. H. Sadler OBE, the brilliant Royal Observatory astronomer and Superintendent of the Nautical Almanac, a genius of great modesty. The *Air Almanac* was the foundation for the revolution in astro navigation and was finally accepted by the nautical diehards, though only after much deliberation and many years' hesitation.

The staff of DDT Nav were relentlessly goaded on by Kelly, our rumbustious iconoclast and illustrious, ever-inspiring Deputy Director, whose critical faculty made a deep impression on everyone. Dismissive of bumbledom and highly contemptuous of all reactionaries, whom he was quick to dub as 'constipated', he naturally made few friends among his seniors; but he it was I unconsciously always tried to emulate. He taught us to beware of clever fools – persuasive officers with smart ideas but no commonsense and consequently extremely dangerous. On posting away, they often left a trail of disaster behind them.

He had just returned from incarceration in Iceland. Having clandestinely simulated engine failure in a Sunderland flying-boat and taxied it into Reykjavik, at that time still a neutral Danish port, he had then deliberately returned the aircraft to the UK after carrying out 'repairs'. For this breach of international law, he was duly sent back to internment by the Foreign Office, to languish in Iceland 'for the duration', though he had been secretly briefed to keep an eye out for covert U-boat activities. To help endure the boredom of a six-months' arctic night, Kelly married and took his wife with him into exile; but the Germans shortly afterwards invaded Denmark and brought his expectations of a long honeymoon to an abrupt end. Kelly's effect on his staff was dramatic and galvanising. He was nothing if not positive and we followed him with great admiration.

My scribbling constantly clashed with other tasks that filtered into my office – often, it seemed, demanding priority. A case in point was the arrival of Flight Lieutenant Anthony Armstrong Willis, alias 'AA' of *Punch*, to occupy the next-door office. As editor of *Tee Emm*, he asked to be fed regularly with copy for his unique and humorous training magazine. Everything I supplied would be so tranformed by his wit as to be almost unrecognisable in print. He had a fantastic gift with a pen!

It had been late 1940 in the Savage Club, of which Willis was a member, when, wearing the uniform of a reserve Captain in the Royal Engineers, he had been introduced (at the latter's request) to Air Marshal Sir Guy Garrod, Air Member for Training, who was looking for a humorist to create a monthly training memorandum (T M) that would be avidly read by our aircrew. Judging by Willis' long record at *Punch*, Guy Garrod thought his style would fill the bill to perfection and, over lunch, asked if he would care to take on the job.

Anthony, whose talents were not being fully exploited by an Army wartime job, liked the idea and, for the sake of convenience when working in the Air Ministry, readily agreed to transfer to the RAFVR as a Flight Lieutenant in the A&SD[1] branch. Garrod regretted that there would have to be a routine appearance before a Selection Board; but this was purely a formality – he wanted Anthony to start as soon as possible.

On the appointed day Anthony, impeccably dressed in the uniform of a Sapper Captain, stepped through the door to the Selection Board and delivered a full-blooded Army salute, to which the chairman barely nodded in reply. Anthony was then waved condescendingly to a chair.

The chairman happened to be a 'dead-beat' Squadron Leader recently recalled to the colours and he looked the part. He was flanked on each side by faceless officials and began riffling through piles of papers, searching for Anthony's c/v and application form. Anthony sensed the vibes were not too promising, but was quite taken aback by a sudden outburst of sarcasm from the chair.

'Hmm! See you call yourself a writer. Had anything published?'
'Oh yes, lots' said Anthony, cheerfully.
'Where, may I ask?'
'In *Punch*', replied Anthony, beginning to prickle.

'Did you say *Punch*? Hmm! Can't remember ever seeing any articles by Willis in *Punch*. See you say you write plays. Ever had anything produced?'

Anthony felt he could now score a bull's eye, for with his brother 'Chris' (then head of Military Survey in the Air Ministry and later Director General of Ordnance Survey) he had written *The Ten Minute Alibi* which had had a very long run as a West End whodunnit.

'Yes I have' replied Anthony, diffidently.

'Oh!' said the Chairman in obvious disbelief. 'And what was it called?'

'*Ten Minute Alibi*' replied Anthony, mustering up his most self-deprecating, throwaway tone of voice and quite expecting the chairman to concede defeat. On the contrary, turning to one of the officials at his side, the old dunderhead whispered 'Ten Minute What?'

This might have been the end of the story, but Anthony had given Garrod his word and in due course the Selection Board's summary misgivings were swept aside and the RAF gained a star performer. The first fruit of this happy marriage was a prize buffoon called Pilot Officer Percy Prune whose flying exploits appeared in a blue cover monthly magazine, illustrated by the two outstanding cartoonists of the day – Fougasse and David Langdon – as well as by Bill Hooper (Percy's doodling midwife), Roberts, Wyndham Robinson and Lee.

It would be no exaggeration to say that Willis had hit on a way of putting over vital lessons of the developing air war so effectively that the latest stories of the blundering anti-hero PO Percy Prune and his equally cack-handed aircrew were eagerly awaited in aircrew messes all over the world. The concept of 'Prune' was a brilliant winner. To add an air of verisimilitude, Willis gave Prune a desk, back-to-back with his own. A worn-out RAF cap hung on the office hat-stand. On the empty desk, an In tray full of files overflowed into a Pending tray which in its turn spilled on to the desk. Prune's name was on the door and, when it rang, Willis answered Prune's extension number, now in the Adastral telephone directory.

Prune's permanent absence soon led to a minor problem. The heavy casualties of Front Line operational pilots were becoming so difficult to replace that all HQ staff posts throughout the entire Service were combed to find any active pilots who could be spared for ops. Organisation and Methods 'experts' appeared in the 'Air Box' to scan the scene and report urgently to the Air Member for Personnel. The one sent to investigate the Flying Trainers, under the then Air Vice-Marshal Sir Ralph Cochrane, was a rather bogus-looking reserve Army officer with the highly improbable name of Major Skit. His habit was to arrive unannounced and ask what was going on and why. He stayed as long as he thought necessary, first to be convinced that the job needed to be done at all and second to discover if it needed the expertise of the pilot concerned. He took copious notes and gradually compiled a large plan showing who was doing what and where. Being a 'Brown Job' made his task more difficult with the sceptical and light-hearted Light Blue brigade and he made slow progress through very heavy weather for some weeks.

However, the day he stepped into the *Tee Emm* office seemed to Skit to mark a watershed. Willis, not himself a pilot and thus immune from Skit's direct inquisition, could see what was coming but he kept a straight face and started to enunciate at great length all the things he was trying to do himself. Skit began to wonder why the RAF needed such pampering, when the Army had to put up with an unimaginative recital of hard facts in a black and white 'TM' handout on foolscap. All this fancy fuss was a little beyond his grasp. Apart from the *élitist* activity of the Flight Lieutenant, what was PO Prune doing, he wanted to know? When pressed, Willis seemed to become uncomfortably evasive.

At 11.30 one morning, Skit was told that Prune had just left for lunch in the sub-sub basement refectory. Next day, Prune had gone to the dentist. He seemed to spend hours at the barber's and then, without warning, might go off on a staff visit. He was frequently absent sick. Once, he had not returned from lunch even when it had gone half-past three! Major Skit could never track down PO Percy Prune and Willis clearly had no proper control over his junior and needed reminding of his responsibilities. Even if Prune was resting after the recent Battle of Britain, as Willis had said, there was no excuse for such sloppy behaviour. Prune was redundant and Skit marked him down as a scalp on his plan.

In the end, Skit had to be told by ACAS(T), A V-M Sir Ralph Cochrane, that his leg had been pulled and that the jobs of Willis and Prune were indispensable and literally inseparable. After that, little was heard of the Major – rumour had it he had been posted to an active overseas front; but that may have been wishful thinking. All the pilots I ever came across 'flying desks' in the 'Air Box' were simply itching to get away to fly aeroplanes instead.

One day a Major Guy Prendergast of the Royal Tank Regiment arrived unannounced in my office. By coincidence I had known Guy in Cairo in the 'thirties. He was now being seconded to the already famous Long Range Desert Group founded by Bagnold, operating

LSE undergraduate F C Richardson in 1932 with his cherished Austin Seven *Hiccup*, which he had to abandon in Park Lane after a fire under the bonnet.

Having disembarked her RAF 'sprogs', RMS *Ranchi* leaves Port Said for Bombay – July 1933.

B Flight at No.4 FTS, Abu Sueir, with its Avro 504Ns.

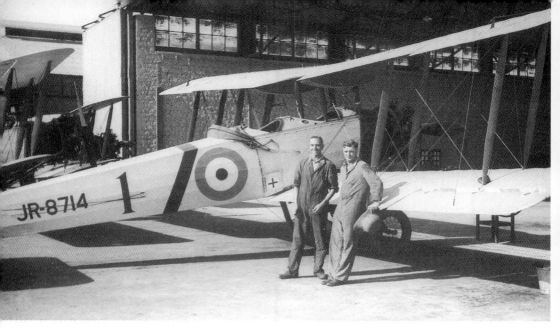

ABOVE: Avro 504N wih fitter and rigger – the groundcrew who kept them in the air.

LEFT: 'Bog rats' changing places in an Armstrong Whitworth Atlas – its engine still running.

BELOW: 'Bog rats' waiting their turn to fly – with mugs of very sweet 'shai'.

Parading for 'four solid hours of lectures'.

Jaguar engine of the Atlas (which 'flew like a lump of lead') being started up for the day's programme.

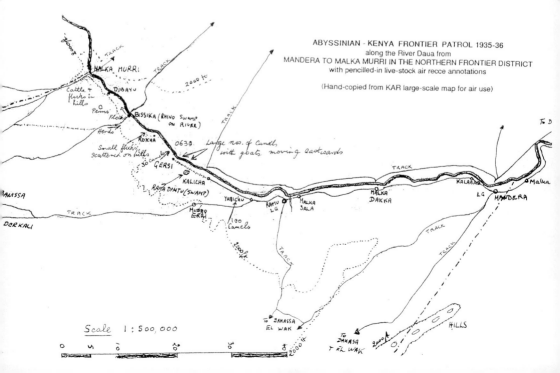

ABYSSINIAN - KENYA FRONTIER PATROL 1935-36
along the River Daua from
MANDERA TO MALKA MURRI IN THE NORTHERN FRONTIER DISTRICT
with pencilled-in live-stock air recce annotations

(Hand-copied from KAR large-scale map for air use)

Scale 1:500,000

RAF Heliopolis – looking west towards the No 216 Sqn hangars.

Officers' Mess, RAF Heliopolis.

No 216 Sqn Vickers Victoria Mk V flying towards Suez.

Pilot Officer Richardson with Egyptian Frontier Police at Bir Gattar landing ground (2,400 feet above sea level), Sinai.

BELOW: Refuelling with four-gallon cans – which 'had to be carefully strained through chamois leather while being poured by hand through a large funnel into the top tank'.

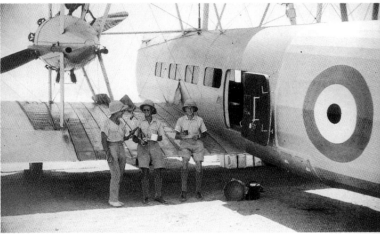

A well-earned 'cooler' from the ice-box.

BELOW: VIP honeymoon beach party, Mersa Matruh: *from left*, Flt Lt Colin Cadell, ADC; Lady Lampson; HE Sir Miles Lampson; Sqn Ldr Philip Mackworth; and *(far right)* Maj 'Bimbashi' Green, Commandant, Royal Egyptian Frontier Force Police in the Western Desert.

Inspection of Heliopolis in 1935 by Sir Philip Sassoon, Under-Secretary of State for Air. The tall figure on his right is Gp Capt Raymond Collishaw, the Station Commander.

Victoria VI of No.216 Sqn, with Bristol Pegasus engines and four-bladed propellers, during the Kenya detachment.

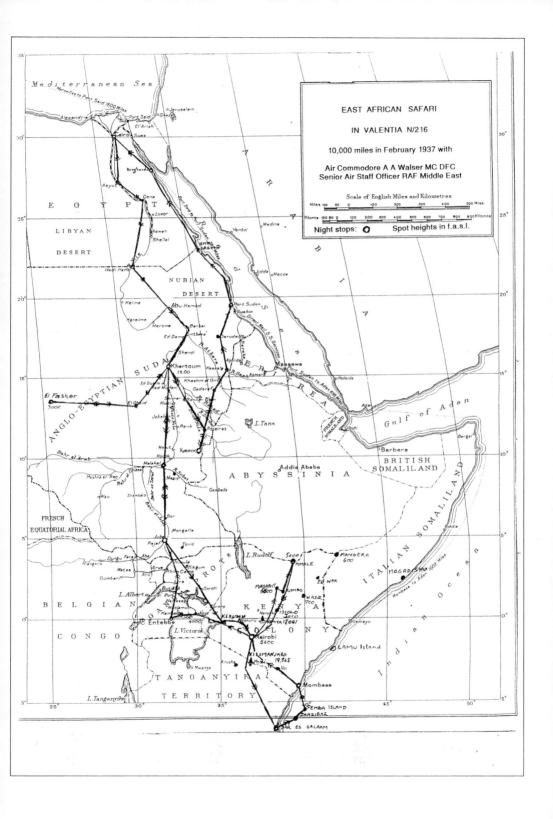

Aircraft strength on the Kenya detachment – five 'very old' Fairey IIIFs supported by two Victoria VIs.

Deutsche Gesandtschaft
in Ägypten

May 2nd 1936

Dear Mr. Richardson,

I have let some time slip by before doing what I had long intended to do, – write to you in person to thank you once more for what you have done for me. I felt more shaken, than I had expected for the first few days – in fact – quite unable to do my work properly; then came the King's death. But, please accept my thanks, though late. I hope, when my wife arrives toward the end of this month, she will also be able to thank you in person.

Yours sincerely

L. Stöhrer

Letter from the German Minister to Egypt, Baron von Stöhrer, to 'Mr Richardson' thanking him for his desert rescue in April 1936.

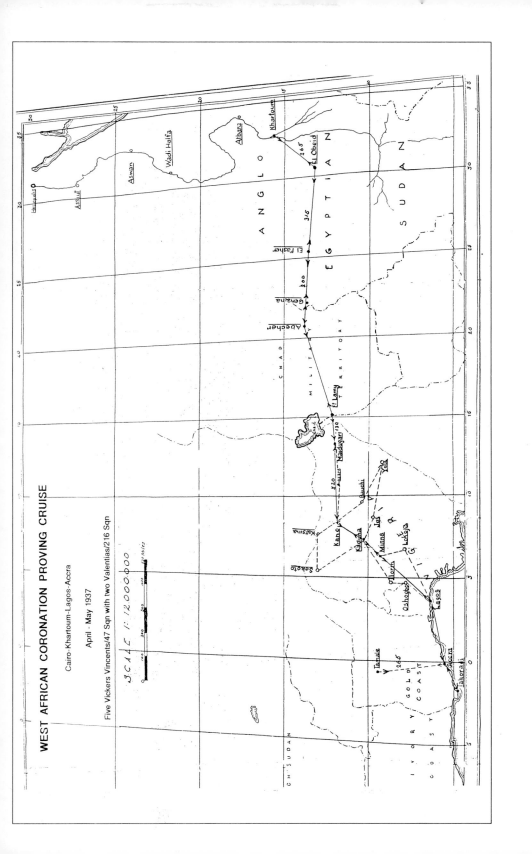

WEST AFRICAN CORONATION PROVING CRUISE

Cairo-Khartoum-Lagos-Accra

April - May 1937

Five Vickers Vincents/47 Sqn with two Valentias/216 Sqn

SCALE 1:12,000,000

'Large aeroplanes were still something of a novelty' – Dickie Richardson's Valentia and members of the Colonial Governor's staff on Entebbe's grass airfield in 1937.

West African Cruise – the No 216 Sqn component. Air Cdre Walser is in the centre of the front row with Flying Officer Richardson on his left.

Royal West African Frontier Force troops ready for an emplaning exercise during the West African Cruise.

Whitleys Mk VII BD572 (airborne) and BD569 of No 502 (GR) Sqn at St Eval in 1942. This type was the first operational aircraft to be equipped with ASV Mk II air-to-surface radar, and auxiliary tanks increased its fuel capacity to 1,100 gallons.

Last rite for a Whitley on 16 November 1942 – ditched by its crew, who can be seen leaving it in their dinghy.

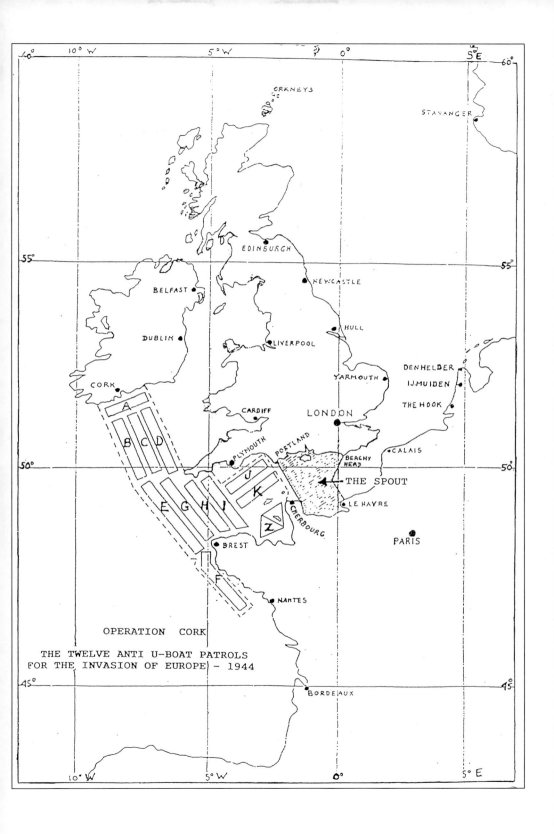

OPERATION CORK

THE TWELVE ANTI U-BOAT PATROLS
FOR THE INVASION OF EUROPE – 1944

Coastal Command's Chief Navigation
Officer 1942–44 – Gp Capt F C
Richardson.

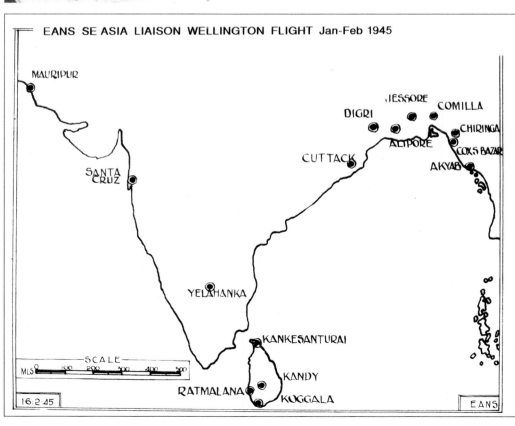

EANS SE ASIA LIAISON WELLINGTON FLIGHT Jan-Feb 1945

MAURIPUR

JESSORE

DIGRI   COMILLA

CHIRINGA

ALIPORE   COXS BAZAR

CUTTACK   AKYAB

SANTA
CRUZ

YELAHANKA

KANKESANTURAI

SCALE
MLS 0   100   200   300   400   500

KANDY

RATMALANA   KOGGALA

16:2·45   EANS

Converted Lancaster *Aries* and crew before the first trans-Polar flight of 1946.

Aries returning to Shawbury – mission accomplished. *(Daily Sketch)*

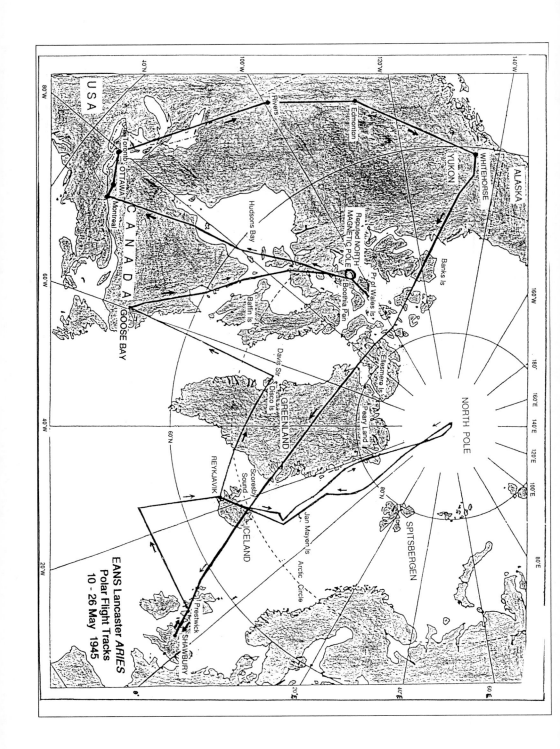

EANS Lancaster ARIES
Polar Flight Tracks
10 - 26 May 1945

armoured cars adapted to cope with the heat, lack of water and soft sand of the Western Desert. The LRDG reconnoitred the southern flank of the Italians in Libya to enable surprise attacks to be made from an unexpected quarter. This task involved problems of navigation and Guy had come to ask for help. He was at once made welcome and was soon sorted out, returning to Egypt with a consignment of our latest Mk IX bubble sextants, copies of the *Air Almanac* and the RAF Astronomical Navigation Tables, sight-reduction proformae, navigators' watches and a file of users' instructions – an astro-by-numbers correspondence course.

We had been only too delighted to lend a helping hand, little thinking that these bits of equipment and paper would become something of a *cause célèbre*. Two years later, the war was still raging when Finance caught up with the 1941 free inter-Sevice hand-outs and began asking on whose authority they had been made. The greatly expanded Training Department had by then left Adastral for Alexandra House; but official minutes began to pass to and fro and kept on recurring every month with no let-up. Meanwhile, the LRDG had made good use of astro in the Western Desert. T Nav 1, then Wing Commander 'Nick' Richard T. Gething, began to tear out his hair. Nick had been the lead navigator of the 1937 record-breaking Wellesley Long Range Flight commanded by the then Squadron Leader Richard Kellett who, together with Nick, had been awarded the AFC. No wimp, Nick now voluntarily donned the cloak of 'Action Man'. When next the inquisitive Finance file turned up in his In-tray, Nick put it with a sense of relief straight into the blazing coal fire in his office.

Later, over a lunchtime beer with DDT Nav, he confessed what he had done. Kelly Barnes was still in the chair and laughingly reproved Nick for not simply slipping the offending file under his office carpet – the approved disposal method for annoying files. There are more ways than one of killing a cat and Nick's choice had been perfect – for his cat was never seen again. Far from being penalised, he went from strength to strength and finally retired as an Air Commodore with a CB and a CBE.

But to return to T Nav 3 in April 1941, there came another unexpected interruption to my writing. I was appointed, in the simple guise of 'An Officer of the RAF', to broadcast two talks to schools, each of half an hour, on the BBC Home Service and had to spend several precious hours preparing the necessary scripts. This was, of course, an interesting if unwanted diversion, the more so when I told the BBC Presenter, Lloyd Williams, that I was due for a spot of leave in May. Most obligingly, he at once suggested recording my second talk on a '78' disc so as to let me get away as planned. But I was in for quite a shock.

I was sitting in a state of acute expectancy in a hotel room in Bournemouth on the morning of 13 May. This was the first time I had ever heard myself speak, let alone broadcast. When the talk began, I was aghast at the unrecognisable, up-stage voice that came out of the radio. Did I really sound like that? I could hardly believe my ears and vowed to try to tone my voice down several social notches before I opened my mouth again to speak in public. Not for the first time, the BBC had taught me a useful lesson, albeit at some incalculable cost by delaying for several days my own contribution to the training of air navigators and pilots. Happily, this interlude proved to be the last of all my official distractions.

By the end of May 1941 I had actually finished the first six chapters, which dealt with the basics of navigation terminology, mathematics, maps and charts, time, dead reckoning and position lines, about which there had been very little to debate. However, six other chapters resolutely refused to lie down and followed me around, nagging that there was more to say than I had given them credit for. They could not be completed because there were always things happening in the pipeline for which I had to wait and they always had cross-reference implications in the text.

Nevertheless, I had already developed close contacts with S5(b), the Ministry secretariat that liaised with HMSO for publications, both of whom couldn't have been more helpful to this struggling author. With only raised eyebrows, they immediately fell in with my plans for multi-coloured diagrams and text. I could settle for black, white, red and light blue and they didn't even jib at my request for a normally-bound quarto hardback, to depart from the stereotyped official publication held together by boot laces.

A swatch of blue-dyed linens for the cover was offered for consideration and my choice was accepted without demur. They then discussed some pleasing if sober mock-ups for the front cover and I was given a call on the services of their professional draughtsman to polish up my rough diagrams which formed the majority of the manual's 233 illustrations. My need for specially-miniaturised maps presented no problem.

Every morning in the Air Box, Kelly Barnes started with a thought-provoking prayer meeting with all the T Nav staff in his office. Before discussing the day's programme we usually exchanged quick comments on the night's *blitz*. One day Kelly related how, when dancing with his wife at a club in the West End on the previous night, it had taken a direct hit and some of the nearby guests had been killed. This sobering thought made no difference to our proceedings, for his experience had been by no means unique, though not exactly commonplace.

Kelly now started piling on the pressure, repeating a wise saw that has since often stood me in good stead. To my pleas for more time, he would remind me that the Best is the enemy of the Better, from the French: *Le Meilleur est l'ennemi du Mieux*. He insisted I should wait no longer to draw the bottom line.

The time had come to accept what technology I knew was going to be available within the next few months. There was no advantage in further delay, since the march of progress would continue apace. The new equipment wouldn't be issued across the RAF simultaneously and the last places to receive it would be the navigation schools themselves. In such a fast-changing world, the book would be out of date anyway on publication day!

I was glad to be able to include the eagerly awaited Astrograph, an invention of Pritchard and Lamplough from the stables of the Royal Aeronautical Establishment at Farnborough, on which we were pinning such high hopes of simplifying and thereby enhancing the operational use of astro. Tubby Vielle was now a Squadron Leader and had been instrumental in its rapid development. I assigned a photograph showing an Astrograph in a mock-up over a navigation plotting table as the most prestigious frontispiece for the manual. A new sun compass Tubby was also working on had to be omitted for lack of a firm production date.

Rapid progress with the book had been impossible while I was coping with the staff job; besides, travel to the Air Box wasted two hours of every day. So I now worked frantically at home and my family kept well clear of their bear with a sore head! Fortunately, word processors were unknown in 1941: the book would never have been finished if re-editing had been as easy then as it is today. I had to make do with only two drafts before copy went off to the printers *via* S5(b).

At some point during gestation, I had recalled a book on banking, listed for reading in 1928 for my BCom Intermediate. Written by Dr Robertson, a don of the Cambridge economics persuasion, it was very readable because every chapter bore a quotation from the Rev Charles L. Dodgson, the Victorian Oxford mathematics don, alias Lewis Carroll. I decided to follow Robertson's example and a little re-reading of my infant daughter's copies of *Alice* and *The Hunting of the Snark* soon yielded 12 apt chapter headings.

Kelly also took a hand and together we discovered a suitable 'logo' of an old manuscript woodcut of an ancient mariner taking a sun sight with a back-staff. We then coined its now-famous and hopefully terminal motto for the end page of the manual: *Man Is Not Lost*.

At a 1991 lecture in the RAF Museum at Hendon, Dr Karl Karwarth related how, after a tour of duty as a KG FW Condor navigator/captain in 1942, he had been asked to translate a captured copy of AP1234 for the *Luftwaffe*. At first he was told he could not have the book on loan to work on it because it was Secret! (In fact it was only Restricted.) But at Hendon he admitted the only parts that had defeated him were the quotations from Lewis Carroll.

I made another, but this time surreptitious, departure from protocol which ensured the only person's name credited in any Air Publication was that of A. W. Street, the Permanent Under Secretary of State responsible to the Air Council. My wife's first name, Mary, in clear, and my own name and initials in a very simple anagrammatic code, stared up from Chapter I on page 21 but were never spotted.

S5(b) thought a visit by the author in uniform might hearten the printers who were doing a fine job despite the *blitz*. So I went for a day to Whitefriars Press in Tonbridge to call on the Managing Director and to meet the operatives who seemed quite pleased to chat with me over their printing presses. Compiling an eight-page index was tedious, but at last, on the 8th anniversary of my own commission and the precursor of D-Day by three years, the nine months of gestation had ended. I was able to pen a glad memo to all my T Nav colleagues as follows:

More Bumph! 26 tons of paper and five miles of linen cloth, representing the first 50,000 copies of AP1234 (1941) will at last be rolling off the presses for distribution by Air Pubs and Forms Store which will take another month or two. I know we only pretend to read our manuals, but the cover of this one is unusual, the coloured diagrams are eye-catching and the text will be only slightly out of date by September! It will have been with the printers for only four months, which is quite a record for HMSO in these days of blitz.

F. C. R., T Nav 3, 6 June 1941.

Within three weeks, Hitler launched his ultimately fatal mistake, Operation Barbarossa, which would bleed the Germans white after three years of grappling with the Russians. We were not to know that outcome for a very long time, but were now cheered to some considerable extent by no longer standing alone. Our own home-grown Communists were naturally disconcerted by this turn of events and had to put a very brave face on the *volte face*. One effect of the

German move was a noticeable easing of the nightly *blitz* on London. Another, and less obvious, effect was the reduction of the threat of invasion. Operation Sealion was at least put on the back-burner.

For my part, I continued to answer the office 'phone, develop ideas with Francis Chichester, feed Tony Willis with titbits for *Tee Emm* and shuffle paper as fast as possible from my 'Air Box' In tray into my Out tray. I felt strangely shy and self-conscious when an advanced copy of the brain-child arrived prematurely well ahead of ETA in late August, with its 817 paragraphs and 328 tightly-packed pages. I had a sense of tangible relief tinged with anxiety. Was it going to be any good?

There was, however, no time to wait for reactions, as the text was urgently needed by the Commonwealth Air Training Scheme already in full swing. To avoid shipping the finished bound article, first 'pulls' from the presses were rushed to Canada, South Africa, Australia and New Zealand for their local presses to copy and publish as required. In Australia, fortunately unknown to me until quite recently, it reverted to a ghastly loose-leaf format between cardboard covers tied up with string. So much for my hard-won cherished readability intentions, down under!

A letter came to the Air Box from Frank Debenham OBE, Cambridge Professor of Geography and former geologist on Scott's last 1912 Expedition. He was gallantly trying to teach navigation to Cambridge air and naval cadets without the benefit of a manual or any training aids. He had therefore been obliged to prepare a treatise on the basic principles of navigation and had resorted to Lewis Carroll to entice his readers to study it rather than frighten them away.

Having got wind of the new *Alice in Wonderland* RAF manual, he wanted to know if there would be any official objections to his own strangely coincidental quotations on the grounds of poaching? The letter found its way to my desk and I replied that we were greatly complimented to have the full backing of such a distinguished scholar. The more Alice, the merrier! Hodder and Stoughton eventually published Frank's *Navigation with Alice* in 1961, handsomely illustrated by Anne Scarisbrick.

I am sorry I never met the Professor. I was away on an investigation of navigation practices on the Burma Front in South-east Asia in January and February 1945, just when the plans were being made for pioneering trans-polar flights by *Aries*, the modified Avro Lancaster from RAF Shawbury; so I missed the briefing visits my staff made to the Scott Polar Research Institute at Cambridge where

Frank was then Director. But many other events were crowding in on me at Adastral House. For one thing, my short 15 months' tenure of Squadron Leader rank was ended abruptly with promotion in September!

Then I was invited by my former T Nav boss and friend, GeeGee Barrett, to visit him at Oban where he was commanding No 210 Catalina Sqn and could fit me into a maritime operational sortie. There being no airfield at Oban, I went by train and encountered a rather muted welcome from the squadron navigators who had probably been overly-briefed by GeeGee.

Appointed a supernumary member of one of the crews, I was flown off down the Firth of Lorne late the following night in heavy rain, setting out on a 15-hr sortie to meet and escort a homeward-bound convoy some 200 miles south-west of Ireland. Using the Met forecast wind, we skirted round the coast of Donegal and at midnight set course for the convoy from a lighthouse in County Mayo, flying south-west over a dark and stormy Atlantic.

Occasionally, a flame-float was dropped overboard and, for lack of a drift sight, the rear gunner then tried to measure the drift by pointing his guns at it while our Catalina waddled along at 95 knots into the headwind. As I have already mentioned, Dead Reckoning as a system of air navigation is notoriously inaccurate; but with no good drifts, no astro and with D/F loop bearings on far-away beacons highly suspect, our progress was inevitably very questionable.

Little wonder, after flying some 200 nautical miles into the ocean, there was no sign of a convoy or any ships in the welcome light of day. By then we were possibly 50 miles adrift in any direction; but so also might have been the convoy. Apart from position errors which it may have acquired on passage, it might have had its course altered on secret Admiralty orders, in the light of intelligence on the U-boat threat.

If this change had been ordered while we were airborne, we would not have been informed for fear of alerting the enemy; but we would still have been expected to rendezvous with our elusive and vulnerable friends. We couldn't win!

We began at once what is known as a square search, flying in ever-increasing distances, outwards from our starting point like a square-sided corkscrew, while the crew scanned the heaving waves 1,500ft below on either side and out through the haze to where the ragged clouds and sea merged into a grey mist about a mile away.

Wind velocity could be guessed from the tell-tale streaks on the surface called 'sea lanes', but this did not exactly apply to us 1,500ft

166

up above. The search was unrewarding and was aborted after two hours, when we had reached the prudent limit of our endurance, having only enough fuel left to reach Oban with a following wind.

Ours was just another 'Not Met' sortie of the many that were then dogging Coastal Command. Only one in four convoy air escorts had been making their rendezvous during this very crucial period of our grave maritime misfortunes, a depressing statistic which was not much noised abroad!

As a fly on the walls of the 'Cat', I had been impressed by the fact that, while the two pilots in the crew had 'George' to help fly the aircraft, the solitary and ill-equipped air navigator had no respite at all and his professional activity dwindled to a totally inadequate level. Before taking off, he had been busy for an hour planning the flight and, once ashore, faced another hour's de-briefing. This was far too long a stint for any single navigator, with such primitive equipment, yet the crew lacked a comprehensive co-operative system. Was there not scope here for a general air navigation directive, I wondered? AP1234(1941) Chapter XII had suggested some sort of answer.[2]

We reached Oban quite safely, after first making an unidentified landfall in Eire. The weather had improved at base, though it was now almost gloaming. I would not have much cared to be onboard had we been returning in a storm and at night. The Catalina captain, who shall be nameless and with whom I had been in the air for 15 hours, had made the occasional visit to look at the navigation plot but had had precious little idea of where we were for most of that time. The clouds covering the coasts of Eire and Scotland are notoriously 'stuffed' with mountains and had already claimed many a maritime aircraft.

On returning to London, I heard that Coastal Command were negotiating for me to take over one of their two maritime Whitley squadrons, as soon as I could get myself 'converted' at No 3 Operational Training Unit at Cranwell. My old colleague Moseley had recently joined Kelly's team as T Nav 1 and I was definitely *de trop* as a Wing Commander. So I left the Adastral toilers soldiering on through the nightly *blitz* and headed for the keen fresh air of Lincolnshire: Atta Boy! But it was more than a few weeks before I could take over my squadron and when at last I was in the chair, I found more than a spot of fresh air was needed to blow away all the Adastral cobwebs, let alone the new ones that began to entangle me.

Kelly now disclosed a tender side of leadership that he had carefully hidden beneath his brusque manner. In spite of the relentless pressure he was under, he found time to dash off a heart-warming note in his own fair hand on an office memo pad. It reached me in

December and I have kept it ever since. Little did he or I appreciate the irony of his gambit!

25. XI. 41 Air Miny.
Dear Richardson,
Now that you are at last being allowed to settle down to your new post and get on with it, it is opportune for me to write to wish you fortune and to thank you for your diligent services here. We miss you very much – rather cunningly we do more than use the 'contacts' you established – we allege it's still you speaking!

For your sake I rejoice for you – and I take comfort that there is one more potential relief for myself!

To your Lady and yourself best wishes – you will ever be a welcome caller.
Ventios semper agitemus
L. K. Barnes

Just after the War, leukemia claimed Kelly, then a budding Air Commodore. He had been the RAF's brightest navigation star and a born innovator. At his own passionate request in 1942, as a gesture of support and to boost the prestige and morale of the generally under-esteemed RAF air navigators, the Air Council authorised him to wear the one-winged air navigator's brevet in place of his own two-winged pilot's badge. In this action he has remained unique.

There could never have been enough Kellies for the good of our Service and any close and anxiously-informed observer of some of today's policy developments might come to the disturbing conclusion that Kelly may well be turning in his grave.

Notes to Chapter XI

1 Administrative and Special Duties.
2 This was the chapter on Applied Air Navigation.

XII

Whitleys at Sea

AT No 3 OTU, Cranwell, I walked into another world, peopled by flying nomads living out of suitcases; of physical endeavour and spells of predictable 18-hour daily stints and of equally unpredictable relaxations from duty; years of 365-day toiling and years of universal camaraderie; a world of organised chaos.

The shambles had really started in 1926 when Hitler marched a symbolic token of the *Wehrmacht* into the Allied-occupied and demilitarised Rhineland. It was then he called the bluff of the French and British who both showed complete lack of resolve and dared not react positively while the Americans were busy rebuilding the former industries of Germany under the Dawes and other Plans. They had no will to back up mere verbal protests.

Ever since that gamble, Hitler had held the initiative and we British were left to flounder, year after year, with off-the-cuff improvisations. Even our declaration of war in 1939 on behalf of Poland, whom we could never help directly, was merely an expression of intent, in defiance of Der Führer of a nation of maniac Nazis. The British loathed the *Herrenvolk* and the myth of the Master Race, of which, to my personal regret, Richard Wagner had been adopted as its musical genius and has for ever lost much of his shine for me.

Hitler continued to call the shots till in late 1941, with God-sent overconfidence, he embarked on Operation Barbarossa and, as we were to find out later, finally over-reached himself at Stalingrad. In early 1941 we were still plugging holes in our dykes after he made them. We had turned the tables a little in the 1940 Battle of Britain and for a time had secured our Base; but we weren't sure we could 'repel boarders' and believed Hitler's Operation Sealion had only been postponed. Our military resources were totally inadequate to wrest the initiative from him and it seemed in 1941 we would go on dancing to Der Führer's tune indefinitely.

It is often forgotten that on 3 September 1939 U-boats had made their first strike against civilians – the liner SS *Athenia* was torpedoed without warning and the Battle of the Atlantic had started.

Crocodile tears shed since then on behalf of the Germans for their later sufferings must be seen in the bright light of reality to be simply hypocritical nonsense. Clearly, the U-boat war was intended to re-run Germany's WW1 attempts to subdue us by starvation. But our Masters now failed to recall a really vital Principle of War – the total security of one's Base is a prime necessity and a pre-requisite for ultimate victory.

Throughout the next three years, far too little effort was allocated to protect our maritime lifelines by providing offensive air forces for their effective defence. Top priority was invariably accorded to Bomber Command, who mistakenly rejected as of secondary importance many suitable and highly important targets like the very vulnerable, half-built U-boat pens in France in January 1941. Their 18ft-thick ferro-concrete roofs had become absolutely impregnable by the time they were bombed in desperation, two years later.

More ships were being sunk than could possibly be replaced, but we needed food, oil and raw materials so as to live and fight for life. It was a shock to the Admiralty when their much-vaunted ASDIC[1] was found to be fairly useless in early battles at night against half-submerged undetectable U-boats, which sank our battleships and destroyers with impunity and took such devastating toll of our merchant fleet. By mid-December 1940, the War Cabinet was well aware that food stocks were at rock bottom, down to 15 weeks' supply of wheat, two of meat, eight of butter, three of margarine and 27 of bacon, with no imported fruit at all. All other essential supplies remained very much touch-and-go until May 1943, a turning-point in the struggle. We clearly had to win the Battle of the Atlantic if we weren't to lose the entire war. This deadly and unpublicised ding-dong 'high-tech' struggle only ended with the collapse of Germany in May 1945. Another round in that contest would have certainly gone to the pre-fabricated, truly submersible Mk 22 U-boats which were then making their debut and to which we had no proven answer.

With no thought of defeat or wish for a negotiated peace, we stood alone, teeth gritted and waiting for the Commonwealth to hasten to our side. The 1941 advent of neutral America as a super ally, after Pearl Harbor, was a completely unforeseen bonus. Translated into everyday life, our political and military Masters had been living from hand-to-mouth since well before 1939. Now, as pawns in the game, we had to learn how to survive one day at a time. In such chaos, any short-term personal plan was a very welcome, if brief, relief from great confusion.

Thus, as CO designate of the AuxAF No 502 General

Reconnaissance Ulster Squadron based at Limavady in County Londonderry, I would soon have charge of 24 crews, 20 Armstrong-Whitworth Whitley V mid-wing bombers (powered by two liquid-cooled Rolls-Royce Merlin Xs) and of several hundred ancillary troops. Other things being equal, from 6 November I could perhaps peer ten months ahead. I went to No 15 Group HQ in Liverpool to meet my new AOC, A V-M J. M. Robb CB DSO DFC AFC and his Senior Air Staff Officer (SASO), Air Commodore K. B. Lloyd AFC, with whom I would soon be having daily telephone 'confabs'. They laboured in an Area Combined HQ together with the Admiral C-in-C Western Approaches (responsible for shipping to and from the Clyde and the Mersey).

The normal OTU course lasted six weeks but, true to the then prevailing mayhem, I learnt I was urgently needed at Limavady to replace 'Uncle' Tom Cooper DFC who had gone to HQ Coastal Command as Wing Commander Plans, only to die shortly afterwards in a prang. I had to pare down my ops training to a mere eleven days, insufficient to get well acquainted with the Whitley Vs which flew like lumps of lead, as had the Atlas, a predecessor from the same stable. When I had flown an hour on solo circuits and bumps, it was time to go. The sophisticated maritime ops techniques would have to be picked up on the job – not the most propitious start for taking over command of a high-tech squadron.

By 1941 the Merlin Xs' cylinder blocks had been re-ground to very fine limits in various aircraft shadow factories,[2] after being used elsewhere in the Service. Nobody at Cranwell told me that the Merlins were already playing up very badly and that there had been 17 engine failures since 1 January in No 502 Sqn alone, with the loss of five aircraft – three pranging with only minor crew casualties but two ditching in the sea, with the loss of both crews. Whitleys could not maintain height on one engine and as the dead propeller couldn't be feathered, it tried to windmill the seized-up engine, thereby adding to the drag. Having two such unreliable powerplants only doubled the chances of a crisis. At the normal anti-U-boat search height of 1,500–2,000ft, the loss of one engine involved ditching within 30 minutes. The OTU syllabus gave no practice in single-engined flying, which would have been a waste of time anyway. Besides, who had ever heard of Rolls-Royce engines packing up?

Dinghy drill was practised –the underlying reason for it needing no emphasis to intelligent aircrew. I was amazed that the ability to swim was not a compulsory item in the maritime curriculum. ASV Mk I, a metric waveband airborne radar designed to detect surface vessels, now covered the Whitley V's back, sides and wings with dipoles[3] and large fixed loop aerials. The set was highly sensitive to humidity and temperature and was kept in air-conditioned stores when not installed for flight. Inexplicably, it was always referred to as 'SE', short for Special Equipment. Perhaps this sounded more impressive?

ASV Mk1 was never more than 75% serviceable and often much less in practice. Over rough seas, its cathode-ray screen became cluttered with sea echoes called 'grass' and was quite unreadable. At best, the 'blip' of a U-boat might be seen for a few seconds out to a distance of ten miles on either beam. Half-hour watches on the screen were therefore adopted so as to preserve the operators' visual acuity. Unknown to us, U-boats soon had listening radar detectors called 'Metox' that had a much longer range against searching aircraft and so could at least prepare to dive long before being spotted on our ASV screens.

Apart from the two pilots and one air navigator (in 1941 still called an 'Observer', a relic of 1918) the crew formerly had two Wireless Operator/Radar Operator/Air Gunners who were now increased to three. They were all NCO aircrew and shared spells in the rear gun turret, at the ASV screen and on the W/T set. They were also in charge of a box containing two caged pigeons of suspect homing reliability for release by the crew when ditched. The Whitley's war load comprised only six 250-lb torpex depth-charges or two 500-lb A/S bombs. Depth-charges had a lethal range against a U-boat's pressure hull of a mere 10ft (later thought to be only 5ft) and all six were dropped in a 'stick' spaced at 36ft (changed in 1943 with good effect to 100ft) and laid at an angle of 10° across the target: one of the six might then be near enough to damage the U-boat's pressure hull.

Twelve attacks had already been made by 502 Sqn in 1941 without a kill, but two DFCs had been awarded in appreciation of the huge effort involved. The U-boat would usually crash-dive out of range at the mere sight of an aircaft and there would be no chance of having a second 'go', even if there had been any depth-charges to drop. In the light of past failures, these were now triggered to explode at a depth of 25ft instead of the original 50ft.

The Whitley flew for ten hours in a most ungainly, nose-down attitude, due to drag from its wings' high angle of incidence and its stickleback radar aerials. To maximise the element of surprise against U-boats and for air-to-air protection, it was camouflaged white underneath and sea-grey on top. These strange visual characteristics failed to confer any immunity against pot shots from trigger-happy seamen on convoys being escorted or from 'friendly'

172

naval craft inadvertently flown over when in cloud, as I was soon to discover. There had been four such unexpected attacks against No 502 Sqn in 1941, resulting in three ditchings, but the crews had, luckily, all been rescued.

Designed to fly at 200kt at 26,000ft with a clean fuselage, flying at low altitude in such a nose-down attitude deflected the air from the radiators and undoubtedly contributed to our subsequent engine problems. A cast-off from Bomber Command due to its inadequate ceiling, the Whitley, like all maritime landplanes, had never been designed for the AU-B role. It was really unsuitable for two reasons – its range was too short and it carried too few depth charges. Hard to navigate, it had now become a death-trap due to the newly acquired design inability to fly on one engine. Unwieldy, noisy and cramped on the flight deck, contact between the crew, except by intercom, involved awkward crawling on hands and knees in flying kit through the tunnel of the mid-wing centre-section separating the three flight-deck members from the three in the aft-section, with the vital ASV radar screen, the W/T set, the tail gun-turret and the aforesaid homing pigeons. I began to realise why Coastal was universally already known as the 'Cinderella' Command.

At last the afternoon of 23 November came when I sent for an airlift to Northern Ireland from Cranwell. I was more than glad when Squadron Leader John B. Russell arrived in one of my aircraft to take me to my squadron at Limavady. He had been one of the star pupils on the very bright Spec N course that had graduated just after the war began and I could not have wished for a better No 2. We flew across the Irish Sea and shortly I had my first glimpse of Limavady's East-West runway lying parallel to the dangerous 1,200-ft cliff of Benevenagh. This hazard was more or less in the circuit and had earned the appropriate sobriquet Ben Twitch. The safest way to approach Limavady in the normally poor local weather was from the low shores of Lough Foyle.

I was greeted by a bunch of enthusiastic youngsters to whom a Wing Commander of 29 summers may have seemed just young enough to be one of themselves. They had stoically faced the demands of a flying task which never offered a let up, day or night, except when the weather was absolutely 'clampers'. The aircrew looked to me to fight their corner against sometimes incomprehensible and seemingly mental lapses on the part of our Top Brass. The very next day, we had a crash-landing due to engine failure but fortunately the crew were all unscathed. Two days later, Flying Officer Holdsworth attacked a U-boat, with no tangible results. This sequence of events soon became fairly normal.

By 1941 the squadron's AuxAF Anson aircrews[4] had, of course, long since become tour-expired, replaced by aircrew from all four corners of the world. I found with dismay that 14 of my 24 crews were overdue for rest, that the remainder would also shortly become tour-expired and that I had inherited a very rapidly dwindling asset. The aircrew outlook was grim. To add to this sorry tale, the squadron had also been seriously over-employed and had steadily accumulated more aircraft needing major inspections than our maintenance groundcrew were able to service, not only due to an acute shortage of skilled manpower but also for lack of spares.

Pilot Officer C. M. Slatter, our young Engineer Officer graduate from Bristol, had been trying to work miracles since May, but every time a serviceable Whitley was rolled out, it had been snatched up by No 15 Group[5] for a sortie. Upon its return, it could only be turned round again at the expense of the other accumulating servicing tasks. Our maintenance section was being flogged and overwhelmed. This crazy situation continually dogged the squadron and for several months to come I was unable to resolve it. Living from hand to mouth, a build-up of reserves was impossible and nobody had ever thought of planning the flying effort to match the prevailing limitations on maintenance – of which more anon. The SASO at No 15 Group would not, or could not, respond and made me feel guilty whenever my daily state of aircraft/crew readiness fell below six. There was much more stupidity to come; but for the time being I had to remain frustrated, for fear of being regarded as a 'belly-acher'. It was the enemy we wanted to fight, not our own commanders.

Among my newly-arrived pilots was Flying Officer K. J. Bhore, a very slightly-built Indian who needed several large cushions stuffed behind his back in the pilot's seat to help him grip the control column and reach the heavy rudder bar with his short legs. An extremely game young man, he was, unfortunately, physically too small to handle the weighty Whitley and had to be re-posted at the end of December, away from flying duties, to the School of Aeronautical Engineering, despite all his previous flying training.

What with Australians, Canadians, South Africans, New Zealanders, not to mention Bill O'Malley Brayton, our lively Air Gunnery Leader from Eire, together with a majority of English, Welsh and Scots aircrew, No 502 Sqn was a great mix of cultures and personalities. Every meal turned into a battle of wit and riotous repartee which was not only hilarious but also a great boost to morale. It has always been axiomatic in the RAF that the tougher the living conditions, the higher the morale. Life was basically far from comfortable at Limavady and squadron morale was correspondingly high. The Dominions later withdrew their aircrew from the RAF to be absorbed into their own separate air forces – which we in the RAF considered a great loss to both sides. The mixture within No 502 Sqn showed how inter-tribal rivalries stimulated *esprit de corps* against a common enemy: we all spoke the same language when it came to flying and never had a dull moment!

By contrast, many of my technicians and tradesmen were the original Northern Ireland Auxiliaries. Off duty, they played drums, fifes and bagpipes, useful for squadron 'dos' and for occasions like the Glorious Twelfth of July. A mixed bag of Protestants and Catholics, they rubbed along peaceably together. (What devilry has since come between them?) When in our cups, the whole squadron sang *The Sash* (i.e. the one my father wore at the Battle of the Boyne) – but this dirge never produced tribal friction: we had no time for Irish myths – *The Sash* was as much a joke as 502 Sqn's badge, the Red Hand of Ulster.

Our long-suffering, highly-supportive RAFVR Adjutant J. S. N. Sewell, a mature teacher in peacetime, was promoted to Flight Lieutenant on 1 December. His wife had suffered in the *blitz* of Plymouth and became a drug addict, thanks to an overworked GP. The squadron soon boasted a first-class Belfast-trained MO, softly spoken Flt Lt Magill, very popular with the camp-following wives, whose families were in his caring hands.

Pilot Officer Slatter, short, plump and twinkling, could, when properly primed, recite the 20 minutes of *Eskimo Nell* without pausing – a considerable feat of memory. One latent problem which he and I shared was not then apparent – many of the Auxiliary erks had never signed an agreement to serve outside Ireland and some evidently thought they were exempt from posting overseas – including to anywhere outside Ireland! For the time being, there was plenty to occupy us, escorting convoys in the North Western Approaches. The question of leaving the Emerald Isle didn't arise.

For a few weeks before they moved to North Coates Fitties, we shared Limavady airfield with No 53 Hudson Sqn whose officers under Wing Commander 'Tubby' Grant also suffered the discomfort of the Mess at Dreenagh, a dismal, crumbling 18th Century country mansion, damp, cold and rat-infested. It belonged to the McCauslands, a family of Scottish/Irish descent who occupied the only wing they had managed to maintain in reasonable order. We saw little of our resident hosts. Our NCOs messed uncomfortably at Gorteen House on the road to Dungiven, nowadays a thriving hotel.

Dreenagh's only saving grace was a very small bar which some enterprising RAF catering officer had set up in a corner of the labyrinthine cellar, where creamy Guinness was dispensed from earthenware bottles, the like of which put nectar in the shade. As it always seemed to be pouring rain outside, that flag-stoned underground haven succoured many a thirsty soul.

One memory of Dreenagh was quickly imprinted on my mind, for it was in Dreenagh's large and cheerless anteroom that an inter-Service Court of Enquiry assembled shortly after my arrival. This inquest was a joint RN/RAF affair arising from the shooting down of a 502 Sqn Whitley by the convoy to which it had been assigned as escort on 3 October. Luckily, our crew were rescued and had lived to tell the tale; but unluckily for the Royal Navy, Squadron Leader Foster, the aircraft captain, was a highly-experienced Flight Commander who had been shot at before! Bill Brayton, our stalwart Gunnery Leader from Eire, who had joined us in September, had been a supernumerary in the crew and was also in no mood to quibble. The Naval contingent were embarrassed and full of apologies, but as somebody remarked rather forcibly: 'Shit a brick! What can we do with sorry?' By the time Foster had given evidence, spiced with a little anger, it being his third time of being shot at, there was no more to do but wring our hands at the stupidity of confusing a Whitley with a Ju 87 or 88 or a Focke Wulf Condor. The correct identification procedure had been followed and, besides, could anything ever look quite so ungainly as an ASV-equipped Whitley V?

It seemed of little concern to Group Captain Pearce, who was commanding Limavady, that No 15 Group were bleeding us white by using us in the foulest weather looking for U-boats in nil visibility when the sea state was also far too bad for ASV to function effectively. Flying in such conditions really seemed a complete waste of valuable flying time; but there was, in fact, a little method in this madness: the U-boat commanders' expectation of danger from our mere presence hampered their deadly surface actions. It was an unenviable choice and a matter of very fine judgment how best to use the Group's slender flying resources.

I turned my efforts to arranging some degree of staggering of the programme of crew replacement which nobody, including my esteemed predecessor, had apparently so far addressed. It was far too late to restore a complete balance of highly-skilled crews against new 'sprog' crews; but I was able to spread the process of crew replacement over a slightly longer period by asking for voluntary tour extensions, so that, at least in time, my successor would not face a similar dramatic loss of expertise when it was my turn to hand over the reins.

Occasionally, Professor (later Lord) Blackett, the recently-appointed Scientific Adviser to AOC-in-C Coastal Command, would pay us a flying visit, to sit over cups of tea with one of my captains, Flight Lieutenant 'Wizzy' Weizmann, a star physics graduate of Blackett's from Imperial College in the University of London. Wizzy had joined us on 25 November from the Coastal Command Development Unit in South Wales. Together they devised a transponder radar beacon to work with our ASV. Sited on the runway, it produced two 'lobes', dots on one side and dashes on the other, interlocking in a narrow beam for the approach path. From a range of ten miles an ASV operator could 'con' the pilot down to the runway threshold. Provided the ceiling wasn't below 800ft and visibility was at least 2,000 yards, the aircraft could be landed. The strong incentive for this invention was the avoidance of our infamous local flying hazard, 'Ben Twitch', which had already claimed one Whitley in bad weather and had given several other crews the frights of their lives.

The transponder was an instant success and became the first-ever RAF airborne blind approach device. Known as BABS (Blind Approach Beacon System), Mk I, it only needed a radar beacon parked at the end of the runway, combined with a little extra crew flying training. When installed and in good working order, it made an approach in poor weather a 'piece of cake'. We were over the moon!

The days slipped by, but our task paid no heed of such mundane measurements of time. My recollection is of just one continuous activity. As CO, I was not allotted a crew of my own and decided not to displace a regular pilot or air navigator whenever I could escape from my desk. Instead, I took turns with all my crews, flying as a supernumary pilot/air navigator, getting to know them all on the job at first-hand. Deliberately, I did not appear on any formal crew list. Rather than hog the most favourable sorties presented in a series of offensive sweeps, which some squadron commanders seemed inclined to do, I left it to chance as to whether I was lucky enough to pick a sortie that encountered a U-boat. My luck was never in and during my ten months I never saw a single one.

The squadron air navigators were dead keen and I soon spotted an embryonic leader among them, one Flying Officer James Perry RAFVR, who had joined the squadron in June, had above-average drive and was always laughing at something or somebody. When the time came for Flying Officer J. M. Wheeler to leave, I decided to appoint Perry to succeed him as squadron navigation officer. Meanwhile, we three put our heads together to devise a flight routine to keep our navigators on their toes. It was the embryo of the Coastal Command 'Drill', of which much more anon.

In this effort, we were shortly to be greatly helped by the unusual journalistic talents of Flying Officer Dave J. Wright, a witty and stylish Canadian from Edmonton, Alberta, who had come to the squadron in August. Wright was to be inspired to write a monthly broadsheet entitled '*The Cock-(ey)-ed Hat*' (No 502 Squadron Navigators' Own Gen Sheet) – a DIY *Tee Emm* on flimsy foolscap, cyclostyled by the Orderly Room and distributed to every navigator. With such homespun gifts already available, I saw it was going to be fairly easy to sow the seeds of professional enthusiasm into such willing and receptive minds.

Notes to Chapter XII

1 A name derived from the Allied Submarine Detection Investigation Committee of 1917, during the First World War anti-U-boat campaign.
2 The creation of which was designed to increase productive capacity during war. They were one of the 'pieces of preparatory work' to strengthen the UK air defences announced by Prime Minister Neville Chamberlain in May 1938 (see *Per Ardua*, by H. St G. Saunders; OUP, 1944).
3 I.e. twin aerials, H-shaped.
4 No 502 (Ulster) (B) AuxAF Sqn had originally been equipped with Avro Ansons.
5 Whose HQ was at Liverpool with the C-in-C Western Approaches from February 1941.

XIII

The Atlantic War (1)

O UR MASTERS now displayed a significant change of tactics and I was ordered on 28 November to send ten fully-trained crews and serviceable aircraft with groundcrew on detachment 'for a few days' to RAF Chivenor in North Devon. No 19 Group[1] was about to mount a concentrated offensive against U-boats based on the French ports as they transited the Bay of Biscay on the way to and from their Atlantic hunting grounds.

To round off the month in the brightest of ways, U-206 was sunk in the Bay on 30 November by Flight Lieutenant Holdsworth; while on 1 December, U-563 was seriously damaged by Flying Officer Cave, for both of whom I very happily cited immediate DFCs.

It is a well-known fact that the smallest viable organised unit in the RAF is a squadron. Apart from services such as messing, technical and personal accommodation, fuelling, motor transport, parachute storage, Intelligence, meteorology and other such basics provided by stations, a squadron is designed to stand on its own feet and, when occasion demands, to be able to shed a flight on detachment for a strictly limited period.

A squadron is a living, tangible entity and a focus of *esprit de corps*. What it cannot do is survive for very long, split into flights or even smaller numbers, for these sections tend to disintegrate quickly when separated from their central organisation. This was just what Fate had in store for 502 Sqn: the time-honoured tenets of RAF organisation were about to be utterly ignored.

A wet November passed inexorably into a wet December and for a few days what was left of the squadron in Limavady continued with its routine tasks day and night, usually in close support of convoys in the Western Approaches, sometimes on fruitless offensive sweeps into the Eastern Atlantic. We were now slowly re-equipping with Whitley VIIs but they didn't have any noticeably improved features other than ASV Mk II, against which the U-boats, unknown to us, were quickly equipped with 'Metox', a radar listening device that nullified its usefulness.

All our sorties were designed to seek and attack U-boats alleged to be in specified areas as prompted by top secret intelligence based on 'Ultra' and the 'Y Service', sources of information that were always scrupulously concealed from us.[2] From our limited point of view, a ten-hour flight over the ocean, in and out of the ragged base of low cloud, with nothing to show for the sustained effort, demanded a strong tenacity of purpose and endless patience, especially when it had to be repeated *ad nauseam*.

The monotony was broken every now and then in the North-Western Approaches by encounters with reconnoitring enemy long-range bombers whose job it was to report the position of our convoys to Admiral Dönitz and his U-boats. Any air-to-air combats which ensued had usually been inconclusive exchanges of fire except for one, on 17 July 1941, when a shoot-out with a FW Kurier by Q/502[3] had resulted in three of the crew being wounded and the Whitley having to ditch. They had, luckily, all been rescued.

December had, however, begun well with the award of a DFC to Flying Officer Cave for his damaging daylight attack on a surfaced U-boat. On 7 December, the Japanese attacked Pearl Harbor and our immediate gut reaction was one of huge relief, for we then realised that the half-hearted and often covert help we had been receiving from the USA would in future be replaced by unlimited support from an official ally. No more 'cash on the barrel' to pay for re-armament out of our dwindling national wealth. Lease-Lend had been invented!

Our reaction of guarded optimism was reinforced when Hitler had the temerity also to declare war on the USA! Within a few months, the US was converting the UK into a European offshore unsinkable aircraft carrier. The sleeping, inward-looking giant had been rudely woken and now began to listen to its well-informed journalists such as Ed Morrow and Walter Kronkite who had been sympathetically monitoring our war since September 1939.

At first, our new Allies ignored all warnings and paid very heavily for set-piece daylight raids relying on the defensive fire-power of formations of Flying Fortresses, which were no match for the Me 109s and 110s. They learnt from their bitter losses and later developed long-range Mustang fighters to escort their bombers.

Now, at the end of 1941, providing the USA would give war in Europe a higher priority than the defeat of Japan – which was by no means certain for some time – we knew that Hitler, Mussolini or Hirohito hadn't a hope in Hell of winning, however long and hard the struggle was going to be. These heartening assessments were naturally repeated to the listening world by Churchill *via* the BBC on every possible occasion.

After reorganising what was left of my squadron at Limavady to continue with No 15 Group's tasks, I flew down to Devon for a quick visit on 8 December to see how the boys were coping. Chivenor was a pleasant and comfortable station and they were excited to be involved in this new venture. The Blind Approach Beacon System (BABS) Mk I had been installed to reduce the hazards of low cloud on the surrounding cliffs. Next day I joined a sortie into the Bay and was grateful to have our home-made radar aid available when we returned in the dark and found clouds sitting right down on the cliff-tops at Hartland Point.

Obviously, the Bay offensive was potentially very profitable. The trouble was that my Engineer Officer couldn't be cut in half! All our main servicing facilities and records were 200 miles away at Limavady; time-consuming ferrying was unavoidable. SASO at Liverpool was very sympathetic and buoyed up my hopes that, one way or another, No 502 Sqn would soon be re-united. But on 12 December I was told that the Chivenor detachment was to go at once to St Eval in North Cornwall, to be nearer the Bay. This augured ill for reunification back at Limavady but I was assured that the split was still only a temporary one, even though we were now further apart than ever.

Meanwhile, Flying Officer Cave continued his good work and had two night sightings in the Bay on 17 December and bombed a tanker on the night of 24 December, illuminating the scene by parachute flares, one of which caught up on his tail wheel, setting fire to the tail for a short time! He had found the tanker lying up a creek on the Biscay coast, half beached and simply asking for trouble.

That same day, one of my officers reported that a rumour was circulating in the bar of Limavady's Alexandria Arms, reputedly run by a Sinn Fein supporter, that the whole squadron was about to leave Ireland for good! To me it seemed a very likely piece of 'duff gen'.

The weather had taken a turn for the worse and according to the Limavady Met Officer flying would not be possible for 48 hours; so I rang SASO at No 15 Group and repeated what had been heard at our 'local'. He replied that he'd been discussing our future that very morning with the AOC. There was no grain of truth in the rumour; on the contrary, steps were now being taken to end the St Eval detachment immediately.

In the light of this reassurance, I suggested that, as it was now Christmas Eve and the weather looked impossible for two days ahead, he might feel like standing down the Limavady half of the squadron for a short break? He readily agreed, following up with a signal from the AOC, wishing us the compliments of the season and confirming the grant of 48 hours stand-down. The Adjutant spread the glad tidings and by midday we were happily celebrating the prospect of a rest-break over Christmas.

The local Auxiliary erks were sent off with 48-hour passes and those who could not get home made the most of the NAAFI, while I did the rounds with recently-promoted Squadron Leader Barclay to engender the seasonal spirit, as far as a very wet and stormy night alongside Ben Twitch allowed.

Sometime later that evening, I reached the shelter of Roe Park, another rat-infested but very pleasant manor house belonging to a widow, Bunny Ritter, where my wife and infant daughter shared rooms with Flying Officer Richard Holdsworth, his wife Mary and Flying Officer George Buchanan (the novelist) who was an Intelligence Officer at Limavady. They had just finished chasing rats with hockey sticks as I came in, but the 'phone rang almost at once and I was summoned back to the Ops room because a message had arrived from No 15 Group which could not be read out to me over an open line. In 15 minutes I was holding the signal in my hands and could hardly believe my eyes. It was an order to despatch all available aircraft and crews to St Eval at once. The squadron maintenance gear was to be loaded into rail trucks and, as soon as possible, my headquarters, groundcrews and equipment were to take the train to Docking, a satellite of RAF Bircham Newton in Norfolk. Three unservicable Whitleys sitting at Limavady were to be serviced as and when spares could be found and were to be left in charge of my Flight Lieutenant Egerton. Two Whitleys were to be detached to Docking for unspecified operations under No 16 Group, Chatham. So the Limavady pub rumour had been 'pukka gen' after all!

Talk about chaos! Even the impossible can be done when necessary. On 10 January 1942 a train with five passenger coaches and ten laden goods trucks, fitted with more or less square wheels, trundled off at the crack of dawn from Limavady. The road party under now-promoted Flying Officer Slatter had already left for Norfolk the day before. At Larne the goods trucks were lifted into a waiting ship and the squadron officers, NCOs and men of the rail party climbed on board for the short sea crossing to bleak Stranraer.

Here we found other rail coaches waiting in a siding to carry us onwards as soon as our ten freight trucks could be hitched on. It had started to snow and by the time we reached Preston we could see the country was under a thick white mantle. Some elderly ladies had turned out in the dark to revive us with buns and hot tea on the platform, our rations having long since disappeared. They were angels.

It made a welcome change to get out of dimly-lit carriages to stretch legs and make acquaintance with these kindly folk; but it was all too brief and we were soon on our complicated cross-country way, chugging through the snowy, blacked-out Midlands until at last in the early hours, more dead than alive, we came to a halt in a god-forsaken white wilderness at a place called Heacham Junction.

We still had two miles to go to find our destination huts, sitting in the middle of a white and frozen field. We must have been taken there by Bircham Newton transport and helped by the drivers to find our allotted quarters; but of those details I have not the slightest recollection – it was a nightmare, best forgotten.

Here was I, based in No 16 Group for administration and for future unspecified operations, commanding a triangular-shaped squadron with 200-mile sides, located in three separate Groups and under the operational control of two of them! I didn't ever really know where I ought to be at any one time and was left to decide this for myself. Instinct drew me towards St Eval where intensive ops were in progress; but my squadron headquarters and all the records were parked on the stark Norfolk satellite, together with the heavy maintenance gear.

The scale of this crazy arrangement was clearly beyond the scope of any of the Groups concerned to have thought up and I realised the plan must have been conceived and ordered by some half-wit on the Air Staff at Command Headquarters. I had no contact with HQCC except through No 16 Group and even had I known anyone to protest to, I could not possibly have done so over Group's head.

As a small sideline, numerous Ulster Auxiliary airmen who had taken to the hills when they heard we were moving had to be rounded up in Ireland and escorted for summary jurisdiction to Docking during the coming weeks. We were truly glad to have them back, so I had to let them off with a caution.

Our bleak and frozen grass snowfield was four miles from Bircham, itself just able to keep its runways clear for use by two other squadrons and an experimental torpedo development unit. All its hangars were full and the Docking satellite had no shelter at all, much to the dismay of Slatter, my Engineer. Next morning I thumbed a lift to Bircham with my remaining Flight Commander, Australian Squadron Leader James Barclay RAF, and went to seek help from the Station Commander. I must refrain from naming names, but I have never encountered such a useless specimen of a Group Captain in all my life. He had been recalled from retirement and hadn't the foggiest idea of what was going on in the maritime war. When I asked him to provide a minimum of shelter for daily inspections – called in RAF jargon DIs – he replied that I had a de-icer van, so what more did I want? The war was quite beyond his grasp and he had decided his best contribution would be to raise chickens, fed on the swill from the Messes, and to publish the daily egg count in Station Routine Orders to boost morale.

In this novel war effort he was ably supported by his Squadron Leader Admin, who really hadn't got a clue but, to be fair, could boast only few months' service background. No doubt they both felt their existence was more than justified.

Tearing out my hair, I requested a runabout for myself and a 30cwt van for Slatter and then headed for the Ops Room from where I rang the Wing Commander Ops at Chatham HQ. I gathered that the two serviceable Whitleys from St Eval would be needed for night anti-E-boat operations in the North Sea; but as we had no means of illuminating targets other than by parachute flares, which had been proved quite useless, every prospect seemed rather dim. It was difficult to see any way out of this particular wood. Unable to shed much light on my situation, he advised me to pay a personal call on one of the naval Commanders on the staff of the Admiral C-in-C Nore stationed at Great Yarmouth; he might be able to supply some gen. The Wing Commander was sorry to be so clueless. I made an appointment with the naval Commander for the next day then went in search of my Adjutant and Engineer Officer whom I had abandoned somewhere in the middle of the Docking snowfield. With Jimmy Barclay, we four waifs then returned to the crowded Mess at Bircham and stared gloomily into the bottoms of several preprandial 'jars'. Fortunately, I felt sure John Russell had everything under control at St Eval.

I tracked down my naval Commander informant in Great Yarmouth and heard that German E-boats, fast heavily-armed launches with torpedoes, lurked on the Dutch and Belgian coast and made night forays through minefields to attack ships plying between London and north-east ports. They outstripped our fastest naval craft and it was hoped our ASV Whitleys might be able to attack them. When I pointed out the problem of night illumination, if and when we ever found our quarry in the dark, the idea lost a modicum of feasibility. After a discussion of possible weapons, it was decided we should use depth charges dropped from 100ft.

With our inaccessible and frozen Docking airfield in mind, I pleaded for the maximum notice for dispatching aircraft on sorties. I was naturally very keen to have a go at such a well-worthwhile task but said I was far from sanguine at the prospect of inadequate night illumination.

I drove back to Docking through the snow and next day we began to prepare the necessary pyrotechnics. I signalled John Russell at St

Eval to ask for two crews to fly over and Flying Officers Holdsworth and Cotton duly arrived, none too pleased to exchange the balmy coastal greenery of Cornwall for the white wastes of Norfolk.

We already knew parachute flares were far from effective for visual sighting from the air at night. To get maximum value before they fell into the sea or burnt out, they had to be dropped from 4,000ft to give about five minutes of useful light. But a Whitley could not dive to attack quickly and a target could only be seen when looking away from the flares.

It followed that two aircraft were needed, one to drop the parachutes and the other to be flying below 1,000ft, ready to pounce. This may sound simple but in practice the tactic required intensive training by the two crews involved if they were to co-ordinate their separate actions in the dark.

By 7 January we were ready for the fray and that night I went up with Jimmy Barclay to lead the search from 4,000ft. Somewhere off the Suffolk coast we picked up ASV echoes, flew to where we expected them to be and fired off a green Very light. This alerted Flying Officer Edward Cotton, following in our other Whitley down below. Then we dropped a string of flares and tried in vain to see through the brightly-lit haze which they created. Cotton's crew were equally dazzled and could see nothing. After a fruitless five-minute search, the flares died and I fired off a white Very light to signal a return to our original flight plan.

Off we went towards the Dutch coast, hoping for better luck but there were no more ASV echoes. After two barren hours I called off the sortie with another Very light and we returned to Docking for an inquest. The tactical co-ordination of the two aircraft had been difficult, though it would not be impossible to improve with a lot more practice. But the flare illumination had been quite useless, largely due to the prevailing smog. We would need very clean polar air for this kind of lighting to work.

We tried again on four further nights with no better results and I had reluctantly to report to No 16 Group that the idea was proving to be unworkable. I recommended suspending any further anti-E-boat night air sorties until much brighter and longer-lasting parachute flares or some other more effective means of lighting the target became available.

Meanwhile, the working conditions in the open air at Docking became quite atrocious and Slatter and I made another bid for hangar space at Bircham, for we had heard that the experimental torpedo boys were packing up. This time we were luckier and were allotted their hangar when they departed.

Slatter took all day to clean up the mess left behind and when the Station Commander paid him a surprise visit he had only just finished mopping up pools of oil off the concrete floor. He was made speechless when the Group Captain remarked in all seriousness that Slatter had evidently taken over the hangar in spick and span condition – adding 'So you just see you keep it that way!'

Two Whitleys were now undergoing major inspections sitting in the snow at Docking and had been lifted up on jacks to allow the undercarriages to be retracted. One day there was a slight thaw and the jacks began to sink unevenly into the ground, threatening both aircraft falling off their perches with their wheels up. The thaw was followed by a hard frost, freezing the jacks into the ground, where they stuck hard. Two Whitleys suspended drunkenly over the snow might have looked funny in other circumstances, but it was a disaster waiting to happen. After frantic scrounging back at Bircham we unearthed large inflatable air bags to place under the wings to enable the undercarriages to be lowered again.

Meanwhile at St Eval on 1 January 1942, P/502 with Pilot/Flight Sergeant Bell at the controls and Flight Lieutenant Bill Brayton as rear gunner, attacked an enemy ship with depth charges and gunfire and appeared to damage it severely. The squadron was now patrolling over the Bay by day and by night.

News came from St Eval that Squadron Leader N. S. F. Davie had made a forced landing in Occupied France when he lost an engine while flying at 4,000ft on a daylight anti-U-boat patrol over the Bay of Biscay, close inshore, on 4 February. Ironically, his posting to No 3 OTU for his operational rest had only just been received at my Docking HQ!

Three weeks later, the International Red Cross reported that all but one of his crew had escaped injury and had all been 'put in the bag'. They had been lucky to survive. Both John Russell and I had previously formed the impression that Davie had a premonition of some sort of incident like this, for he had given a vague impression of having slightly cold feet. This marked the start in No 502 Sqn of a rising incidence of engine failures which culminated during my tenure of command in a total score of 26 cases, four of which ended in ditchings from which only one crew of six young men were rescued.

We were now struggling well into February, deep snow still lying all around us at Docking. For light relief, we sometimes drove to a Hunstanton pub adopted by the RAF. Membership of the bar required uniform ties to be cut off just below the knot, the two ends being pinned on a shelf to join a row with many others.

Suddenly, we were pitched into real drama. During January and early February, Bomber Command had made thirteen night attacks on the German battleships *Scharnhorst, Gneisenau* and *Prinz Eugen*, which had been waiting in the French port of La Pallice, ready to put to sea as convoy raiders. All three had been slightly damaged by Bomber Command and Hitler decided to sail them back to the comparative safety of Kiel.

Taking clever advantage of the progress of a deep depression moving up the Channel, with its attendant cover of very foul weather, the ships left La Pallice unobserved by air recce and made an audacious daylight dash up the Channel, past Dover. The Royal Navy and the RAF were rather caught with their pants down, though no really adequate naval forces were available to stop the enemy battleships. Nos 19 and 16 Groups became involved in succession and Fleet Air Arm and RAF torpedo bombers at once went in to attack. Those crews that managed to find their targets in the heavy storm were easily shot down. All three battleships went through the Straits at full speed and reached the North Sea by midnight on 13 February.

Enter No 502 Sqn from Docking! We had two Whitley VIIs standing by for the E-boats and were ready to undertake maritime reconnaissance. No armour-piercing bombs were available for us at Bircham, so attack was out of the question. Flight Lieutenant Holdsworth (just promoted) and Flying Officer Cotton were duly briefed in the Bircham Ops Room to shadow and report and the hundred and one other items of pre-flight planning were hastily completed. Hot for the chase, we all jumped into waiting trucks and trundled off as fast as possible towards Docking, four miles away. The road to our snowbound aircraft went over a level-crossing and unbelievably, when we arrived at the railway, we found the gates were closed against us.

I jumped out and ran towards the adjacent one-eyed railway halt, shouting for the road to be cleared. A solitary man in railway uniform appeared out of the dark and was persuaded in the strongest possible language to get cracking with the gates, because we were going to war and hadn't a moment to spare. Talk about 'Fred Carno's Army'! British Rail were on the warpath.

At last we were airborne and headed for the Dutch coast, our ASV picking up the battleships at 12 miles. We were able to follow them as far as the Frisian Islands but lost contact in the shore echoes. The enemy was now home and dry and further shadowing was called off. Squadron Leader Barclay followed up with a dawn recce and more recces were made on 17, 20 and 21 January. While this was going on,

No 19 Group, in the panic and unknown by me, ordered three of my Whitleys to RAF Langham, 15 miles east of Docking, to support No 16 Group. Again, unknown to me, they were all returned the next day to St Eval without ever being used!

The derisive escape of these highly dangerous ocean raiders, able to menace our worldwide shipping routes, caused severe political and inter-Service recrimination. A scapegoat of high rank usually seems to be required for such a 'cock-up' and for a time one of the most farsighted, imaginative and staunchly irrepressible architects of Coastal Command, none other than Air Chief Marshal Sir Philip Joubert de la Ferté, found himself in that hot seat. In the event, however, blame was pinned fairly and squarely on the weather!

Fortunately for the success of Coastal Command's future maritime efforts, Joubert survived the inquest and steered many important plans to fulfilment before handing over the reins to Jack Slessor a year later. 1942 had started badly in our maritime world and things would only get much worse during the coming months.

On 29 January 'Gremlin' Hill had been forced to land at Portreath, 20 miles short of St Eval, after a hazardous struggle to reach land after one of his engines blew up. There had been no warning, just a puff of black smoke and then seizure. Then on 10 February the detachment had the disaster of losing our star performer, Flight Lieutenant Wizzy Weizmann, who took off on that very stormy night in J/502 to patrol the Bay. Wizzy lost an engine while close to the French coast and sent an SOS before ditching; but he didn't have a chance, going into that turbulent sea in the pitch dark. To make matters worse, *Scharnhorst* and company now began their dash up the Channel and the No 19 Group controller had to rule that it was too dangerous to go searching for a dinghy, even if there had been any aircraft resources to spare.

Six hand-written letters of condolence were duly penned from Docking the following day, expressing the whole squadron's deep sense of loss. One letter went to Wizzy's father who was his next-of-kin. Dr Chaim Weizmann became the future Israel's first President.

Investigating 'Gremlin's' seized-up Merlin showed the engine blocks had cracked internally, allowing the glycol coolant to enter the cylinders. This failure was well beyond the grasp of Flying Officer Slatter and of the combined engineering facilities of St Eval to remedy so No 19 Group arranged for Rolls-Royce to send an expert to St Eval where he became a fixture. For weeks on end he did his best to resolve our trouble but the fact was that previous reborings had made the cylinder walls so paper thin it was impossible to anticipate seizures on any of our 40 Merlin Xs. As if to emphasise this verdict, more sorties had to be curtailed in flight on 26 February and again on 1 and 22 March, each time because of engine trouble.

Notes to Chapter XIII

1 With HQ at Plymouth and responsible for coverage of the South-Western Approaches.
2 Ultra was the yield from the German Navy's Enigma cypher and the Y Service was radio surveillance of enemy Intelligence.
3 Q Queenie, one of 502's aircraft.

XIV

The Atlantic War (2)

SHORTLY AFTER this dénouement, I was relieved to receive orders to move from Docking after enduring six weeks of snow, to abandon the unserviceable hulks at Limavady and to reunite the squadron at St Eval. Some guardian angel at Command must have been at work!

Neither I nor my Engineer, Slatter, could have been happier and there were smiles on many faces when I arrived at No 502 Sqn's cliff-top airfield in North Cornwall on 23 February amidst the flowering daffodils and pink feathery tamarisks blooming in sight of the grey-blue Atlantic.

Compared to Docking, this was fantastic. However, one cloud on the horizon was the posting away of recently promoted Flight Lieutenant Richard Holdsworth on tour-expiry. He had been a tower of strength and little did we know this bright Cambridge graduate would shortly come to grief when a new parachute flare he was testing wrapped itself round his aircraft's tail at the Command Development Unit where he had gone for a rest from operations.

No 502 Sqn could set up shop in well-built accommodation with our aircraft dispersed on hard standings and with a large maintenance hangar. Although it had already been bombed, the Station was in excellent shape. Its organisation was efficient and the staff most co-operative, following the lead of their diminutive and chirpy Group Captain Bentley.

Wooden-hutted Messes provided food and drink on the station where my erks lived in pre-war married quarters and barrack blocks. The officers had a commandeered four-star Watergate Bay Hotel, ten miles north of Newquay, with a fine surfing beach. My own room overlooked the rollers on the Bay; but a landline to the Ops Room at the bedside meant almost nightly calls which were invariably critical. I began to hear ringing in my sleep and would wake to find it was only a bad dream. My NCOs had the run of Bedruthan Steps Hotel, overlooking picturesque Trenance cove, a natural amphitheatre with only a few bungalows and practically no visitors, even in the summer.

St Eval, 12 miles north of Newquay, had become the busiest air-field in the RAF, with seven mixed squadrons of Whitleys, Hudsons, Blenheims, Hampdens and Beauforts and a detached Flight of photo-recce Spits. In the spring, No 10 OTU with non-ASV Whitleys, was 'lent' by Bomber Command, at first under Wing Commander Pickard of *F for Freddie* film fame. Its staff and pupils – the valuable seed corn of Bomber Command – were to be withdrawn to participate in the 'thousand-bomber' raid on Cologne on 30 May and suffered heavy losses. St Eval also had a very thriving transit air traffic with Gibraltar.

Together with two RAAF Sunderland flying-boat squadrons at Mount Batten, two more flying-boat squadrons at Pembroke Dock and, in March, a Leigh Light[1] Wellington squadron at Chivenor, there were two Wellington squadrons, No 311 (Czech) at Talbenny and No 304 (Polish) at Dale in Pembrokeshire. No 19 Group had thus assembled as potent an air force as possible concentrated on offensive sweeps in the Bay of Biscay and these were to continue day and night, under the command of A V-M Geoffrey Bromet CB CBE DSO. In hard fact, all these aircraft lacked long range, effective weaponry and adequate navigation capability.

It was usual every day at St Eval to see two or three U-boat symbols displayed on the secret Ops Room wall map of the Bay, where 'black market' Intelligence indicated U-boats were on passage. It also showed what patrols had been laid on by the Group controller to seek and attack these targets. By forcing U-boats to submerge when crossing the Bay, the efficiency of their crews was steadily undermined and their time on patrol effectively cut by the slower underwater speed. Sinking the U-boats was our aim, but damage inflicted by a near miss was a feather in our caps and we steadily became a serious threat.

Details for each sortie would be assembled by the Duty Intelligence officer, one of whom, in 1942, was Flight Lieutenant Eddie Shackleton, later to be posted to Command HQ and destined for much higher rank as an anti-U-boat planner. (After the war, he enjoyed a brilliant career in the House of Commons, in Commerce and in the promotion of learned societies, before being translated to the House of Lords where he led for his Party and rendered many other important services to the nation.)

The vital 'Ultra' source of information on enemy movements and intentions, which remained a close secret until well after the war, had, unfortunately, dried up in February 1942 when U-boat Enigma machines were changed, thereby defeating our brilliant code-breakers at Bletchley Park until December 1942. During these ten

Intelligence-blind months, the U-boats had a terrifying field day, sinking nearly eight million tons of irreplaceable Allied shipping and threatening our prosecution of the war.

Crews in the AU-B squadrons at St Eval conjectured that the U-boat gen came from fishing boats which a 'salty' Lieutenant Commander Luard RN controlled from St Eval. Some suspected he had spies on the cliffs overlooking the U-boat pens, reporting by clandestine radio. We didn't ask. For safety under possible interrogation, we were deliberately kept ignorant, knowing nothing of 'Ultra' or of the 'Y Service' which busily sifted all W/T signals passing between the U-boats and their controllers working in Lorient under Admiral Karl Dönitz.

At all our pre-flight briefings, we were always warned of a highly treacherous Wing Commander H. M. A. Day, himself an early PoW, whom we had to avoid like the plague if we found ourselves 'in the Bag'. It seemed to me almost unbelievable of the fun-loving, champagne-drinking 4 FTS ex-Marine Adjutant I had known; but his pose was evidently an elaborate double-double-cross and the induced reactions of PoWs helped his subterfuge. 'Pricky' alias 'Wings' Day gained the enemy's confidence and managed to leak highly valuable gen throughout the war, before being dramatically rescued from the SS by American troops in the Dolomites where, with a group of political VIPs, he was being held as a bargaining pawn! As already related, most unusually he was awarded the DSO for his services in captivity.

St Eval, 600ft above sea-level, was often under low cloud, and Predannack, on the comparatively low-lying Lizard, made a very useful diversion. If it was also 'clampers' down there, a new runway built on Davidstow Moor was almost certainly clear. This was 1,000ft high on the treeless marshy slopes of Brown Willy, the Cornish mountain I had once climbed on a family holiday as a twelve-year-old. Crews disliked the discomfort of being diverted from Base and because the next day's flying programme was also disrupted, diversions were used as last resorts by my Flight Commanders. As long as there was 800ft clearance below cloud, No 502 Sqn's crews therefore hoped to fall back on BABS; but the threat of a lower ceiling had to be taken seriously by all concerned, of whom perhaps none felt more uneasy than the Squadron and Flight Commanders who knew their crews' limitations in tight corners.

Take-offs were seldom affected by low cloud; but nail-biting last-minute decisions had to be made when weather became touch-and-go for landings. In certain atmospheric conditions, a drop in air temperature of as little as half a degree Fahrenheit at St Eval could rapidly produce 'clampers', sometimes to the embarrassment of the local Met boys. Unable to see out of their Ops Room office, they sometimes thought it clear when, in fact, 'vis' was Nil. On such occasions I invited the Duty Met officer to step outside for a quick 'shufti' at the sky. We were greatly helped in shepherding crews back to Base by the national defence radar system, backed up by the Coast Guards. Crews approaching from the south-west were instructed to switch on their IFF (Identification, Friend from Foe) to be monitored and their positions were then fed into the Ops room.

As previously related, the squadron detachment was well placed to perform effectively against the U-boats. Richard Holdsworth had sunk U-206 and Robert Cave had seriously damaged U-536 for which they were awarded DFCs. On 17 December Cave sighted two more U-boats travelling at high speed at night, but they dived before he could attack. On Christmas Eve, he tried to attack a U-boat by the light of a parachute flare, while on his way to find and attack a tanker beached up a creek on the French Biscay coast, which he then bombed successfully. On 1 January Flight Sergeant Pilot Bell in P/502, with Flight Lieutenant Bill Brayton in the rear turret, had attacked and damaged a small enemy ship with depth charges. So the 502 Sqn detachment in No 19 Group had been showing its paces. There were, however, two very significant impediments to full success. The first was the unnerving incidence of engine failure to which I have already referred. The second was the propensity of our masters at Group to squeeze the squadron beyond its sustainable output.

Shortly after my own arrival at St Eval on 23 February, Group Captain Rex N. Waite, whom I had previously met, took over as Station Commander from the ever-cheerful, helpful and diminutive Group Captain Bentley. Everyone was at this time still alert to the possibility of a German invasion, though it was believed the threat had somewhat receded when Hitler went to war with Stalin. Cornwall, with its deeply penetrating estuaries cutting into the coast from both south and north, offered natural advantages to an invader who would have to seize only small strips of land to lop off great chunks of the peninsula. St Eval was scattered over a huge area and the camp was very vulnerable to ground attack, offering a most attractive prize. The airfield was always thronged with parked military aircraft and in constant use as an operational base.

In mid-March, when we had recovered from the traumas of February, I suggested to Rex Waite that he probably couldn't stop a group of my own officers and men from 'blowing up' all the aircraft parked on dispersal sites. He gladly accepted the challenge of a defence exercise, for the security of the Station was a big headache and needed to be kept under constant review. On the appointed day, the Station defence plan collapsed and Waite had to admit defeat, the defenders being easily evaded and every aircraft being 'destroyed' by infiltrators in broad daylight. This only added to our sense of unease, for it became very obvious that only a mere handful of trained saboteurs, landed clandestinely on the Cornish coast, could easily cause havoc.

A few days later Rex Waite took his revenge: he sent for me and showed me a letter from a firm of St Austell lawyers who were acting as Executors for the Will of a certain German Count who had evidently been a fugitive from Kaiser Wilhelm in 1914. The Count had settled down happily near St Columb Major, in time becoming a much-respected member of a rural community which has never been noted for friendliness towards foreigners, that is anyone not born in Cornwall. The Count had had two wives – in succession – and these good ladies had been leading lights in support of local charities and village fêtes, so much so that their eventual demise had been much deplored.

When Hitler came to power, the Count was even less enamoured of his Fatherland and nothing would have given him greater pleasure than to live to see the end of that tyrant. Alas! He had just died, a lonely and despairing old man. But his last wish had been for his ashes to be scattered from the air over woodlands of his beloved Cornwall, and unfortunately, it was no longer possible to charter private aircraft. The solicitors had written to ask if RAF St Eval could help. As 502 Sqn had numerous tests flights every day, I unhesitatingly offered to take on the job, if Rex Waite wished. So saying, I went back to the war and forgot all about accepting such an unusual task.

About a month went by – an age when every day was packed with compelling events and was seldom less than 18 hours long. Then the Station Adjutant rang to say he had a package for me to collect sometime please. I drove over to SHQ and as I entered Flight Lieutenant Cooke's spotless office, he exclaimed 'Mind the Count, Sir!', adding as an afterthought, 'and his two Countesses!' I had nearly tripped over a large cube-shaped cardboard carton with 12-inch sides. On its lid was the well-known logo 'Harrods' and underneath, in discreet lower-case, were the words Funeral Dept. Looking quizzically from the box to the Adjutant, I couldn't recall a previous encounter with any Count or, come to that, with Harrods.

'Don't you remember, Sir?' Cooke prompted: 'You told the Group Captain you could help by disposing of a Count's ashes. Well, Sir, there they are; except that he had two wives who have been exhumed and cremated with him. They are all three in that box.'

I was dumbfounded. I suppose I'd originally had visions of a small urnful. Gingerly picking up the box, which must have weighed a good 20lb, I left a square of grey dust on Cooke's highly polished floor, where the contents had seeped from under the four-sided lid. In the silence of shock-horror I carried the box with its dryly rattling contents to my staff car and drove back to my office, where I put it in one corner and retreated behind my desk to consider the next move. No good taking up a small sample, decanted into a paper bag to drop out of the pilot's window and then digging the rest into somebody's vegetable patch – I could see too many risks in that idea.

After a few minutes I remembered 'Ted Thread'. Of course! Flying Officer Edward Cotton, alias Ted Thread, was just the man! Ted had discovered the secret of Life – he never took any situation, even Death, very seriously. What was more, his whole crew were equally imbued with his light-hearted philosophy: everything was potentially a joke. If put to it, they could laugh their way through Hell. They were a great tribute to his leadership.

I picked up the flying programme for the day and saw he was marked down for an Airframe and Engine test that morning. So I asked my Adjutant to arrange for Flying Officer Cotton to report to me before he took off and by and by there was a knock on the door and in came Ted, his eyes twinkling, his fair hair escaping from under the jaunty set of his fore-and-aft forage cap, his beaming face one huge grin as he stepped in and saluted.

'Ted', I said, as I stood to greet him, 'I've got rather a tricky job I think you and your crazy crew are very capable of, er, doing' – I bit back the word 'undertaking' just in time! 'I see you're on an A and E test this morning', I continued. 'Well, will you kindly take that box over there and dispose of its contents as I will try to explain'.

Ted waited for more. 'The box contains the ashes of a German Count and two Countesses and I want you to scatter them over the woods just behind Newquay. See here' I said, pointing to a wooded area on the large-scale local map hanging on my wall. 'I'm sorry there's no time to explain all about it now. I'll tell you later. So off you go and please, Ted, do your best for the Count.'

'Yes Sir', he replied, 'certainly Sir,' and picked up the box with obvious relish. Was he thinking that jobs like this didn't come every day? I might have just been asking him to have a drink for all the effect my unusual request seemed to have on him. Smiling from ear to ear and with the box now tucked under his left arm, he gave a smart salute and went on his way. Minutes later, I watched him cycling gaily off to his Flight, the ashes perched rather precariously on his handlebars.

A couple of hours passed and I went over to the Mess for a bite of food. In the far corner of the anteroom, where a small window gave on to a little serving bar, I could see a group of my chaps, all rocking with laughter. Beer was going down the hatches as if to celebrate something important. I strolled over to pick up the gen and a sea of amused faces turned my way. Short-arsed Gremlin Hill, one of my highly esteemed captains who was due perhaps some day to be re-incarnated as a garden gnome, volunteered the question:

'Haven't you heard, Sir? About Ted Thread and a Count?'

'No I haven't, Gremlin. What's been the problem?' I asked, keeping a straight face.

'Well,Sir. You know what a mad crew Ted's got. Well, the W/Ops had this large box, Sir, full of ashes, to scatter over some woods, Sir. Ted told them to open the rear escape hatch in the roof and to put handfuls of the stuff out when he said. Well, Sir, they made such slow progress they kept running out of woodland and the pilot had to keep turning the 'plane round to fly back again. So Ted went aft to supervise and he told the chaps to get a move on.'

I nodded understandingly. I could see them down at the stern, crowded and uncomfortable, listening for the pilot to say when to hand out the ashes and when to stop; and Ted getting more and more fed up as the ashes went on coming out of the box.

'Well,' Gremlin went on, gleefully: 'You see, Sir, they got a bit impatient. So they picked up the open box and just jerked its contents out of the hatch, thinking the ashes would fly out in a big cloud of dust into the slipstream. Only they forgot the air always blows IN, not OUT of an open hatch. So all the remaining ashes – several pounds of them – blew back into the aircraft, all over their faces and down their necks, just everywhere, Sir. That's why Ted's very thirsty, Sir. He says he doesn't much fancy any lunch today.'

At the end of the month, when I came to sign Ted's Pilot Log Book with all the other flying log-books, I saw he had added in the 'Remarks' column, against an A and E test flight, the laconic words: 'Burying a German Count and Two Countesses. Dusty job.' I wrote to the Station Commander that the scattering of ashes had been completed. Rex Waite in turn informed the Executors that the Count's wishes had been observed with all possible decorum, if not with ceremony.

Officially the RAF was being discreet, but it has to be admitted we were also being economical with the dusty truth. Far from posing a grim problem, it had all been quite extraordinary. In return, Rex

Waite received a letter of gratitude from the Executors in St Austell, together with a splendid silver cup which lies with many other trophies in the Squadron's safe-keeping in Ulster to this day. It bears the inscription:

To No 502 Squadron in appreciation of the courteous fulfilment of the last wishes of Eberhard Count von Fabrice, formerly Royal Saxon Chamberlain and Captain in the Royal Saxon Horse Guards, 1942.

Wryly I recalled my rescue of Baron von Stohrer and Herr Klein from the Western Desert, when they were lost in a very dusty *khamsin* in 1936. As Nazi Ambassador to Kings Fouad and Farouk in Egypt, the Baron's rather churlish lack of tangible gratitude to the RAF, and to No 216 Squadron in particular, for saving their lives compared very poorly with this elegant wartime gesture to No 502 Squadron, six years later. *Autres temps; autres moeurs!*

The squadron's saga of engine failures grew by five in April. Two aircraft had failures at night on 24 and 25 and both crews were lost, although they had ditched in the close vicinity of the Scillies. The first crew to go was captained by Flying Officer Lonsdale, flying the unpopular P/502 to which my predecessor had fitted extra fuel tanks to extend its range. The fuel couldn't be jettisoned in emergency. N/502's crew was the second to be lost, captained by Pilot Officer Brown. One of their engines stopped while they were searching at night unsuccessfully for signs of P/502's dinghy, a cruel irony indeed.

In May we had eight more; three more in June; three more in July; and five in August, one of which (Mackay's) became a rescued ditching and another (Hunt's) a forced landing on the beach at St Ives, injuring three crew, after failing to reach Predannack. During ten months in charge of 502 I had altogether 26 cases of Merlin failures, causing three forced landings of which one was in Occupied France, and four ditchings, three of which were fatal to the crews.

Very naturally, we had all become somewhat disconcerted and inclined to spend far too much time on patrol anxiously watching for signs of engine trouble instead of looking for the enemy. It behoved me to try to bolster hope by joining the more timorous crews on their sorties; but as the record shows, the wretched breakdowns continued unabated.

It was on one of these morale-boosting sorties on 19 March at 1500 GMT, in position 51° 25'N 03° 25'W, looking through the astrodome into the clear blue sky at 4,000ft over the Bay, I noticed that I could see not only the declining Sun and the rising Moon, but also, after a careful search between these two, the faintly shining planet Venus. They made an unusual trio for astro. With a Mk VIII bubble sextant, I took two shots of Venus which was too weak to be seen through the bubble of a Mk IX sextant but could be 'juggled' optically with both eyes open using the Mk VIII. Then I shot the Moon three times and the Sun twice. The resulting 'fix' was impressive and the Venus average error was the best of the lot. I still look proudly at that plotted data in my records.

Added to the nagging engine unreliability, the excessive and relentless demand for aircraft by Group slowly and surely overwhelmed our maintenance resources so that we regularly had more crews available than aircraft to fly. Maintenance was badly held up by the faulty Merlins but neither could we obtain other essential spares, including ASV^2 parts. The daily requirement of Group for six aircraft and crews every twenty-four hours, not to mention those needed for essential extension flying training of aircrews, progressively ran our aircraft resources into the ground. As usual, I couldn't get it across to the Air Staff at No 19 Group that they were killing the goose that laid the golden eggs. But help was at hand.

Out of the blue came Dr J. M. Robertson FRS, a Professor of entomology at Aberdeen University whom we immediately and affectionately dubbed 'Professor Joad' after the popular BBC Brains Trust member. The Professor was sent by Command from the recently-formed Operational Research Unit to look into the troubled servicing of No 502 Sqn! This turned out to be one of AOC-in-C Sir Philip Joubert's most incisive contributions to operational efficiency.

I was immediately impressed by the fact that the Professor actually listened as I related all the problems of aircraft maintenance which had only been compounded by the insatiable demands of all three Groups that from time to time had controlled my squadron's flying during the past four months. Little by little the facts spoke for themselves and the Professor's conclusion was that the shortage of spares, delays in the pipeline and limited resources of trained manpower, all meant that the daily output of serviceable aircraft would be far less than previous uninformed expectation.

Never before had I been so pleased to be 'investigated'. Had I been alone in trying to rationalise the use of maritime resources? We had to meet a steady 24-hour all-the-year-round task, without peaks or troughs, except rarely when attacks on blockade runners were needed or when extreme weather dictated events. Unlike the bombing campaign, there were practically no set-piece engagements in our maritime war. Unlike the fighter battles, our adversary was always there. I had the ear of a powerful ally and a highly skilled analyst.

In a very short time, the Professor evolved what became known as Planned Flying and Planned Maintenance, a calculated system of anticipating operational needs matched to the constraints of wartime maintenance resource shortages. Incredibly, the calculated requirement for No 502 Sqn, with its 20 aircraft and 24 crews, given the practical problems of aircraft maintenance, was henceforth halved to only three aircraft operationally available per day, every day! It must have seemed absurdly small to the Air Staff, but now we could plan continuation flying training for the less experienced crews, organise aircrew leave and anticipate tour-expiry in full co-ordination with the output programme from the OTU. On the maintenance side, the whole range of inspections could be programmed on a regular basis without the frustration of waiting for spares and at the same time avoiding gluts and famines of manpower.

We had been very willing guinea pigs and were finally vindicated when, in August 1942, this rational procedure was applied to every squadron, by a Command ukase to the sceptical Air Staff at Groups. Then the Professor went on his way; but he had earned the deep gratitude of the entire squadron.

Long before he had started his enquiry, I had to bid farewell to my trusty No 2, John Russell, whom I had gladly backed for command of No 172 Wellington Sqn, then forming at Chivenor and equipped with Leigh Lights and Mk II ASV, not to mention highly reliable engines. He left on 4 March after a great send-off from the inmates of Watergate Bay. With a new, powerful and accurate radar, for which U-boats had as yet no warning receiver, John Russell's Wellingtons could approach a small target unseen in the dark and illuminate it with a dazzling Leigh Light slung under the wing in a pod, when only 400 metres away, pre-set and focused for that range. The surprise achieved was absolutely deadly and was a brilliant combination of radar and the light with, later on, a radio altimeter enabling safe descent in the dark and under cloud below 200ft and to within 20ft of the sea surface. The Wellington could also fly on one engine, though it still lacked navigation capability, was comparatively short-ranged and carried only a small load of depth charges.

John had been highly supportive and added an air of genial stablility whenever it was most needed. A man of large stature and immense mental capacity not to say of outstanding stamina, I often saw him go through a day as Flight Commander, coping with a thousand and one tasks; then, after a pre-flight meal of bacon and eggs and a briefing, fly off on a ten-hour offensive patrol into the Bay. On his return, after de-briefing and a wash-and-brush-up he polished off another aircrew meal and went back to his Flight to carry on, until finally standing down in the evening at the end of a 30-hour stint. On the other hand, when opportunity presented itself, he could fall asleep at the drop of a hat, a truly 'Churchillian' gift.

His command of No 172 Sqn was predictably, in more ways than one, a brilliant success, his Leigh Lights being the first to surprise and light up many unsuspecting U-boats on their sudden journey to Davy Jones's Locker. His and other squadrons operating in the Bay were credited with ten kills in August, ten in September and 16 in October. Altogether, Admiral Dönitz lost 65 U-boats from July to December 1942, 35 of them being the victims of air attacks. Luckily, I still had Australian Squadron Leader Jimmy Barclay as a seasoned Flight Commander and when a replacement arrived for John on 1 April, also bearing the name Russell, I began to wonder if 'They' were now also running out of surnames.

Ramsay Russell had already flown a maritime operational tour in the Whitleys of No 612 AuxAF (City of Aberdeen) Sqn. Endowed with the attributes of a sturdy Dee-side Scot, he proved to be a fine replacement Flight Commander. Like his namesake predecessor, we became life-long friends.

Our anti U-boat sweeps into and across the Bay by day and night were complicated by a number of somewhat distracting events. We were often flying well within range of various types of enemy aircraft and encounters took place with Ju 88s, He 115s, FW 190s, Arado 196s and other unidentified hostiles, none of which singly were a match for us. If, however, we were outnumbered, we could either take evasive action in cloud or alternatively fly at sea-level. Altogether we were engaged five times in air-to-air attacks.

Sometimes our patrols unexpectedly came across enemy motor vessels which opened fire, usually with rather poor aim. Thus WO/Pilot Vic Pope DFM had had a brush with what appeared in the darkness to be an enemy convoy 12 miles north of Ushant on 7 February. On 1 March Flying Officer Cave DFC attacked two motor vessels with depth charges and sank one of them. On 25 March Sergeant Pilot Coates in F/502 was attacked by an M-class minesweeper of unidentified nationality. Coates and another crew member were wounded but he was able to crash-land back at St Eval. On 3 May, the redoubtable Flying Officer Cave used depth charges to sink a ship and damage two others in a group he had unexpectedly run across at night.

In the course of combing the Bay up to the end of August, no fewer than 24 U-boats were sighted by No 502 Sqn but most were ASV contacts which 'disappeared', probably because the U-boats, unknown to us, had Metox radar receivers and dived before being seen. Thus only 13 attacks developed and only three of these were kills.

One of the most disturbing factors frustrating our patrols was the presence of fleets of Spanish and French fishing boats and tunny-men. They provided a useful screen for the U-boats and were a constant source of irritation to us in our searching, especially as they carried mast-head lights at night. It was impossible to differentiate between the fishing boats and U-boats by ASV and they became such a frustrating nuisance that we began dropping leaflets warning them to keep within strictly-defined areas of the Bay. When they were found outside these limits, we shot up their sails and rigging as a warning to keep out of the way.

It would be tedious to catalogue all the squadron's maritime activities, but what has already been described may give a fair idea of how we were engaging the enemy. Not a week passed but we encountered maritime activity of one sort or another though it must be emphasised that much of the time we were condemned to fight with our hands tied behind our backs, thanks to our treacherous engines.

Part of the squadron was always absent, being on short leave, resting after sorties or detached for special training. Sometimes compassionate leave was essential when family war casualties occurred. New crews arrived, to be welcomed and detailed to their Flights. Tour-expired crews departed after due celebrations. There was a constant bustle between the squadron Adjutant and his orderly room, but he had practically no Service crime to handle. The war made models of us all. But life was far from all doom and gloom, albeit at times a trifle macabre. Its worst feature was the monotony of our operational task, relieved only exceptionally by U-boat sightings leading even more rarely to an encounter. Occasionally, we found some shipping to attack and we had a few encounters with hostile aircraft.

The one luxury we dared not indulge was to become bored. My one-time Manston air navigation mentor, Wilf Oulton,[3] himself a former flying-boat captain, in 1943 became CO of No 58 Sqn with four-engined Halifaxes operating from St Eval. He notched up the highest personal record of success in the Bay offensive – two U-boats killed and one 'shared' with another squadron's aircraft. He describes Coastal Command operations as typically very demanding but essentially unglamorous, without the satisfaction of the prospect of an encounter with the enemy. 'For most people', he has said, 'it meant getting up at an ungodly hour, going out in the pouring rain, waiting for your aircraft to be made serviceable, flying out into the Atlantic in foul weather, not seeing anything at all, and coming back . . . to somewhere like Ballykelly, with your heart in your mouth, missing 'Ben Twitch' by inches. This happened not once but a thousand times for many people; for three years they would see nothing. Then, for one fleeting moment if they were lucky, they might actually see something. For many people, one sighting in the whole war was better than average.' That is an excellent summary of what had to be endured.

The major challenge to anti-U-boat operational efficiency was the monotony of continuously repeated and basically similar offensive sweeps of the Bay of Biscay that very seldom resulted in action. Although in 1942 we had ASV Mk I which we hoped would give us a slight edge on the U-boats, it was far too liable to fail and at best gave only very brief glimpses of our targets. As a result, taking Coastal Command's total experience at that time, ASV accounted for only one so-called 'sighting' as against every nine by 'Eyeball Mk I'. It wasn't until February 1943 that anti-U-boat aircraft were fitted with the greatly-improved centimetric ASV Mk II.

But in early 1942 our lack of sightings was also due to the U-boats being ordered by Dönitz to submerge when crossing the Bay in daylight. This precaution necessitated their recharging their batteries at night, running on the surface on diesel engines with their hatches open for four out of every 24 hours. We sometimes caught them at it and the attacks in 1942 by No 19 Group's day patrols had a cumulative effect on the U-boat crews' morale. Our daylight patrols were therefore kept going at full tilt.

The U-boat commanders thought they were safe at night and began running the gauntlet in the dark at speed on the surface. Without any means of illuminating them before they dived and because we could not rely on aneroid altimeters to descend safely close to the sea surface in cloud or darkness, night attacks were very rarely successful. But sometimes there was enough moonlight for a low-level attack.

Operating over the Bay with the minimum of navigation aids had untold repercussions. The attempt in August to pin-point the position of 'Baldy' Mackay's dinghy, which is described later, was a good example of defective maritime air navigation and of its consequences. When No 19 Group sent out aircraft on interlocking patrols, hundreds of miles away, there was no way of ensuring that gaps or overlaps didn't develop. Apart from astro, which needed reasonably clear skies, the main aid for our air navigators was UK-based M/F D/F[4] which, because of geography, could not give much more than general indications of direction – useful for homing but not for fixing positions remote from the UK. Likewise, the aircraft's loop aerial gave D/F bearings on radio transmitters but in practice readings were susceptible to even more numerous errors and were often impossible to plot accurately. But the air navigator still frequently needed to know exactly where he was and he was left guessing.

He was, therefore, forced to rely on his own fallible deductions drawn from imperfect observations of the angle of drift which he applied to calculate the wind velocity and the courses to be steered by reference to far from perfect magnetic compasses and to measurements of distance flown obtained from inaccurate airspeed readings. This deductive process, known as Dead Reckoning, is inherently unreliable because all the observations required to provide the basic data are subject to error. In addition, the air navigator's own calculations suffer from the effects of noise, discomfort, lack of space and fatigue. He is only human! At best, 'DR' provided only a rational guess of where the aircraft was at any one time and hence which way it should proceed and for how long. DR in practice was subject to a cumulative error of 10% of the distance flown from the air navigator's last fix of position.

An anti-U-boat patrol, starting from a DR position, perhaps 200 miles from the last fix, and aiming at a DR-based turning point, say another 300 miles further on, would certainly be many miles adrift at each end. Two vital actions flowed from this harsh fact: first, a correcting fix had to be obtained whenever possible – such as when a chink in the clouds gave a chance for astro; second, the numerous aircraft navigation instruments, and other related equipment which provided the basic DR data, needed repeated calibration, often with the aircraft on the ground.

The navigators could be encouraged to undertake these bread-and-butter precautions and Flying Officer J. M. Wheeler, our Navigation Officer, had a powerful reason for inspiring their enthusiasm. His efforts never failed to meet a fulsome response. Our air gunners also became keenly interested in calibrating their rear turrets to measure the drift, an all-important vector used in DR, by sighting smoke floats by day or flame floats by night, dropped into the sea as required by the navigator. Success or failure depended on crew co-operation and it helped to foster a team spirit.

We started up a competition among my navigators to see who could produce the best-kept navigation log and plot every month. This proved to be so stimulating that I sent Flying Officer James Perry over to Mount Batten to challenge No 10 RAAF Sqn to join in, the winner being judged monthly by No 19 Group's staff navigator who had the rather painful job of analysing the data and adjudicating. With Group's help, I also arranged for my pilots to visit Royal Navy submariners whenever they were in port in Plymouth. It was extremely valuable to get to know the submariners' point of view and to have some idea of their unenviable environment.

Life for the squadron aircrew was a succession of advanced training, recurrent sessions of standing-by in suspense for operations, briefings and flight planning, ten-hour sorties, de-briefings and of accumulating fatigue relieved by periods of leave. The daily round was enlivened by engine failures, ditchings, encounters with hostile aircraft, rare U-boat sightings and sometimes an attack, which could be lethal only if one of the stick of six depth charges exploded very close to the U-boat's pressure hull.

Unlike the traumas of our bomber colleagues, our lives were comparatively humdrum. Unlike typical young bachelor fighter pilots who could relax at night from the strain of combat by mixing briefly with civilians at their 'local' but for whom survival was fairly uncertain, anti-U-boat aircrew were not subject to such intensive attrition, could take a more moderate view of the immediate future and were able to accumulate a lot of general flying experience. About a quarter were married and some lived off the station in hirings that were easy to find in semi-deserted neighbouring seaside holiday resorts.

Except for *Kamikaze* shipping strike squadrons with the heaviest RAF losses and correspondingly very short ops, maritime operational tours were long enough to encourage aircrew to live as normally as possible. Indeed, the Command's policies, unlike those in many other Commands, did nothing to discourage camp followers. However, apart from providing family medical services, official back-up systems like wives' clubs wilted for lack of transport but efforts were made to support the wives, whose role in maintaining *esprit de corps* and morale proved invaluable.

502 Sqn had developed a strong family feeling and misfortunes as well as successes were there to be shared by all. Outside St Eval lay a coastal paradise of quiet secluded coves, romantic windswept headlands, huge rollers from the Atlantic tumbling into roaring surf, swirling past strange twisted pillars of rock that rose here and there out of empty beaches of golden sand where the undulating hills of North Cornwall ended abruptly in cliffs of granite and shale. The seascapes were enthralling and, thanks to wartime travel difficulties, few summer visitors invaded our Cornish Garden of Eden: we had its wild beauty all to ourselves. With so many resources of Nature on our doorstep, it was easy to pretend nothing untoward was hap-

pening! But harsh reality permeated the bracing sea air and threatened us every hour of the day and night. Such a contrast defies description to those who have not experienced it. There was no escape: war presided at the top of the hill.

Notes to Chapter XIV

1 A powerful illuminating beam named after its innovator, Squadron Leader H. Leigh.
2 Air-to-Surface vessel.
3 Subsequently Air Vice-Marshal W. E. Oulton CB CBE DSO DFC. In 1957 he commanded the Operation Grapple thermonuclear weapon trials based on Christmas island in the Pacific Ocean.
4 Medium Frequency Direction Finding.

XV

Maritime Men

I FIRST met Gunnery Leader Flight Lieutenant William O'Malley Brayton RAFVR at Limavady in November 1941, by which time he had been flying in 502 Sqn for two months. He had an imposing, saturnine face with bright penetrating brown eyes that exuded quiet confidence. A citizen of Eire, he had joined the RAFVR in 1939 because he hated the Nazis.

Actually, Bill Brayton was a German linguist and had been drafted, against his wishes, into the Administrative and Special Duties branch to serve in Intelligence. His skill and natural inclinations made him a very effective interrogator of German PoWs whom he used to entertain, dressed in mufti, as part of a softening-up process. This frequently took the form of lavish *tête-à-tête* dinners in the West End during the London *blitz*.

Bill had other ideas and escaped from Intelligence and from a boss who he always contemptuously insisted had manufactured condoms in peacetime! Having now trained as an air gunner, though still an A&SD officer without flying pay, he wangled a posting to operational flying with No 502 Sqn where he quickly showed outstanding zeal. By November 1941 he was greatly respected by our 70 WOp/AGs and frequently joined a crew on the spur of the moment to take his turn in the rear turret.

On the night of 1 April 1942 he was crewed up with Warrant Officer/Pilot 'Vic' Pope with whom he had already previously been attacked by enemy shipping 12 miles north of Ushant in the very dark night of 4 February. This time there was a half moon, the sea was slight and they were dodging in and out of light cloud at 2,000ft as they swept along on patrol, all eyes either on the ASV screen or scanning the sea surface.

Bill was busy keeping himself alert in the rear turret, swinging his guns to and fro and generally peering down at the dark, receding sea below him. Suddenly, he spotted the wake of a submarine ploughing at speed, fully surfaced, across the Bay. It had been unseen from the flight deck, the Whitley having flown directly over the top of it. By skilfully conning the pilot from the rear turret, Bill managed to put Vic Pope into visual contact, without alerting the U-boat. A copybook attack ensued, with six depth-charges straddling the still-surfaced target. The U-boat completely disappeared, much to the delight of the crew who returned to St Eval in high spirits.

I was always looking for a chance to obtain battle honours for my crews and sent off for immediate awards of a DFM for Vic Pope and a DFC for Bill. Ten days later the Admiralty Submarine Plotting Room confirmed that the U-boat had been seriously damaged and had returned to port for repairs. In recognition, on 14 April Vic Pope received a DFM as captain of the crew, the first DFM to be awarded to the squadron in the war. But for Bill, a pillar of strength in the squadron for eight months and whose zeal was directly responsible for the attack, there was nothing. I felt furious at such myopic injustice.

Shortly afterwards, he fell ill and was admitted to Newquay Hospital with double pneumonia, probably brought on by sheer exhaustion. Fortunately, he pulled through, but his operational days were over and he was posted back to his old Intelligence job in the 'Air Box' for a rest. I rang up his new Air Commodore boss in the 'Air Box' to say how much we were going to miss Bill and what a fine job he had done, all without any flying pay. I went on to mention my failed recommendation on his behalf for a DFC which he had so richly deserved. The Air Commodore asked for a copy of my citation and I was gratified when, three weeks later, a DFC was Gazetted for Bill. In those days of severe rationing, which even extended to military decorations, it was clearly important who you knew.

After the War, Bill set up a thriving business in Occupied Berlin, of all places! He married Daisy, an attractive German *fräulein* and lived to anticipate, much more accurately than Prime Minister Margaret Thatcher, the early unification of that divided city. Very sadly, my annual exchange of Christmas Cards with Bill and with his erstwhile captain, Squadron Leader Vic Pope DFM, ended ominously and abruptly in 1992.

We carried on as usual through the month and on 14 April Flying Officer Ted Cotton and Sergeant Pilot Ellis both had good attacks, followed by similarly promising ones by Flying Officer Pettit and Squadron Leader Ramsay Russell on 21 and 22 April. Then came the losses of Flying Officer Lonsdale and Pilot Officer Brown and their crews in the ditchings of Whitleys P and N.

At the end of April, Flight Lieutenant Wheeler went on his way to a specialist course at the advanced school of navigation, now at Port Albert in Canada. James Perry took over from him and was promoted to Flight Lieutenant on 1 May, together with 'Baldy' Mackay and bright little South African Dan Osborn.

The next month started well with Flying Officer Cave's successful attack on shipping on 3 May, but three other 'sightings' were abortive and six more engine failures brought May to an unedifying close. There were some indications of possible enemy jamming of our ASVs, possibly a resonance from Metox, which was a counter-device as yet unknown to us.

June was even less remarkable. The squadron suffered three more cases of engine trouble though we enjoyed some vicarious pleasure when, on 3 June, our own J/502 was able to escort Whitley B of No 77 Sqn which was making for Predannack on one engine.

July was much more profitable. It started well with the popular, if tardy, award of a DFC to Ted Cotton for his attack on a U-boat on 14 April and for his efforts in February from Docking when he was shadowing the *Scharnhorst*. Better late than never! On 6 July, recently commissioned Pilot Officer Hunt engaged and drove off an Arado 196. Pilot Officer Brook had a good go at a U-boat on 15 July and on the 17th Pilot Officer Hunt attacked and sank a U-boat, for which he received a DFC in August.

These normally very happy events were overshadowed by the loss of a newly-arrived crew, manned by a keen young Canadian, Pilot Officer John Arbuckle. Returning at night above continuous cloud, after reaching the Scillies his progress was being scrutinised because St Eval was under threat of 'clampers' and there was a strong chance of a last-minute diversion being required. Arbuckle had remembered to activate his IFF and the UK defence radar was, as usual, keeping a useful eye on progress which was being reported to me in the Ops Room. When the aircraft was only twenty minutes flying from St Eval, the radar plot suddenly faded. Shortly afterwards the St Just Coast Guards reported seeing a bright glow in the sky. The coincidence was most unpleasantly significant.

A Royal Naval light cruiser, returning from operational duties in the Med, was sailing up the Bristol Channel. They picked up Arbuckle's Whitley on their radar, flying towards them unseen above cloud, but they utterly failed to notice it was displaying IFF. Taking no chances, they let off some AA rounds at the invisible target on which, with very bad luck, they scored direct hits. Flying on a steady course at 2,000ft, it was a sitting duck. 'Shoot first and answer questions afterwards' had by then become an acceptable AA gunner's trigger-happy reaction in the Navy.

Pilot Officer Penny was washed up between Bude and Barnstable and interred in Chivenor churchyard in the presence of several of his comrades.[1] New Zealander WOp/AG Flight Sergeant Bush was found off the Scillies and buried at St Mary's. It was bitter to recall the Court of Enquiry at Dreenagh in November 1941: was this not exactly where I had first come in? 'Friendly fire' is a hard pill to swallow. The fault was all too obvious but the Forces were now far too busy to set up elaborate enquiries. This time there would be no official conference and no red-faced Naval officers to mutter 'Sorry' – only six more letters of condolence for me to compose.

It must not be thought that life was all work and no play. The Watergate Bay Hotel offered plenty of relaxation after dark if we could let our hair down over a few pints. Someone had unearthed a cache of surf boards in one of the hotel stores and two or three of these had been split lengthways into two. The foyer of the hotel had a flight of marble steps running down from a mezzanine landing which provided a very hard, simulated ski-slope. Standing in socks with each foot on half a surf board, we shuffled towards the crest of the top step and then carefully toppled the 'skis' over the slope. Few skiers ever reached the vestibule floor without a spectacular prang.

When we had sung our songs and played our boisterous games, it being an entirely male affair with not a female in sight, there would be a general shedding of uniforms and a rushing out in pitch darkness to the deserted beach absolutely 'starko', down into the breakers which at low tide were a good 400 yards away. The foaming sea didn't feel cold and we were mostly strong swimmers, but not far offshore the tidal current ran past at a good eight knots and was extremely dangerous. I used to wonder, as I waded ashore, if they would all turn up again. What on earth would I say to the Board of Enquiry if I ever lost my aircrew officers having high jinks in the roaring surf at the dead of night?

Parties sprang up spontaneously whenever night operations permitted, especially when there were promotions or gallantry awards to celebrate. There were several special occasions such as the monumental 'do' at Watergate and at Bedruthan Steps when Baldy Mackay and his crew were rescued from their ditching off Brest. They had been *en route* for the Bay on the summer evening of 5 August in S/502 when they lost an engine. Baldy was one of the few, if not the only, squadron aircrew who couldn't swim.

The ditching procedure required the second pilot and air navigator to leave the flight deck and crawl through the wing tunnel to the after-section, where they would join the three WOp/AGs and brace themselves against bulkheads for the moment of impact, an SOS having been sent giving their position and the Morse key then clamped down for last D/F bearings to be taken by the D/F stations back in the UK. The crew would then release the door hinges, throw out the spare dinghy secured by its painter (lest the dinghy in the port wing failed to inflate) and step into one or the other, carrying the caged homing pigeons for release with their ringed scribbled messages reporting the crew's predicament. Meanwhile, the Captain had to put down the aircraft as smoothly as possible on the sea which would immediately rush up through the bomb-aimer's cockpit. He would escape through a hatch over his head, clamber along the roof, jump down to the port wing and step into the dinghy where his crew would be waiting for him.

So much for theory. In practice on 5 August the sea was calm and there was enough twilight and sufficient ripples for the sea surface to be visible for a smooth touchdown. As the sea rushed in, Baldy was out on the roof without even getting his flying boots wet. He reached the port wing after a few uncertain steps when he nearly tumbled off into the sea out of sight on the starboard side. But, as he stood balancing against the swell, to his dismay there was no sign of the port door falling off, let alone any sounds from within the fuselage. Nor had the dinghy come out of the port wing and inflated according to plan. He began to wonder if he'd knocked out all his crew, leaving himself stranded on the wing, a nasty prospect for anyone, let alone a non-swimmer.

After what seemed an age, the door did fly open and the crew emerged unscathed. Baldy was then able to step into the tethered dinghy, still without wetting his boots. When the pigeons were released from their cage they made a few circuits of the sinking Whitley and then perched back on top of the fuselage where they fluttered about until it quietly went under. Then they flew off roughly in the right direction for home but were never seen again in their loft at St Eval: there were plenty of pigeon predators flying around Cornwall.

Baldy and his crew enviously watched them disappear as they and the sinking aircraft had provided a little distraction from their close view of the heaving ocean; but attention was soon riveted on a large codfish which began formating on the dinghy and tenaciously stayed with them. More importantly, while they drifted for the next six hours, they watched a Wellington of 311 Czech Sqn pass overhead, followed at intervals by two Whitleys N/502 and A/502. Then they saw a Beaufighter chase off three enemy aircraft. At last a No 461 RAAF Sqn Sunderland arrived *en route* for Mount Batten. It had beaten off a *Luftwaffe* FW 200 and an Arado 196 before finally picking them up.

Back at St Eval, I had been alerted to Baldy's predicament and had received two possible positions – one in his SOS and the other a D/F fix taken from his ditching signal. Not surprisingly, the D/F fix was 50 miles distant from the SOS position, due to the unavoidably acute angular intersections of the D/F bearings. The Controller at No 19 Group agreed to ensure that all sorties going out or coming back that way were ordered to look for a possible dinghy. After about an hour of anxious waiting a sighting report came from M/311, a Czech Wellington, but it gave no position. Asked to say exactly where the dinghy was, they replied that it had been seen 'under a large cumulus cloud'! A second sighting report at 2153hr came from my N/502 homeward bound but gave another and even more remote position than the two previous ones. Back to the drawing board! Then a third sighting, this time by A/502, also bound for St Eval, reported yet another position to play with! The night was wearing on and I began to lose heart.

Dawn has never been attractive to me. Though an agnostic, I nevertheless felt the need for quiet contemplation. So I left the drama of the Ops Room and drove round the airfield to the far side where the little square-towered church of St Eval stands on the cliffs among the then fresh graves of some of our colleagues from other squadrons. I believe St Eval church tower had been built there by the Merchant Adventurers of Bristol as a prominent landmark to guide their ships past the dangers of the local wreckers. The door was unlocked and I went in and sat in a pew, pensively wondering what else to do. After half an hour or so I returned to the Ops Room, still feeling subdued; but as I entered, the Duty Controller greeted me by waving a signal he had just received from the Sunderland of No 461 RAAF Sqn. They had found the crew and were heading back to Mount Batten with all onboard! Let joy be unconfined!

As I have already said, there were quite some parties at the Watergate Bay and Bedruthan Steps Hotels, but when our truck returned from Plymouth with Baldy and his crew there were none to compare with those that started on 6 August and finished sometime on the 7th. (When last seen in 1958, Baldy Mackay was running a very nice pub on Deeside and we shared a good laugh over yet another 'jar'.)

Not all events had such happy endings, as we had already discovered in February. Indeed, only a week before Baldy's rescue, just after lunch on 30 July, I was clearing the desk in my office, the main bedroom of an officer's married quarter overlooking the station, when there was an almighty bang, followed by an even louder crump.

Across the airfield I saw a large black cloud rising above something that had evidently blown up in the distance, beyond the runway in use.

I rang the Control Tower and was told it was a Whitley of 502 Sqn which had just arrived from Predannack where, having been diverted owing to low cloud at St Eval earlier that morning, its tailwheel had been damaged and three of my erks had been sent over by road with spares to carry out emergency repairs. The low cloud lifted during the morning and flying at St Eval had been resumed; so the captain had asked for permission to return to Base.

I rushed to the scene of smouldering tangled wreckage, all that was left after six depth charges and the fuel tanks had exploded. The unrecognisable members of the crew were still in their normal work stations. Saturated with fuel, some disconcertingly burst into flames as we gently lifted them out of the fire-smothering foam and carried them to the 'blood-wagons' waiting to take them to the mortuary. A brief inquest was held on the spot with the Flying Controller and Ramsay Russell, the Flight Commander concerned, and it became clear that the immediate cause of the prang had been a stall leading to a spin into the deck about 200 yards short of the runway. The weather was as clear as a bell and the probable reason for the pilot error was fatigue. Recently-commissioned Pilot Officer Leonard Endicott, who had joined the squadron on 24 March 1941, had been upset by breaking his tailwheel and unable to relax properly at Predannack. He was also keen to get his crew back to the home comforts of St Eval.

My next task was to find some of the crew's wives who were living at nearby Trenance and to break the news that they were now widows. The three young women concerned had all heard the prang. Two days later, we laid Pilot Officer Endicott, our zealous captain, to rest in the Roman Catholic cemetery at St Mawgan and paid our last tribute to this fine young man with full military honours, the dour solemnity of an Irish piper's lament and a firing party from his own squadron. The five other casualties had to be sent elsewhere at the request of their next of kin. Squadron life during the war was not a bed of roses.

My own command was drawing to a close and I hadn't yet smelt a single U-boat! The squadron had been slowly rescued from the shambles left by Uncle Tom Cooper DFC, whose flying as regular Second Pilot in one of the crews had undoubtedly been at some cost to squadron organisation during a time of considerable upheaval. Disorder was anathema to me and, rather than risk creating a vestige of chaos, I insisted on flying as a supernumary pilot/navigator and my name had deliberately never been listed as First or Second pilot nor as Air Navigator.

I was still smarting from the senseless trauma of the triple sub-division of the squadron from December to March. On the other hand, I was glad to have helped, in a small way, to introduce Planned Flying and Planned Maintenance, from which the entire Command was now benefitting. I had also managed to nurse the squadron through the months of lost confidence and lowering morale which flowed from grievous crew losses caused by the treachery of our engines.

During the past ten months I had served in three Groups and under no fewer than six different Station Commanders, whose six-weekly turn-over at St Eval had been hastened by the approaching North African invasion, 'Operation Torch' for which one of its planners, Group Captain 'Tubby' (later Air Marshal Sir Walter) Dawson, was installed to ensure the smooth despatch of part of the air armada mounted from St Eval in November. He was the fourth and last Commanding Officer I had served under there in six months. How could any of them have noticed during their short tenures of office that No 502 Sqn under my command had been performing successfully against heavy odds and had been credited with two U-boat kills, one seriously damaged and two 'possibles'?

I have to admit I had been argumentative with the Top Brass at Group from time to time and my absence from crew lists may perhaps have suggested I'd been leading my squadron from behind. So, when some unknown, distant 'Friend at Court' arranged for me to be Mentioned in Dispatches as the retiring CO, I felt I had to be thankful for small mercies. In sober light, however, it might have been construed as a disparagement of the squadron's operational performance which had somehow managed to prosper gallantly through ten difficult months. From a purely personal perspective I knew only too well that careers can be damned by faint praise.

The squadron was soon to be re-equipped with reliable four-engined Handley Page Halifaxes and eventually fitted with micro-wave ASV Mk III. They were able to carry a useful load of depth charges and 600-lb bombs for long distances. Thus, most importantly, they could reach out to where the U-boats were running confidently on the surface, well beyond the range of Whitleys. Frankly, I envied my friend and successor, Wing Commander Jock Halley, a fair-haired, blue-eyed Scot, himself a Spec N. He was in luck with the impending re-equipment and was riding high, in due course, for a well-deserved DSO. A gallant officer, he could be relied upon to lead the squadron on to further glory.

Having learnt a little at the sharp end of the Battle of the Atlantic, I was now destined for a potentially influential post as Chief Navigation Officer at HQ Coastal Command, perhaps thanks to a reputation as the author of AP1234 which was being widely acclaimed. There was much to put right in the Command if we weren't to lose our vital part in the war for lack of adequate foresight, equipment, training and planning and by September 1942 the UK was in very grave maritime danger.

Unfortunately, the U-boat fleet was still growing fast. Having started the year with 100, Admiral Dönitz ended 1942 with 200, at first many of them sitting pretty off the East Coast of America, picking off ships at night as they sailed in silhouette across the brightly glowing background of blazing lights ashore. When the Americans reluctantly adopted the despised British convoy system and also imposed a blackout along their East Coast, the U-boats withdrew, to hunt in 'wolf packs' strung across the convoy routes in mid-Atlantic, beyond the range of shore-based bombers.

Thus, in the one month of November 1942 we lost a colossal 700,000 tons of ships and their gallant seamen and by the year's end a total of seven million tons of shipping had been sunk. On the other hand, the landing of Allied troops on the Mediterranean coast of North Africa, Operation Torch, was accomplished without any effective U-boat interference, largely thanks to the aircraft which were able to find, and attack those that tried to enter the Med past Gibraltar.

I left St Eval with the squadron's good wishes ringing in my ears and with some much-prized mementos, including one I used every day: a napkin ring, fashioned very appropriately from the white metal bearing of a con-rod out of a seized-up Merlin X from Gremlin Hill's forced landing at Portreath on 19 January 1942 and inscribed:

W/COM. RICHARDSON
502 SQDN
1941–1942

My recollection of No 502 Sqn is one of eager thrusting youth, of selfless dedication that still shines brightly across the years, of bravery worn so lightly on the brow, of laughter from the heart, of endless patient endeavour to save this country from a relentless, deadly and pitiless blockade. It was exciting and demanding to live among such determined young men through thick and thin for ten months, a period that, alas for many, was their whole life-span. Yet it was so often enormous fun which was always of their own making and whereby they kept their sanity and compassion. They were truly a great band of brothers and fifty years on I salute the memory of their integrity with gratitude.

Note to Chapter XV

1 Plt Off T. J. Penny was the second pilot of Whitley Mk VII E/502, captained by Plt Off J. A. Arbuckle, which had taken off from St Eval at 1255 GMT on 12 September 1942 on an anti-submarine patrol. At 1950 GMT a message – 'am being attacked' – was received from the aircraft, and at 1953hr a further message. The aircraft failed to return to base and at 2110 GMT the Group Controller informed St Eval Control that a Whitley had been shot down over a convoy. The four other crew members were Sgt Bush, W. O. Barnhill, Sgt Wells and Sgt L. J. P. Lafleur.

XVI
Maritime Headquarters

WHAT an anti-climax it was to exchange St Eval for the bland environs of a north London suburb! But before the ramshackle cluster of buildings had been taken over by the Air Ministry for Headquarters Coastal Command, on the Northwood hilltop in Middlesex, they had acquired something of a shady history. The Château de Madrid, a country club with a nine-hole golf course, was a discreet hideaway for anyone looking for a dirty weekend, run by a lady called Kate, a notable West End night club queen, who was said to have nursed grand pretensions for her daughters, both of whom were rumoured eventually to have married well, if not actually into the aristocracy.

Be that as it may, the Air Ministry had decided, just before the war, to set up three new operational command posts, all within easy reach of London but securely hidden among trees. Bentley Priory at Stanmore, Middlesex, was bought for Fighter Command, to replace the ramshackle set-up at Uxbridge called the Air Defence of Great Britain (ADGB). Fifteen miles to the west, beneath beech trees, on a hill high above High Wycombe, a completely new base was built for Bomber Command. Between these two headquarters and con-cealed under the Oxhey trees on the hilltop at Northwood, the Chateau was converted into offices and an Officers' Mess for Coastal Command, a large pseudo-thatched barn being added on one side of the main building for the camouflaged Operations Room. The AOC-in-C had a hired house on a nearby private estate; the WAAF occu-pied Pinner Hill Golf Club house, half a mile away, while the male Other Ranks lived in the camp in wooden huts under the trees.

In 1939 at Christmas, the Camp Commandant, Squadron Leader Ken Harboard, received a request to reserve the two main bedrooms with an inter-communicating door. He replied that the hotel now belonged to the Air Ministry and the two bedrooms concerned were occupied by the AOC-in-C of Coastal Command and his Senior Air Staff Officer (the Chief of Staff). Moreover, the red light that for-merly hung over the front door had now been moved to the top of the drive.

This was the unlikely setting for the management of a vital struggle for national survival which began with the sinking of the liner SS *Athenia* on 3 September 1939 and continued unabated till 1945, long after the U-boat menace had been temporarily suspended in mid-1943 during a period of re-equipment and re-training. Here at HQCC a combined team of highly skilled Naval and Air Force officers, headed by a tireless submariner, Captain D. V. Peyton-Ward RN, successfully held the fort for six long years. From those two bedrooms and their nearby Ops Room was controlled the see-saw Battle of the Atlantic, in close and harmonious conjunction with the Admiralty Submarine Tracking Room. This most dangerous conflict of WW2 is described in the Official History as 'the most prolonged and complex battle in the history of naval warfare'.

Churchill went further and rather grudgingly declared afterwards (despite the priority he had always given to the use of Bomber Command against targets in mainland Germany at the expense of much less glamorous but more vital attacks on the potentially deadly U-boats) that the Battle of the Atlantic was 'the dominating factor all through the war'.

The first AOC-in-C to occupy that 'best' bedroom in the former shady hotel was red-headed Air Chief Marshal Sir Frederick W. 'Ginger' Bowhill KCB CMG DSO. An illuminating story of his good humour was told of how his name had sometimes been taken in vain by junior staff officers who would ring up each other and pretend to be the AOC-in-C. It was a joke they played once too often. One day the AOC-in-C rang for a junior officer to attend at his office and the staff officer, expecting a leg-pull, replied 'Oh! balls!' and rang off. Whereupon 'Ginger' rang again and furiously demanded his presence.

The officer went in fear and trembling, knocked on the door and entered. Red in the face and red of hair, the Air Chief Marshal presented a terrifying prospect.

'Did you say balls to me?' he angrily demanded.

No reply.

'Did you say balls to me?' he repeated, with rising voice.

'Well, Sir . . .' came a stuttering, shamefaced response.

'Well: balls to you!' replied 'Ginger', with a twinkle. End of story.

No wonder Ginger Bowhill was so popular in the Command, and it prospered under his vigorous leadership. He had become something of a legend by the time he handed over in June 1941 to Air Chief Marshal Sir Philip B. Joubert de la Ferté KCB CMG DSO.

Hitler's strategy to prevent us from attacking Germany by cutting off our supplies very nearly paid off in 1942, when eight million tons

217

of ships were sunk, mostly by U-boats. Without food, industrial and oil supplies, we and our Allies would have been impotent, our ships, aircraft and tanks immobilised. We faced actual starvation and it seemed that any re-occupation of Europe was a mere figment of our imagination.

The epic Battle of the Atlantic formed a dramatic background to my every day at HQCC for the next two years. It involved escorting convoys across the North Atlantic and into the Arctic on the supply route to Murmansk in Russia as well as harrying the U-boat fleet on passage to their hunting grounds. These events are already well documented and I will refrain from reiterating their sequence, blow by blow. It was a see-saw contest between the scientists and the planning staffs on both sides, as well as between the fighting men and their continuously improving weapons. The short-lived euphoria of a concession of temporary defeat by Dönitz in May 1943 was still a long way off in September 1942 when I made my number with the SASO, A V-M G. B. A. Baker CB CBE DFC and took my place as the Command Navigation Officer on his staff.

After a brief welcome I was asked to look urgently into the difficulties bugging No 489 RNZAF Hampden torpedo squadron operating from RAF Wick in Caithness. So, after finding my office in its wooden hut and meeting my deputy, Squadron Leader N. A. Edwards DFC, a Sunderland captain and a pilot Spec N, I asked my new secretary, WAAF Sergeant Savage, to book a DH Dominie for me to fly to Scotland from RAF Northolt the next morning.

I flew up to the windswept north, stopping for lunch and fuel at Dyce on Deeside. At Wick I found the Hampdens had not been equipped for navigation in very low-level formations, a necessary tactic in order to approach Norway below enemy radar to avoid alerting the locally-based Me 109s and to surprise the convoys of ships carrying Swedish iron ore from occupied Narvik to the German Baltic ports as they sailed down the safety of the 'leads' between the Norwegian coast and the protecting offshore islands.

Hampdens were narrow-bodied and hideously uncomfortable; worst of all, I was shocked to find the air navigator had no effective means of measuring drift, a vital necessity for making even the crudest of progress. He could only guess the wind direction by looking at the 'sea lanes' or streaks made by the wind on the surface and judging its speed from the general state of the sea. Not surprisingly, formations were very often miles adrift by the time they had crossed the North Sea and reached their Norwegian target areas.

I reminded the squadron commander of the notable navigation boob that had occurred in the earlier days of the war when a formation of Blenheims had set off from their East Coast base to bomb the naval yards at Bremerhaven. On that occasion they had not surprisingly finished up at Esbjerg in neutral Denmark because the leading pilot had stowed his personal pistol in the shin pocket of his flying overalls where it was only a few inches from the cockpit P4 magnetic compass. The compass needle had consequently deviated by 30°!

Hopefully, that homily would be passed around to all his own pilots. To rectify the lack of drift sights, I explained that his rear gunners could help their navigators by frequently taking calibrated bearings on smoke floats which would have to be dropped overboard regularly, and I promised to ensure plentiful supplies of smoke floats and flame floats (for night use). I also said I would try to organise a proper instrument for measuring the drift when I got back to HQ; though I frankly admitted this latter might take a very long time to achieve.

It was presumptuous on my part to lecture these aircrew who were engaged in this most deadly of all the RAF flying roles. Anti-shipping strikes with torpedoes required the pilot to fly directly at the target which had to be broadside on. He had to approach it flying straight and level, just above the waves, before releasing his 'tin fish'. The pilot was quite unable to turn away from the flak and was committed to flying right over the ship; in fact during this whole manoeuvre, the Hampden presented a no-deflection target to the cannons being fired from the target ship and from all its escorts. It was the most notorious operational task in the RAF and carried an unenviable four-month life expectancy.

In 1941, 46 Hampdens had been lost sinking 15 ships; and in the first four months of 1942, 55 aircraft were lost for only six ships sunk. Like the Charge of the Light Brigade, it was *magnifique mais non pas la guerre*! When, later on, better aircraft and weapons became available, including rocket projectiles and long-distance fighter protection, new tactics reduced these terrible odds; but even by May 1943, only 107 ships had been sunk at the cost of 648 aircraft. Mining from the air during the entire war had a much better 'rate of exchange' – though still pretty bad: 329 aircraft were lost for 369 ships sunk.

I flew back to Northolt in a very sombre mood. There was going to be much more to do than I could manage single-handed. To start with, my staff was too small to be effective and I personally was outgunned in the Air Staff pecking order. There seemed to be no cut-and-dried organisation for bringing the various related functional departments together to ensure we were all working harmoniously in the same direction. I had expected to team-up closely with

Operations, Signals, Armament and Training staffs but I was left to my own devices to find out what was cooking and to co-ordinate policies with my colleagues.

I foresaw fighting from my corner against some who might 'pull rank' if I spoke up strongly on behalf of the users. In my book, the consumer should always have the last word! Clearly, big tussles were also looming with Air Ministry and Ministry of Aircraft Production staff if the deficiencies of navigation equipment and services that needed rectification were to be promptly addressed.

First things first. I set about creating a properly balanced Navigation team, headed by a Group Captain and supported by a Wing Commander as Deputy, two Squadron Leaders and a Flight Lieutenant. He would also have control of the Command Maps Store run by a Captain RE at Northwood Hills. Compelling job descriptions for all six posts were needed to convince my hard-pressed boss and, though I didn't expect to be believed, I offered in writing to act as the Deputy to the proposed up-graded C Nav O.

Unfortunately, there was a serious oversight in my assessment of the situation regarding air navigation, and due to the general obsession with anti-shipping and anti-U-boat operations, I had fallen into the trap of lack of concern for the problems being encountered by No 1 Photographic Reconnaissance Unit at Benson. Their operations were shrouded in the secrecy surrounding every Intelligence activity; no-one advised me of this hush-hush work or I would have realised that the use of unarmed and stripped-down blue-camouflaged Spitfire Vs to make deep penetrations into Europe posed almost insuperable navigation problems for the pilot. He had nothing but a watch, a compass and a primitive flight plan strapped to his knee to complete a sortie of upwards of six hours and return to base with photos of the target to achieve his operational task. This supreme challenge required special and most urgent attention and yet I was unaware of its existence![1]

My somewhat defective planned establishment went to the SASO as an appendix to a withering memorandum on the paucity of the Command's navigation performance which was apparent from unflattering statistics gleaned from Operational Research. Within a day or two SASO Baker indicated Air Staff approval in principle but the AOA, A V-M 'Sammy' Maynard, would have to implement the establishment and not unexpectedly sat on the proposals for some time, partly because it would be a headache to find office space. Nevertheless, on 1 February 1943 I became a paid acting Group Captain with a fourth ring on my sleeves and scrambled egg on my hat.

There were drinks all round and I couldn't help smiling quietly to myself: I was now a senior member of the AOC-in-C's war council and, with the help of a strong team, would be able to pull enough weight to influence air navigation affairs. Only ten years earlier I had been frying chips in North Islington!

In the meantime I had many other plans to hatch. A clear priority for the whole Command was the fitting of the Distant Reading compass, or its American equivalent, in all maritime aircraft. For the Leigh Light Wellingtons, the AYF radio altimeter[2] was absolutely essential for safe descent to 15ft above the sea in all weather conditions and at night. All our aircraft desperately needed an improved drift sight which would have to be optically periscopic, a very ticklish problem for installing in flying-boats. As soon as they became available, the Air Mileage Unit and Air Position Indicator would become other top priorities for maritime aircraft.

Above all, I was determined to get the top secret electronic fixing aid which was on the point of general issue to Bomber Command. Called Gee,[3] it gave the bomber navigators invaluable coverage eastwards over Europe as far as the Ruhr and was potentially useful for our North Sea strike squadrons. Unfortunately, it did not extend to the south-west, where the existing radio aids were useless for AU-B or any other maritime ops. We badly needed Gee in the Bay but that would involve an entirely new Gee Chain being set up on new sites in the southwest.

I cannot recall the exact sequence of events that followed my cataloguing these requirements. To win user approval for the proposed re-equipment programme, I held conferences with Group navigation officers, attended by appropriate Ministry navigation staff. The former were the users and the latter sat in hot seats listening to long tales of woe. Ministerial obstruction had to be overcome, but winning approval was one thing: delivery and installation was quite another!

The provision of Gee posed less of a problem than I had expected, for I think it was Sir Robert Renwick himself[4] who called a meeting which I attended in London to sponsor a new Gee chain in the South West, thus taking some of the wind out of my sails. I was delighted at the prospect, though it was going to take some months for the Chain to come on the air. Little did I then visualise how vital that SW Gee Chain would become for our patrols protecting the Overlord invasion fleets in June 1944. We could not have done that job without it and there were no military-secure alternatives, as will be explained later.

Ted Edwards DFC was my esteemed Sunderland flying-boat

veteran and I pressed successfully for his promotion. I turned to the ever-helpful P staff (who included Wing Commander Leigh, of Light fame, among their number) to find variously experienced and recently tour-expired officers to fill my new posts. Luckily for me, James Perry had just returned from Canada as a qualified Spec N and I was able to grab him to train as an adviser on the unique navigation problems of the land-based new heavy bomber forces.

To cover the needs of anti-shipping squadrons, I was given an expert from strike Beaufighters. Flight Lieutenant Bill Strachan, a hard-boiled journalist by profession, paired up nicely with Perry when we launched our in-house monthly Coastal Command *Navigation Newsletter*. This was not competing with *Tee Emm* – nothing could do that! Nor were we in the same league as the *Coastal Command Review*, which had just made its very valuable PR debut as the brain child of our AOC-in-C. Our flimsy journal helped to create a sense of professional concern and pride among the navigators. It set out to explain new navigation equipment to the users as it became available. Innovative policies such as the application of the 'Drill' and the introduction of the Second Navigators were discussed. Operational lessons were analysed and controversy was encouraged. Covertly, we aimed to make our Top Brass more aware of air navigation and of air navigators and the *Newsletter* was widely distributed to the Command air staff, to Groups, Combined Area Headquarters, stations and squadrons.

My next recruit, Squadron Leader Philip Marsden DFC, ex Hudson squadron navigation officer and a chartered accountant from Yorkshire, had experience in maritime bombing and thus rounded off my staff coverage of maritime roles. As there was still a need for a compass expert, along came Flight Lieutenant Gerry Bristow who had temporarily lost his flying medical category and knew his stuff when it came to current aircraft compasses.

The threatened overcrowding of office space was resolved in a most unexpected way. The obvious vulnerability of the Northwood Operations Room had led to a huge hole being dug in the old hotel golf course to make a new Ops Room, deep underground, complete with all its related offices. The entrance to this dungeon lay at the end of an uncovered, unlit and, in winter, slippery tarmac path, 300 yards down a slope from the main building.

When Sir Philip Joubert handed over command in February 1943 to Air Marshal Sir John Slessor, the latter inherited all the improvements that Joubert had instigated. A brilliant staff offficer, Slessor tended towards an ivory tower or was it the stratosphere? One legacy of Joubert's was an underground operations room which was dubbed 'The Hole' even before it was half-built. Aesthetic little A V-M Baker was replaced by the imposing and impressive A V-M 'Dusty' Durston as SASO. No featherweight, he moved rather ponderously. Always genial and approachable, 'Dusty' robustly absorbed an awful lot of punishment. Such is the irony of forward planning that Sir John Slessor, because he had a gammy leg, was unable and unwilling to undertake long walks from his office in all weathers and often in the dark every time he wanted to see what was happening on the 'Board' or to confer with the Controllers, Intelligence, Planners or with Captain Peyton-Ward RN, the presiding anti-U-boat genius. The 'Hole' was a white elephant from the moment it opened and all the new offices were up for grabs. Guess who filled the best of the empty space! Our new offices were splendidly quiet and proved their worth when the 'doodlebugs' arrived.

Shortly after this general post, while enjoying a pre-lunch drink in the Mess alongside a number of officers of air rank and of more than ample girth, of whom none was more portly than bulbous Air Commodore I. T. Lloyd (always known affectionately as the 'Overripe Officer'), James Perry looked round and remarked to me in a whisper that the Royal Air Force was an excellent example of the survival of the fattest. Many a true word is spoken. . . !

My next move was to establish a qualified staff navigator at every station, from Iceland to Gibraltar and from the Shetlands to the Azores, to forge links, *via* the Group navigation staff, between my officers and each squadron. This took a lot of lobbying with my colleagues, the AOA's Organisers; but No 31 ANS in Canada was now producing sufficient numbers of graduates from its Staff Navigator courses to fill all our new posts, so in the end our persistence won. Within six weeks, a strong navigation organisation had been created.

One of our new AOC-in-C's first actions was to tackle the heavy losses in the anti-shipping offensive being waged off the Danish/German/Dutch coasts but particularly in Norwegian waters, until now out of range of UK-based fighters. Three Wings comprising Torbeaus,[5] cannon-firing Beaufighters and Beaubombers were formed and new tactics evolved to silence the flak from the convoy escorts while the ships were attacked from a safer range using the remarkable new rocket projectiles. The local knowledge of Norwegian pilots flying as outriders was used to guide the attacking Wings over the mountains and into fjords.

I felt at this point that I had muscles to flex for I had acquired the necessary sinews for the improvement, control and direction of the conduct of air navigation in the Command. Not only had I in mind the effectiveness of our day-to-day operations, which still needed to be strenuously addressed; but I also contemplated the longer-term problems arising from the persistent widespread refusal to recognise the vital importance of the element of air navigation which lay at the centre of all planning and air operations.

There was still a lack of focus in the higher echelons of the Air Staff when they touched on anything navigational and we had paid dearly for this myopia. With hindsight, I have to blame my Masters at HQCC for not sending me off post-haste to see what could be done for the 'PRU' boys at Benson. For years there had been navigational illiteracy amounting to the acceptance 'at the top' of unnecessary navigational limitations; and until the Air Ministry itself had a Directorate of Navigation able to seize the initiative and co-ordinate all aspects of air navigation from training to research, from development to procurement and from air staff planning to air operations, the fullest possible application of Science to the objective of air navigation would never flourish properly.

Many senior pilot colleagues and all the unorganised members of the 'Navigators' Union' shared this view for it stemmed from a strong aspiration to resolve a problem that was of concern to us all. I wondered if I might be able to do something radical about it but realised this step would have to wait until I could see a bit more daylight in my own bailiwick; so I put the matter on the back-burner for the time being, to await a more propitious moment.

Notes to Chapter XVI

1 One of the most distinguished exponents of long-range Spitfire photographic reconnaissance, who later became Air Marshal Sir Alfred Ball KCB CB DSO DFC, recalled landing back at Benson with only four gallons of fuel left and that he and other PR pilots 'could . . . fly 500 miles to targets such as Stettin, Berlin, Munich, Genoa or Marseille without a sight of the ground the whole way there and back'.
2 A primary radar equipment designed to provide a continuous indication of true height.
3 'G' standing for 'grid' – a reference to the latttice-work display seen by the operator.
4 Sir Robert Renwick was Controller of Communications in the Air Ministry.
5 Torpedo-carrying Beaufighter.

XVII
Navigator Captains

I HAVE already mentioned that May 1943 saw the turn of maritime aircraft and naval escorts to wield the big stick against the U-boat fleet. For many months in 1942 the enemy had been comparatively free from attack from non-existent escort carriers and beyond the range of aircraft based in the UK, Iceland and Newfoundland.

The so-called 'Gap' in mid-Atlantic had become a happy hunting ground for Dönitz's 'wolf-packs' to waylay convoys with growing effect. Our losses of shipping were still increasing at the start of 1943, when there were no fewer than 40 U-boats at a time hunting in packs in the North Atlantic. By May, the U-boat fleet at sea had grown to 239 of which 60 were now operating in that area.

Admiral Dönitz exercised tight control of his fleet by means of radio-transmitted orders. This was his Achilles heel, for the presence of the packs could still be monitored by our 'Y' Service, de-coding his W/T traffic and so partly able to repair the very awkward loss of our 'Ultra' during 1942, caused by the enemy changing his code. Fortunately, after an enormous effort by its brilliant cryptographers, Bletchley Park was back in business by December. The Intelligence information from both sources enabled the Admiralty to cut some of our losses by astutely re-routeing convoys round the U-boat ambushes.

However, No 120 Sqn started to be re-equipped during 1942 with Liberators (B-24s), which were later also fitted with centimetric ASV Mk III. They carried a useful load of A/S bombs and 250-lb depth charges and could stay on patrol for three hours at a distance of 1,000 miles from base. At last the 'Gap' had begun to be closed and slowly but inexorably the U-boat fleet would be hunted down.

Added to this new equipment, extremely efficient top secret weapons became available in March 1943 from America – Mark 24 Mines. These were torpedoes that homed on to the cavitation coming from the rotating screws of submarines and had a devastating effect. U-boats themselves had not very reliable magnetic homing torpedoes; but Dönitz was quite unaware of our new homing weapons which we concealed with the greatest secrecy, even on RAF stations, where they were literally kept under wraps from leaving the bomb stores until installed in aircraft.

The Mark 24 Mine quickly became our most potent airborne anti-U-boat weapon and largely contributed to Dönitz's throwing in the towel on 24 May 1943 when, in a message to his U-boat fleet, he conceded at least a temporary defeat. This signal was as usual intercepted and, as can well be imagined, caused euphoria among the Allied commanders. Dönitz also delivered a speech at Weimar in which he admitted that radar had deprived the U-boat of its essential element of surprise. The Allies' success was due, he said, to their superior scientific research. However, Dönitz had built up a fleet of 239 U-boats and had sunk 74 million tons of shipping in the previous 16 months and he wasn't going to give up quite so easily.

All through 1942 I had been nursing a pet bee in my bonnet and had luckily been able to give it a whirl in No 502 Sqn. Now, none too soon, seemed to be the time to start applying a systematic navigation 'Drill' to the entire Command.

First, I had, of course, to convince my own staff of its merits and feasibility, being very attentive to their opinions during its formulation. Then, Group staff navigators were summoned to a conference to float the idea in principle and to discuss it in detail. After explanations, argument and some compromise, the Drill's format was finally settled. Air navigators would have to make certain hourly observations such as regular three-course drift measurements to calculate wind velocity to make the DR as accurate as possible at the cost of perhaps five minutes every hour. Position 'fixes' had to be obtained whenever possible, using single position lines to supplement DR when a complete fix was not immediately available.

The air navigators thus had a systematic routine to follow automatically, leaving them free to use their own brains within the framework of the Drill. It was a consensus opinion that an 'Air Plot' should be kept, showing where the aircraft would be in the absence of any wind and was less in error than if a 'Ground Plot' was kept which attemped to show its position on the ground and was always in doubt. The decision to adopt an Air Plot as standard practice was a deliberate anticipation of the future aircraft installation of an Air Mileage Unit and an Air Position Indicator, both having been made possible by an invention for measuring 'true' airspeed by a retired Group Captain Riley at the RAE, Farnborough. The Air Position Indicator (API) and the Air Mileage Unit (AMU) revolutionised the plotting task of the maritime air navigator.

Having launched the Drill, it obviously became necessary to

monitor its adoption by squadrons in the Command. One great advantage of the new system was its ease of analysis, which in turn led to a monthly inter-squadron competition being held without overloading the chain of examining staff navigators, the results being published for all to see in our own monthly *Navigation Newsletter*. There had been nothing like this before, on such a large scale. Perhaps the most important effect was that squadron and flight commanders began to take a really keen interest in their air navigators' comparative performance. To say it stirred up contention would be an understatement. Some of the 'also rans' were quite put out and complained loudly.

A very important by-product of the Drill was, for me, the evidence it produced of the effect of air navigator's fatigue, which became startlingly apparent on sorties that regularly exceeded ten hours' duration. The navigators of Catalinas almost always had to slog away single-handed for 15 hours in the air and were exposed to even much longer endurance at a pinch, the longest recorded sortie being one of over 24 hours' duration. They instinctively adjusted to the demand upon their own strength and unconsciously spread their activity so thinly on such long flights that the navigation became inadequate, often to the point of real danger. It had until now been conveniently overlooked that the solitary air navigator's mental stamina had, after all, finite human limits.

The only answer to this in 1943 was the earliest possible establishment of a Second Air Navigator in all aircraft crews whose operational sorties exceeded ten hours' duration. This change applied to all maritime Wellingtons, Halifaxes, Liberators, Sunderlands and Catalinas. Such a costly innovation had to be tenaciously argued with Air Ministry recruitment and training staffs, not to mention their opposite numbers, my colleagues at HQCC and most importantly the AOC-in-C himself.

Convincing statistics from data accumulated from the Drill analysis records were produced and operational failures and accident reports were already available to support my strong contention that a single air navigator was more often than not unable to cope efficiently with the long sorties that were the norm in maritime air operations. But, surprisingly, the new policy was not universally welcomed by the very aircrew members who had most to gain, namely the navigators themselves, some of whom felt their authority in the crew was being undermined. Change is always anathema, but I persisted. In the end everyone came to accept the obvious – that planned and reasonable rest-breaks had their merits in practice!

One event that prompted me to find the answer to another much longer-term and deep-seated problem was when I cadged a lift from Northern Ireland for a staff visit to Reykjavik. At RAF Aldergrove I joined the crew of a Very Long Range (VLR) Liberator of No 10 RCAF Sqn. They normally operated from Gander in Newfoundland and were returning *via* Iceland to provide an A-UB escort in mid-Atlantic for the *Queen Elizabeth* which was steaming alone at high speed with 3,000 troops on their way to the UK.

We left Aldergrove in the long twilight of 28 July 1943 and after three hours our centimetric ASV picked up the great liner racing towards us when she was still 75 miles away, a very impressive radar range. We patrolled around her in the northern twilight for three hours and then headed north for Iceland for fuel and my own stop-off. This was the signal for the entire crew to pack up and go to sleep, leaving only me and the navigator awake. He kept beavering away at his table until about half an hour short of Reykjavik, when he woke up the Captain for the approach and landing, by which time he himself was nearly 'all in'. It had become obvious to me that this particular navigator had in reality acted during the entire sortie as the captain. The pilot had so far been no more than a 'driver, airframe'. I recalled how many other navigators I had come across in my squadron and elsewhere who had outstanding qualities of leadership which were impossible to exploit fully with their crews. They sometimes excelled their pilot colleagues in intelligence and showed that rare innate sense of authority which is so difficult to define but so priceless to a crew, not only in the air but also on the ground.

On arrival at Reykjavik, where in July the sun shone all round the clock, I caught up with Wing Commander 'Soss' Cohen who had just been awarded a DFC on his 70th birthday – a record that will probably stand for many a year! Soss was a very useful liaison officer at the Admiralty and wore an Air Gunner's flying badge with WW1 medal ribbons. As a boost to morale, he had flown gallantly as air gunner on recce missions in Ansons over the German Navy holed up in Brest in late 1940, which was then a very unhealthy occupation. (When visiting Northwood from London, Soss always had a special lunch consisting of a large plate of shredded carrot.) Like me, he was visiting Area Combined Headquarters, Iceland. When I told him I was arranging to fly on a long Liberator sortie with No 120 Sqn, he begged to come along too. So after I had caught up on some sleep, we took off together on 30 July, flying on a recce of the ice barrier. We skirted the bleak north-west corner of Iceland partly under snow and glaciers then turned north-east to Jan Mayen Island, lying at 71°N 8°W. It was completely hidden below cloud so we circumnavigated it using our ASV.

Soss had asked to fly in the rear turret, but it was very cold at 7,000ft and after a couple of hours he had had enough: his old limbs had frozen stiff and the crew had quite a job to extricate him. It was perhaps lucky we had encountered no opposition! We then turned to port and flew on a course of 235° past Scoresby Sound in Greenland, following and mapping the ice barrier which is an unstable feature and was of great operational importance to U-boats, to convoys and their escorts. The sky had cleared and the distant views of Greenland were impressive. But apart from the sea, the snow and the ice, we saw nothing.

The 12-hour sortie was rather tedious, not having a flying task to perform, but I noted that the professionalism of the crew was high. No 120 Sqn were being consistently very successful against U-boats and their CO, Wing Commander R. M. 'Dicky' Longmore OBE, had graduated with that 1939 Spec N course which had spawned so much outstanding talent. Longmore's brilliant career ended abruptly in the North Atlantic Gap a little later, in a duel with a U-boat Captain who stayed on the surface to fight it out with him: neither contestant survived the encounter.

Back at Reykjavik, apart from my discussions with the Air Staff, there was not much to detain me but I was impressed by the boiling water piped for central heating that a local volcano was providing free of charge to much of the town, a reasonable compensation for the threat of worse things that might come from underground. Living conditions in the RAF hutted camp were on the primitive side and although it was now August I was glad my tiny little cabin had a solid fuel stove glowing almost red hot at night, though it was extremely difficult not to brush against it in the cramped space available.

I was warned of the painful consequences of doing so by an accident that had happened only a few days earlier to Bruce Belfrage, a BBC announcer known everywhere as 'Beautiful Bruce' for his dulcet tone of voice. He was on detached duty in Iceland and, when going to bed a foot had tangled with his trousers. This had caused him to sit back heavily on his stove and he was now languishing in hospital, lying face downwards!

The US Navy were also there in force and their 'PX' store, the American equivalent of our NAAFI, was generously made available to the RAF. I couldn't resist the chance of laying in a good stock of chocolate: the entire UK was starved of sweets and the chocolate bars in our specially-favoured flying rations were always saved for hungry young mouths at home! Unlike George Bernard Shaw's chocolate cream soldier in *Arms and the Man,* the roles had now been reversed!

I also took the opportunity to buy a suit length of tough but sleek Akureyri woollen tweed made from sheep that lived above the Arctic Circle, but gave a wide berth to the notoriously smelly local goats' cheese, for fear of upsetting the young crew, recently trained in Canada, who were on their way to Prestwick and ferrying me back to the UK. As it had the reputation of being able to clear over-crowded railway carriages, it would have been asking too much of my fellow travellers.

Apart from staff visits all round the far-flung Command, I kept my finger on the navigation pulse by analysing the Flying Accident reports which the Command Training staff routinely sent to me for technical evaluation. I had been serving with No 502 Sqn when my friend Tom Moseley became CO of No 228 Sqn. When Air Commodore HRH the Duke of Kent needed to be flown from Invergordon to Reykjavik on a Welfare staff visit in one of 228 Sqn's Sunderlands, 'Mose' had to be in attendance on the Duke and naturally picked his very best available crew for the flight.

Within thirty minutes of take-off, the Sunderland scraped the top of the lower of a group of hills in Caithness. All onboard were killed, except Andrew Jack, the tail gunner who was catapulted out on impact and only stunned. Jack was understandably unable to shed any helpful light on events on the flight deck from his remote position in the tail. The crash was undoubtedly due to a navigation error, though the precise reason wasn't identified at the time and all subsequent conjectures have been unconvincing. The take-off had been delayed and the hand-picked Captain possibly decided to catch up on schedule by 'cutting a corner', a common and normally quite safe time-saving ploy used in four-engined Sunderlands. Having calculated correctly that they had passed the highest hill, the Captain and/or air navigator seem to have miscalculated when it was safe to turn across north-east Caithness, flying at their altitude in cloud. They turned fractionally too soon.

Both before and after this disaster, numerous navigation failures in the Command ended up tragically. The cliffs and hills of the western coastlines of the British Isles were littered during the war with aircraft that had unexpectedly encountered 'stuffed clouds'. I shall never forget investigating one incident involving a Leigh Light Wellington, flying from Chivenor in North Devon in 1943. Taking off in twilight into low cloud, the Captain had asked the navigator on intercom for a course to steer for the Scillies and was given 235°, also over the intercom. But the Captain thought the Navigator had said 135° and climbed through cloud, heading directly towards Dartmoor. Luckily for all onboard, there were breaks in the overcast

230

and the pilot suddenly found himself in a clear patch, staring at a green field rising up steeply in front, like a wall.

The Court of Inquiry recorded the Captain as saying that he then 'eased the control column back and climbed away.' Actually he had probably put both feet on the instrument panel and heaved with all his might to clear the 6ft stone wall surrounding the field! He didn't quite miss the top of the wall, which scraped off the doors of the bomb bay, seen by the terrified rear gunner as they tumbled away into the field. The Captain then turned back to Chivenor, landed and taxied to dispersal, much to the alarm of the waiting groundcrew who saw the gaping bomb bay and its load of depth-charges still hanging there. This accident initiated a mandatory order from my office to all pilots and navigators stating that any air navigation data passed over the intercom was henceforth always to be confirmed in writing. Service message pads were available and this was a case of the pencil being mightier than the intercom.

But the most bizarre investigation which came my way had not resulted in a fatal accident but arose from circumstances quite beyond RAF control. A US Navy Liberator from a squadron based at Dunkeswell in South Devon was returning in daylight from a sortie in the Bay and, at about the expected time, they made a landfall which the navigator at first assumed to be Cornwall. Unfortunately, the ground features didn't correspond with his topographic map nor did the strange country over which they were now flying bear any resemblance to the farmland of south-west England.

He and the pilots decided they had hit off the Brest peninsula by mistake, so an immediate 90° left turn was the order of the day. They quickly found the sea again and, as it looked just like the English Channel, continued flying northwards to make for the south coast of England, happy to have escaped attack. Shortly afterwards, some more land hove in sight and they turned to starboard to fly eastwards. They were, however, again dismayed when close inspection of the ground only increased their bewilderment, for the mountains, lakes and uncultivated land were certainly neither Cornwall nor Devon. Feeling now fairly lost, they decided to break wireless silence to ask for assistance.

Their distress call was picked up by Flying Control in Northern Ireland and they were told to fly to an airfield called Nutts Corner. If such a place ever existed, they had never heard of it – was it all some kind of a sick joke? Unhappily, they continued flying east searching frantically and unsuccessfully for any recognisable feature on their map of southern England. To their final horror, they again ran out of land, but in the distance now espied an island and when they reached its northern tip, were relieved to see an airfield. Was this perhaps in enemy territory? Running low on fuel they decided to land to find out! They had in fact reached RAF Jurby on the Isle of Man, after a long detour from a first erroneous landfall at Mizen Head in County Cork on the south-west corner of Eire. They then crossed Galway Bay and finally flew across the middle of the Irish Republic. All's well . . .? Pilot Officer Percy Prune would certainly have approved.

In December 1942 our Portuguese ally allowed the RAF to open a base at Lagens in the Azores on Terceira Island and No 220 Flying Fortress Sqn duly arrived, led by Wing Commander Pat Hadow who had graduated with me as a Spec N at Manston in 1937. After their first landing on the island, the whole squadron had rolled up their sleeves and built themselves a runway of inter-locking steel plates laid on the soft ground. Just before Christmas, Pat made a break-neck visit to HQCC and insisted on returning to Lagens despite suggestions that he should stay over with his family for 24 hours until Boxing Day. He arranged for an urgent return to his squadron as a passenger in a USAAF DC-3 (Dakota) but for unknown reasons it had to ditch into a dark and rough Bay of Biscay on Christmas Eve with the loss of all onboard. This was one flying accident that didn't come into my office for analysis.

One of my colleagues at Northwood, Jimmy Pike, a son-in-law of J. B. Priestley, took over Pat's squadron at short notice and they went on protecting shipping against U-boats and surface raiders in the North and South Atlantic oceans where Pike won a DSO and DFC. With No 220 Sqn in the Azores was their sister Flying Fortress squadron, No 206, both being controlled by No 247 Group commanded by the efficient and suitably diplomatic A V-M Geoffrey Bromet CB CBE DSO who had been transferred there from No 19 Group. The Azores base made up for our lack of long-range aircraft and enabled us to close the infamous North Atlantic Gap from the south, just as the bases at Reykjavik and Gander were helping from the north. Lagens in 1943 was an unspoilt small Portuguese colonial town and made a very pleasant place for a staff visit in the Spring!

We had been taught by hard experience that the few radio aids to navigation in our maritime roles were of very little use. Until the South-West Gee Chain came on stream and was supplemented over the North Atlantic by 'Loran', the American long-range aid to navigation, maritime air navigators virtually had only astro for fixing position which was seldom available in the North Atlantic when flying at about 1,500ft to obtain cloud concealment in the hunt for U-boats.

The dearth of reliable position lines to remedy the inherent inaccuracies of maritime Dead Reckoning remained a critical factor in our fight for survival. One day in late 1943 when I was at my desk in the 'Hole', my secretary announced the unheralded arrival of a Squadron Leader from No 80 (Signals Intelligence) Group at Medmenham, carrying a captured German chart covering the south of England and the Channel. It depicted position lines radiating like the Sun's rays from locations at Quimper near Brest, Petten in Holland and Stavanger in Norway.

This grid was based on a previously unknown system of MF radio fixing, producing incredibly accurate audible signals which were inherently discrete. To obtain a position line, all that was needed was a tuneable MF radio receiver and the ability to count dots and dashes. The Germans called it *Die Sonne* and were apparently busy building two more transmitters in Spain, one at Lugo and another at Santander to extend the system's coverage of the North Atlantic and into the Mediterranean.

Because radio waves travel round the world on paths known as great circles, the position lines from this system printed on the chart made up a grid of great circles! I was assured the signals remained in narrow bands even at ranges in excess of 1,000 miles; hence U-boats in mid-Atlantic had only to hoist a small aerial above the sea surface to hear the transmitters and acquire their position from the intersection of two, three or even more easily-counted signals already depicted on the chart as position lines. To demonstrate its simplicity, my visitor took me up to the surface and switched on the Mess radio which he then tuned in turn to two different frequencies. Each produced a clear series of dots followed by another of dashes which I counted for a minute or two. Then a quick look at the German chart pin-pointed us at HQCC Northwood. It was very impressive.

This new, enemy radio development had been referred to Whitehall whose knee-jerk reaction had been to recommend the War Cabinet to have the transmitters in Occupied Europe bombed and insist through diplomatic channels on their removal from Spain. Fortunately for us, Dr R. V. Jones, head of Scientific Intelligence in the 'Air Box', saw there were other options. My visitor had come to pose two urgent questions: first, should the bombing go ahead? Second, should Franco, an alleged neutral, be persuaded to close down the transmitter at Lugo, which he had ostensibly bought for a song, and stop any further construction at Santander?

I pondered the situation and slept on it for a night by which time the answers were loud and clear: what was good for the U-boat prey was invaluable for the hunters. With an accurate knowledge of position far out into the Atlantic, Coastal Command, the Navy's hunter-killer groups, the convoys and their naval and air escorts would all be far better able to rendezvous and we could also position our harassing patrols with great precision, thereby saving flying time and making better use of information about the enemy's whereabouts.

A careful look at the German chart which had been left for me to study showed it could be greatly improved. Thanks to the unparalleled co-operation enjoyed with ADI(Maps) and to the instant reaction of the Survey staff at Bushy Park, Teddington, our Maps Officer was able, within weeks, to supply the maritime air forces with a new series of multi-coloured charts, using an improved gnomonic projection on which the bearings were straight lines. They had a cleaned-up graticule and were on exactly the same scale as our own air navigation plotting charts to ease transferring fixes of position from one chart to the other. We thus stole a double march on the enemy and on his rather ham-fisted German cartographers.

To facilitate the slight task of training our navigators in its use and as a gesture to what is nowadays called 'Public Relations', it seemed advisable to use a less Germanic name for the system we were about to adopt. Again I pondered . . . *Die Sonne*: hmm . . . 'With the Sun'. What about 'Con Sol'? From then on, we were on to a winner, courtesy of the enemy! The name stuck and Consol continued in peace, slightly re-deployed, providing all and sundry travellers with a first-class long-range radio fixing aid to navigation at no cost to the users.

By 1943 there was something of a ground swell of doubting reaction developing among our war-experienced air navigators who, after four years' active service, were beginning to question their Service career prospects and their chances of advancement beyond that of being active Flight Lieutenant members of an aircraft crew. The most they could see were the few posts at Squadron Leader level as staff navigators at Group and Command HQ and at training schools. They looked with understandable and suppressed envy at their RAF pilot colleagues for whom the sky was obviously the limit.

On considering the situation objectively, it became clear that the air navigator did not have the basic opportunities enjoyed by the pilot for gaining experience as a leader in the air in order to demonstrate any latent ability in that vital sphere of Service activity. I recalled many air navigators I had come across in No 502 Sqn and elsewhere, who possessed obvious qualities of leadership but had never been allowed to exploit this rare talent in the air. Not only did they often excel in intelligence over some pilot colleagues but they sometimes showed an innate sense of authority which, like other human attributes, is so difficult to define.

I recalled the Canadian VLR Liberator navigator on the sortie to Iceland *via* the *Queen Elizabeth*. He had been in charge of the whole operation save for handling the flying controls for take-off and landing. The pilot had been little more than a helmsman, though he carried the prestige of Captaincy. The recent acceptance by the Air Council of the policy of providing a Second Air Navigator in a large crew would greatly facilitate taking another important step for improving operational efficiency: it would enable our best leaders to be trained as Captains, be they pilots or navigators.

I foresaw that the really important long-term gain would be that Captaincy, hitherto the sole prerogative of pilots, would become a most important first step on the ladder of promotion for navigators. It would open the door to equivalent careers with pilots in the executive General Duties branch of the RAF when such a policy could be accepted. (That innovation finally happened with the publication of Air Ministry Order No A410 on 20 May 1948, by which the Air Council offered equal career opportunities to pilots and navigators. The change was to the everlasting credit of M R A F Sir John Slessor who was then the CAS and to whom many navigators owe exalted rank during the past 45 or so years. Just over 30 years had passed when, in 1980, the first air navigator took his place on the Air Council itself.)

I knew the idea of non-pilot Captains would be regarded as a gross heresy in a Service where, unlike other air forces such as the *Luftwaffe*, the pilot had automatically always been regarded as 'king'. It was essential for the principle to be agreed that the best man should lead the crew regardless of his aircrew category if the imbalance between the careers of the two most vital members of a crew was ever to be corrected. Captaincy of a crew is a most important and practical way for anyone to display leadership, being a vital stepping-stone in the career of a General Duties (executive) officer. Leadership does not start to be shown in the air but first becomes evident on the ground; for it is there that a good Captain exercises his talent for instilling the best training into his colleagues. It would be too late to wait for a crisis to occur in an aircraft in order to exercise leadership. A tough struggle loomed ahead, but as a disinterested, if heretical, pilot I would obviously pull much more weight than had I been a navigator.

Having first tried out my suggestions 'on the dog', namely my own staff of captive navigators, I had naturally also lobbied as many Coastal colleagues as possible, not least the Personnel boys, the Trainers and the Operational Planners. I still had access to Kelly Barnes in the 'Air Box' who was, as I had expected, an enthusiastic supporter. Fortunately, I had the ready ear of my amiable SASO. A V-M 'Dusty' Durston, who readily passed on to the AOC-in-C, Sir John Slessor, the various papers I now began to pen on the ticklish subject of Captaincy, after adding his own endorsements.

The AOC-in-C had consistently shown a keenly incisive interest in air navigation. As Group Captain adviser to the CAS in 1938, it was he who had pointed with alarm to the poor training of air observers who were then joining their squadrons. He had later instigated a revision of the confused official operational roles of air navigators. Not surprisingly, therefore, I now found my initiative was fully supported so I could expect my next hurdle would be a push-over, for there was a natural tendency for the Air Council, then engrossed by much more weighty matters, to look benignly on the mere whims of their operational commanders. No doubt in the stress of war, the appointment of a non-pilot to Captaincy appeared to be of little consequence to 'Their Airships' and could easily be passed off as an experiment.

In these favourable circumstances I was quickly given the go-ahead. Now it was up to me to set the stage. Helped by a willing P Staff, a promising RAFVR air navigator candidate for training as captain of a Liberator was selected for interview in my office. Bob had already, and most remarkably, survived two tours in anti-shipping strike squadrons – our most lethal task and the nearest thing the RAF had to *Kamikaze* – and he was wearing two hard-won DFCs on his tunic. When he arrived, I found he was a handsome, freckled, fair-haired gentle giant, only one year my junior. I didn't know at that time that he was a Wykehamist, a graduate of New College, Oxford, and also of the Royal College of Music. He modestly exuded quiet confidence and listened with evident appreciation as I explained what I had in mind for him.

Bob quickly understood the potential effect on the career prospects of his brother air navigators which a tour as a successful Captain of a Liberator might have. I said I was keen for him to make RAF history if he was game to have a go. Being a man of action, he could hardly refuse the offer of an exacting future. I was most favourably impressed and we parted after an hour or so with my assurance of full confidence in his ability to overcome the prejudices he was bound to encounter. We both knew the venture carried an estimable responsibility towards all RAF career air navigators.

In due course Bob was flown to the Liberator OTU at Nassau in the Bahamas, where he was met by a reactionary Commandant who asserted that a mistake must have been made: Air Navigators could never be crewed up as Captains. A signal from No 111 OTU to Northwood to this effect was immediately countermanded by my colleague, Group Captain 'Crackers' Carey, in charge of all maritime aircrew training. The OTU Commandant was bluntly told to obey orders.

When the trained crew returned to the UK and joined a squadron, our guinea pig Air Navigator Captain Bob again distinguished himself as I had so earnestly hoped he would. His progress had been most carefully monitored during his Liberator tour of ops and everyone concerned from squadron level upwards admitted that he had been an excellent Captain: the trial had been an unqualified success and the door to Captaincy for air navigators had been flung wide open. Henceforth, Air Navigators, like pilots, could now win their spurs. It was very gratifying to the 'Navigators' Union' and an encouraging red-letter day for all RAF Air Navigators.

A year later, towards the end of the war, I sent for Air Navigator pacemaker Bob who was then serving under me as a Squadron Leader at RAF Shawbury and asked him if he would care to stay permanently in the RAF after the war. On instruction from the Air Ministry I was looking for very keen types like himself and if I recommended him, he would be awarded a full regular commission. He gratefully but diffidently declined, saying he was hoping one day to become a conductor! I recalled seeing him poring over musical scores while listening to a radiogram in one of the Mess anterooms and regretfully wished him the best of luck in such an esoteric career.

After a start in 1945 with the BBC Scottish Orchestra, Bob became conductor for the Royal Ballet at Covent Garden for nine years. He was then appointed permanent conductor of the New York City Ballet Orchestra, making innumerable records and composing music for films. In America he even ran a string of race horses as a hobby. Some Air Navigator! I often wondered, sitting behind his flowing white hair and slightly bent frame, when he was sometimes guest conductor at Covent Garden, how many in the audience would believe that the elderly and distinguished conductor waving his baton in front of them was once a renowned 'fire-eater' in the RAF with a DFC and Bar? Few indeed would consult *Who's Who* to read of his wartime exploits.

None would ever know that it was he who, as a 30-year old Flight

Lieutenant, had opened the door in 1943 for pilots and air navigators to share equal permanent career opportunities in the RAF. As he had always wished, he had now won fame as 'plain Mr' Robert Augustine Irving, proving once more that you can't keep a good man down. I say with the greatest regret that Bob Irving is no longer around to delight our ears.

XVIII

Overlord

B Y JANUARY 1944 we had seen the back of a year of crisis during which, after the U-boats had at first inflicted devastating losses on our shipping, the combined efforts of the naval air and hunter-killer craft and of land-based maritime aircraft resulted, by the end of May, in forcing them to stay submerged and to surface and attack shipping only at night. The U-boats' caution so hampered their movements and ability to attack that our convoys now sailed with comparatively lighter losses.

Sir John Slessor was so convinced the U-boat menace had now been seen off for good that when he handed over to his successor he wrote a farewell message in the *Coastal Command Review* saying as much. Most of my colleagues including Captain Peyton-Ward RN and his anti-U-boat experts felt distinctly uneasy that such over-confidence should greet our new Air Officer Commanding-in-Chief, Air Chief Marshal Sir William Sholto Douglas.

Undoubtedly, in the end it was a losing battle for the present U-boats and it is true that during the whole of 1944 they sank only (!) 1 million tons of ships, less than a seventh of their 1942 sinkings and of which only 175,000 tons – a mere sixth of the total – were lost in the North Atlantic. But the most testing campaign still lay ahead: the protection of the Allied invasion armada as it crossed the Channel, facing *Schnorchel* U-boats able to use their diesels submerged and having high underwater speed and great endurance.

We also knew that enemy E- and R-boats[1] were lying in or near the Channel, poised to strike. But we were most fearful of the new types of pre-fabricated U-boats being constructed in Hamburg, Bremen and Danzig. Designed as true submarines, they would be very difficult indeed to find and sink, so our scientists began to consider new technologies for combating this unpleasant prospect. One method was to detect the displacement of the Earth's magnetic field by a submarine; another was aptly called 'Autolycus', as it found minute trails (Shakespeare's 'unconsidered trifles') rising to the sea surface from a submarine. Sonobuoys dropped from the air were already on trial and were most likely to be our first line of defensive detection in these circumstances.

In the event Jack Slessor's optimism proved to be illusory, for Dönitz's earlier safety tactics had been so unprofitable that he had now shrewdly withdrawn his U-boats to re-fit them with more deadly anti-aircraft weapons. His crews were also re-trained for active defence and were to act in groups on the surface against attacking aircraft. This 'false dawn' was however a useful hiatus in the latter half of 1943, for it coincided with the planned rearmament of our Whitley squadrons with four-engined Halifaxes, carrying bigger loads of depth-charges, mines or bombs for much longer distances. They almost matched the effectiveness of the Liberators which continued to harry and destroy U-boats everywhere. We were also able to undertake important sea trials in conjunction with the Royal Navy to develop new combined tactics with their hunter-killer craft.

Equally important to our new weaponry was the welcome installation of high-resolution centimetric ASV Mk III for which the enemy had as yet no warning radar-listening device. Our microwave radar was made possible by the earlier invention in 1940 of the multi-cavity magnetron at Birmingham University by Messrs Boot and Randall. The fitment of the deadly Leigh Lights and of radio altimeters for night attacks also proceeded apace. The Command also intensified advanced aircrew training and happily I could now fairly confidently lay my hand on heart and point to a growing competence among air navigators. Their basic technical needs were being slowly met and, consequently, morale was rising; indeed all the flying categories in our crews, as well as the Air Navigators, were becoming highly efficient professionals. Britain had struggled through the 1943 winter, still suffering losses at sea; but aircraft were now inflicting havoc on any U-boat caught on the surface. We could no longer smell the peril of defeat even if we were still under serious threat. The process of growth and rearmament seemed endless and engulfed the headquarters staff in ceaseless and intense activity. We had to run hard to keep up.

Every now and then a colleague at HQ managed to escape to an operational posting. One such was 'Mystery' Meade, a tall Group Captain whose round, freckled boyish face and golden hair belied a tough and war-hardened officer, though how and why he had acquired his nickname was never explained. At any rate he was very pleased to be posted to command Holmsley South, a recently-opened airfield near Christchurch, Hampshire. On his station was a new, very long-range squadron of Halifaxes and Meade had not been long at his desk before he was tempted to take an operational flight as supernumary pilot on a sortie far out into the North Atlantic, an ambition which he had acquired in his former staff post at Northwood.

When the aircraft had reached a position some 900 miles west of Land's End, a surfaced U-boat was found and attacked. Although mortally damaged, its crew had fought back so determinedly that Meade's aircraft was severely damaged and had to be ditched. The aircrew were fortunately not desperately hurt and were able to take to their dinghy; but they were a very long way from home and had only their Mae Wests for protection against the elements. Thirteen days later, a Polish destroyer just happened to be passing and picked them up. Mystery Meade and his companions had won the RAF's WW2 longest dinghy endurance record; it must have been a story of fortitude and drama which I believe has never yet been chronicled.

The change of Commander-in-Chief had been accompanied by the arrival of a new SASO. Air Vice-Marshal Aubrey B. Ellwood CB DSC, a pilot from the RNAS in WW1, was a highly accomplished if seemingly extremely relaxed officer. He made a fine No 1 for the ebullient and approachable Sholto Douglas and was known to us as 'Tired Aubrey'. In one of the less frenzied moments of March 1944, therefore, I decided the time was ripe to fly a most important kite, namely a partial reorganisation of the 'Air Box', no less!

I have previously mentioned that at Air Ministerial level there was a serious lack of focus on all matters air navigational and a crying need for a central authority to formulate navigation policy, drawing together all the currently separate activities of manning, R and D, procurement and training. Such direction would obviously require an outstanding quality of vision. Even more critical was the absence of expert navigation advice at the highest level, namely in the Chief of Air Staff's operational department. The nearest the Air Ministry ever came to meeting this need was a nebulous advisory gathering called the 'Air Navigation Committee' which met infrequently, had no legislative authority and cut no ice.

Daily contacts were made with navigation staff scattered in the 'Air Box' and with my Spec N 'oppos' in the three other operational commands; and both Group Captains John Searby at High Wycombe and Bob Brittain at Bentley Priory indicated that the needs and implications of air navigation were not fully compre-hended nor adequately represented in the top councils of the Air Staff. Bob Brittain had not unexpectedly found it hard going to interest anyone at Fighter Command in matters navigational. He jokingly told me the average fighter pilot (often somewhat disparag-ingly dubbed by his brothers toiling in heavy bombers as an 'upward twiddler') only used his cockpit compass for wiping the mud off his boots as he climbed on board. The highly decorated John Searby was no mean exponent of bomber operations. He had acted as Master of Ceremonies for such massed bomber raids as the famous attack on Peenemunde in the Baltic.[2] Yet, both he and his predecessor had been trying for two years to convince the Bomber Top Brass that the only way to improve results was to concentrate the best air navigators and the very scarce advanced equipment into an élite force, able to mark targets for the remainder to attack. It had taken all that time to overcome inter-Group jealousies and for the Air Staff to agree to the formation of the Pathfinders and the adoption of a Master of Ceremonies to oversee the bombing.

A body of informed RAF navigation opinion, the unorganised Navigators' Union, began to press for a radical change to enable the vital user, the operational Air Navigator, to be heard above the rather hesitant Training staffs and technical clamour mainly of the Signallers, not to mention the growls from many of the still rather blinkered Top Brass. What now prompted me to act was the exciting wave of forward planning that had begun to surge throughout the RAF even though the war was still far from won. It was strange that the creation of an advanced Air Navigation School, led by an Air Commodore, had already been agreed in principle by the Air Council in early 1944 but no-one could see how it would work when the navigation Training Officer in the 'Air Box' was only a Group Captain. Who, it was wondered, would issue the School's directives and monitor action?

For an advanced Air Navigation School to prosper, a Directorate of Navigation would be essential to define broad policy in the Air Ministry, just as one had long since been recognised as a naval requirement in the Admiralty. More importantly, in the last analysis the problem of air navigation lies at the core of all effective military flying, extending to the precise placing of a bomb, the striking, or photographing, of a target or the delivery of supplies or passengers exactly where and when required and by a designated route. It would be an essential remit of such a Directorate to ensure these facts were appreciated by all commanders of air operations, from captains of aircraft at the bottom upwards to their AOCs-in-C. It would take leadership, time, patience and determination to eradicate air navigation illiteracy wherever it existed.

I broached the problem with SASO who suggested I drafted a letter for 'Sholto' to send to the US of S for Air. In those days of severe paper shortage, in-house memoranda at HQCC were typed on the back of obsolete plotting charts cut into very large (14×9in) pieces. It was impossible to make any typescript on such material look moderately readable, let alone attractive. I'm not, therefore, now surprised my draft received a polite brush-off! In any case, it was far too long-winded!

Sholto's hand-written reply dated '3/4/44' said he was sorry but 'try as I may, I simply can't see how a Directorate of Navigation can be fitted into the Air Ministry structure. . . . I am afraid I cannot support your case by writing to the Air Ministry as you suggest. WSD'. This was very disappointing because I was not alone in seeing the need for a substantial change at the top. As I have already said, my equivalent colleagues in other operational commands and in Flying Training Command all felt the same way, as did the CO of the Central Navigation School, which had recently returned from Canada and re-opened at RAF Cranage. We were all pilots, qualified as navigation specialists, and could not be accused of trying to feather our own nests. I had, moreover, felt it incumbent upon Coastal Command to show a lead as we were alone in having steadfastly carried the glimmering torch of air navigation between the wars. Coastal had nurtured air navigation from its earliest RNAS and airship days to where it now stood, second-to-none among the air forces of the world and playing a leading worldwide role. However, for a vigorous future it needed forward-looking direction. The existing disorientation was utterly incompatible with its objectives.

This general opinion proved to be too strong to ignore and a Directorate of Navigation was created under ACAS(Ops) in CAS's department in June 1944. I suspect that Philip Mackworth, Jimmy D'Aeth, 'Chillie' Chilton, David Waghorn and Kelly Barnes had all been pulling strings in high places. There was naturally much rejoicing in the Navigators' Union.

First thing almost every morning at Northwood, the AOC-in-C presided over a Council of War at which the latest Intelligence was presented. The Senior Air Staff Officer, attended by his heads of sections, among whom I was one, then discussed the short-term situation. The AOC-in-C would consider what action was required and frequently announced far-reaching decisions. Those attending mostly smoked pipes and the room became thick with blue fumes, creating an air of relaxation even on the most tense occasions. Nobody complained of pollution, but I don't expect the pipe-smokers would get away with it today!

For some months we had been considering strange developments which had been monitored daily by the Command photographic recce boys from No 1 PRU at Benson and interpreted by specialist staff at RAF Medmenham. What appeared to be concrete 'hockey sticks' were being built all over the Pas de Calais, with the handles pointing in our direction! Intelligence recognised them as similar to some being photographed by the PRU at the Peenemünde weapons development centre on the Baltic, and before long the hockey sticks were identified as launching pads for V1s or 'flying bombs', the first of Hitler's vaunted war-winning terror weapons. To reduce their obvious threat, Bomber Command and the USAF turned their attention not only to Peenemünde but also to the static launching pads aimed at Britain, wherever they could be found in France and Belgium.

The enemy countered our bombing by developing mobile 'hockey sticks', hidden in woods and carefully camouflaged. To say we were intrigued would be to understate our deepening concern; for the more we learned of the trial performance of the V1s, the more we saw their potential for upsetting any prospect of a Second Front in western Europe. Thanks to 'Oboe', a new electronic navigation aid, pin-point bombing had become possible in the Pas de Calais and indeed wherever mobile launchers were discovered within Oboe range. In addition, the increasingly heavy bombing of enemy industrial centres also helped to delay the production of the V1s and V2s. Meanwhile, rather tentative plans were drawn up to cope with an onslaught, if and when it ever came. It was impossible to do more than guess at their accuracy and other operational features but a fair number of people were well aware of what was afoot and the Press were under orders of silence so as not to cause unnecessary alarm.

The secret remained intact until the first V1s arrived over London during the night of 15 June, their 1,000kg warheads causing considerable havoc at the receiving end among civilians who were becoming distinctly war-weary. Aimed at Downing Street, most V1s fell about a mile short on poor, suffering Wandsworth. When on that June night a V1 flew low over Northwood in the dark on its way to Buckinghamshire, having overshot its target in London, it sounded just like a very noisy 'flying tractor' and I instinctively recognised it as a 'doodle-bug' from its grotesque clatter. So this was what we had been waiting for!

At first it was very hard to stop over-eager suburban ack-ack gunners bringing V1 'overshoots' down on top of their own heads, when they were already heading harmlessly for open country! But the delay in the deployment of Hitler's terror weapons had been extremely valuable during the Allied build-up of invasion forces which would otherwise have been seriously impeded. The casualty departments of the London hospitals were quickly overcrowded with victims needing surgery: near misses shattered windows and flying glass cuts badly; consequently everyone lived with their windows wide open and fortunately the weather was dry. My own contacts in the 'Air Box' spent a lot of time diving under their desks on the approach of a V1, often leaving me holding on to an inter-rupted telephone call until danger had passed or fallen short. On coming up from my bomb- and sound-proof office in the 'Hole' for lunch at the Northwood Mess I would ask my staff colleagues in their surface offices if they had had a disturbing time and on a few occasions I received some dirty looks!

However, long before the V1s had arrived on the scene, at a mem-orable April meeting of his Council of War, Sholto announced that the Allies were going to invade Europe in early June. He said it was no longer possible to withhold the secret from us as there would be a great deal to do before D-day. The exact crossing area, known as the 'Spout', would remain Top Secret but he confirmed that the prin-cipal threat to the Allied invasion would come from U-boats based in the Brest peninsula. Another and secondary threat could be expected from the east from the E- and R-boats, mine-sweepers and destroyers in occupied ports.

To counter this situation, 60 squadrons from the RAF, RAAF, RCAF, the Naval Air Arm, the US Navy, USAAF and other Allied Air Forces would be available, 25 of them operating against U-boats from bases in the south-west under No 19 Group at Plymouth, with calls on Nos 15 and 16 Groups and on Gibraltar for reinforcement if needed. For protection against possible fighters, there would also be two squadrons of cannon-firing Mosquitoes and Beaufighters.

The anti U-boat task would be 'to sweep an appointed area of sea by ASV every 30 minutes, day and night, regardless of weather, start-ing two weeks before D-day and continuing until further notice'. The area to be swept covered the approaches to the English and St George's Channels and stretched from Portland and Cherbourg westwards for a radius of some 160 miles from Land's End, as far north as Ireland's Mizen Head and south to Nantes in the Bay. This area totalled 50,000 square miles.

Combined Services trials carried out during previous months had shown that the application of almost continuous air surveillance would ensure any U-boat in the area would sooner or later be found and attacked. Those fitted with *Schnorchels* could also probably be detected by such high-intensity patrols and probably be unable to attack the invasion fleet.

To counter interference from German naval surface vessels lying in the Biscay ports, two squadrons of Beaufighters, a flight of

Wellingtons (to drop the latest type of parachute flares) and a flight of Albacores would be deployed to No 19 Group. East of the Invasion Fleet's Spout were 30 E- and R-boats in French ports and others in Belgian and Dutch ports. Armed trawlers, mine-sweepers and destroyers were also ready to intervene. So a flight of flare-dropping Wellingtons, five squadrons of highly-effective rocket-firing Beaufighters, flights of RAF Albacores, Avengers and a Fleet Air Arm squadron of Swordfish would be deployed to No 16 Group and be controlled by No 11 Group, as in the Battle of Britain. The Group also had on call the two long-range fighter squadrons of Mosquitoes and Beaufighters in No 19 Group, if they could be spared in the light of events.

The meeting broke up after an hour or so, with everyone almost reeling under the contemplation of such a massive redeployment of force. Peter Canning, the Group Captain Operations, tugged at my sleeve and asked how I proposed to design a plan for the half-hourly ASV sweep. I felt a bit stunned and we went down to my office in the Hole to discuss the problem quietly together.

It was greatly complicated by the fact that there would be such a mixed bag of ASV-equipped aircraft. At one end of the scale were the Catalinas, comparatively slow in attack, not yet equipped with ASV Mk III but only partly fitted with Leigh Lights. They could stay on patrol for a very long time. In the middle range of operational usefulness were Sunderlands with a medium range, a useful bomb load, good ASV and reasonable speed. Some had Leigh Lights and were invaluable for night sorties. Then came the Wellingtons with similar speed and range, two squadrons with ASV Mk III and Leigh Lights and two without lights. Next we had higher-speed Halifaxes with long endurance, some with Leigh Lights but all with ASV Mk III. Then came the Liberators with ASV Mk III, excellent endurance, high speed and Leigh Lights. Some of these aircraft were more vulnerable to air attack than others and might be better kept well away from the French coast intercepters.

To get the most out of each anti U-boat squadron, it would be necessary for patrols to take account of their different operational profiles. I asked Peter for a schedule of exactly what he expected to have available in No 19 Group by squadron, type, location and daily operational availability and he went off, hugging his head, back to his office on the surface.

Then I sent for my deputy, Wing Commander Edwards DFC, who agreed that the problem was right up our bright Squadron Leader James Perry's street. Perry leapt at the challenge and I told him, when the data arrived from Operations, to go away with a wet towel round his head and not come back until he had designed a series of rectangular patrols of different shapes and sizes to take into account the disparate ASV ranges and different speeds of the various aircraft types involved. Endurance might be part of the equation but it seemed to be a factor we could initially ignore.

Two days later he reappeared with a triumphant look in his eye and a smile on his face. He spread out a chart on my desk and pointed to a pattern of twelve interlocking 'boxes' that fitted the area exactly. They were of differing lengths but of equal widths, for he had taken a cautious line over ASV ranges and wisely plumped for the lowest common denominator. According to the aircraft speed, each could be flown round the perimeter of the allotted box in an hour, so two aircraft allotted to each box would achieve the specified half-hourly routine. A name for the design at once leapt to mind, for it resembled a 'cork' stuck into the neck of a bottle – the Channel.

James Perry's chart was accompanied by a detailed 'bus timetable', designating what type of aircraft should be allocated to which of the twelve boxes and how many each 'box' needed per day for nonstop half-hourly coverage, taking endurance, speed and squadron location into account. A feature of the plan was its great flexibility: each self-contained box could easily be reinforced, while the whole structure could be moved around the area at will. With Gee and Consol fortunately now available, I knew the patterns were viable propositions for our air navigators to deliver. It was a splendid piece of imagination and I congratulated Perry on his ingenuity.

The Cork operation then began its long process of endorsement by the Air Staff. Peter Canning was my first hurdle, but he was only too relieved to have anything in his hands. We went to SASO who gave the plan a quick approving look and took us to the AOC-in-C. Sholto was duly impressed. Then it was No 19 Group's turn to be persuaded, since it would be their job to put Operation Cork into action. So Peter Canning and I flew down to Plymouth and showed the plan to the Group SASO, Air Commodore Jimmy D'Aeth, himself a Spec N and quick to appreciate its finer points. We then explained it to the AOC, Air Vice-Marshal B. E. Baker CB DSO MC AFC, who was content to accept his SASO's opinion and agreed the whole proposition – subject, of course, to approval by his naval opposite number, the Allied Admiral C-in-C, South Western Approaches, for whom we then arranged a presentation after lunch.

Admiral Ramsay received the now enlarged RAF deputation in an elegant Georgian conference room with its high ceiling and large windows overlooking the Sound. A long, highly polished mahogany table ran the length of the room and the Admiral sat at its head, with the RAF on his left and his own Naval staff facing us. We spread out our charts and papers in front of him and he listened attentively as the features of the plan were described and explained. Straining forward on the edge of his chair to examine some remote detail on a chart, the chair tipped up and suddenly shot off along the polished floor, while the Admiral disappeared under the table! He was laughing ruefully when he reappeared and the RAF took this as an irresistible cue to join in. We thereby inadvertently 'put up a black' and some of the more senior faces opposite us, horrified by their Admiral's loss of dignity, registered their pained disapproval. Tut, tut! No sense of humour.

Of course this didn't prevent the jovial Admiral from giving our Cork his blessing. This was a great relief to me for time was beginning to run out. With only some four weeks to go to mid-May, I couldn't visualise any better scheme being cooked up at the last minute.

These activities were Top Secret and most of the Services, let alone the public, knew nothing of what was being planned. However, stacks of military hardware were being piled up in every nook and cranny in the southern counties and troops, tanks and trucks were on the move everywhere. They couldn't be hidden and the enemy knew for certain an invasion was on the cards. What he didn't know was when and where.

To prepare to intercept the Allied fleet, some 130 U-boats were accordingly deployed in their pens in France or in bases in the Baltic and Norway and another 70 could be scraped up from reserves. It wasn't going to be easy to neutralise such massive naval opposition to Operation Overlord's seaborne attack on Europe. Life at HQCC had always been highly active but the approach of D-day raised the temperature even higher. Occasions for humour grew fewer and farther apart as April and May wore on. Everyone was bracing for the great day and nothing was being left to chance.

Then a panic call came to my office from a squadron based at RAF Thorney Island, near Portsmouth. Evidently, some functional problem had cropped up in some of their American distant-reading compasses. Could my expert please lend a hand? I sent for Gerry Bristow and asked him for his programme of trouble-shooting visits. It turned out he was due to cope with a similar snag that had arisen at nearby Lee-on-Solent. With an early start from Northwood, he could kill two birds with one stone; but as he wasn't a pilot, it meant a long day's drive by car for which he would need petrol coupons dispensed for such occasions by the AOA's staff.

His application for the six gallons required was blankly refused because both these RAF stations could be reached by train, albeit after making several tiresome changes. Using public transport his two visits would take two days and I could ill afford to lose his time. However, the Deputy AOA was deaf to my appeal: rules were rules and avoidable car journeys were strictly *verboten* due to a petrol shortage. Had Bristow been a pilot he could, of course, have flown there and back from Northolt using ten times as much high-grade aviation fuel as the six gallons of low-grade petrol his little jalopy would need!

So off he set by train, carrying his despatch case on a journey he would certainly be unlikely ever to forget. Arriving at RAF Thorney Island quite early he managed to finish his job there before lunch. Over a beer in the Mess, the grateful squadron commander asked him where he was going. Bristow said he faced a train journey to Lee-on-Solent *via* Southampton where he would have to change. The Wing Commander asked if he would like a lift across the ten miles of water by air? He had a new pilot, just arrived from Canada, who needed a little local familiarisation flying in the 'station' Moth.

Gerry jumped at the offer for he could then get back to Northwood that night. He had no flying kit but the weather was fair and all he really needed was a parachute which he could presumably borrow. He met his pilot, they clambered into the Moth, Gerry sitting in the rear open cockpit and they took off into a north-westerly wind. Gerry realised he had no means of communicating with the pilot but visibility was good and he could make out the line of the Solent where Lee was waiting for him, over to port just beyond the large expanse of Portsmouth Harbour.

However, instead of turning towards Lee, the pilot flew straight ahead and they were soon skimming over the New Forest until they passed just north of Southampton. Then they turned a few degrees to port and the New Forest re-appeared beneath them: nothing but trees in all directions.

Gerry tried unsuccessfuly to reach the pilot over the windscreen of his cockpit to tap his shoulder and point the way. He couldn't remember seeing the pilot carrying any map and at this low altitude he could only guess where they were. It was painfully clear that the pilot hadn't a clue so he sat back in resignation and was surprised when they flew over a large unrecognisable clearing in the forest, simply packed with aircraft all bearing the special black and white Allied invasion stripes.

The pilot made a circuit, then landed and taxied towards some airmen, one of whom came over and was asked where they were. Unbelievably, he replied it was a Top Secret location and he was sorry but he couldn't say! So Gerry asked which way he thought Southampton lay? The erk waved an arm in a vaguely south-easterly direction and shouted 'Thataway!'

They took off again and turned in the direction indicated. After a while Southampton reappeared and Gerry was delighted to see they were now flying towards the Solent. Soon Lee came into view at the end of the east side of Southampton Water and Gerry prepared for a landing. This was not to be. The pilot continued across Spithead to the Isle of Wight, turned to starboard at Sandown, flew to the Needles and, running out of land, turned sharply to starboard and flew up the Solent towards Lee.

The Solent was chock-a-block with frigates, destroyers and mine-sweepers, all assembled for Operation Overlord; and as the pilot flew past them at mast height, Gerry thought his end had come. Surprisingly, they were not immediately shot down as he expected, and lo, straight ahead was their destination! Gerry plucked up courage, loosened his flying harness, half stood on his seat in the slipstream and leaned far enough forward to tap the pilot's head. He pointed frantically to the airfield and the pilot nodded in reply. At last, thought Gerry, after an extraordinary hour, we've arrived! They made a preliminary circuit and Gerry began to pull himself together for his staff visit.

But when he looked out again, he saw with horror they were not on an approach to Lee after all but were about to land at neighbouring Gosport which lay so near that the two airfields had interlocking circuits. As soon as the Moth stopped rolling, Gerry stood on his seat and banged on the pilot's helmet, demanding to stop.

Having clambered down to the ground, he removed his despatch case from the Moth's locker, put his parachute in and shut the door. He then informed the pilot, in case he didn't know, that this was Gosport. He, Gerry, had had quite enough and was going to walk the rest of the way. If the pilot wanted to get back to RAF Thorney Island, it was over there, eight minutes' flying, thataway, across Portsmouth Harbour. He'd be sure to see the airfield from 1,000ft.

With that, Gerry waved him goodbye and set off across the airfield to cadge a lift from the Gosport MT section. A very ruffled Flight Lieutenant Bristow returned to HQCC. Having once been shot at by the Royal Navy and missed, he felt very lucky still to be alive. To his pals, however, it was a good laugh – especially as he was always boasting about being a native of the Isle of Wight!

In the middle of May, Admiral Dönitz tried to move more of his reserve fleet quickly from Norway, all the way round the far north of Iceland to the pens in the Brest peninsula, ordering them to travel fast on the surface. But he was forestalled by Ultra and the Coastal squadrons in Iceland and Scotland were waiting for him. In the long daylight hours, a total of 51 U-boats were easily found and attacked, eighteen being sunk and nine seriously damaged during the next two months, during which Operation Overlord had begun. This preliminary action cost nine aircraft and many more were badly damaged because the U-boats now fought back ferociously. Two of our captains won the Victoria Cross in these encounters but the enemy's planned reinforcement of his Bay of Biscay fleet was foiled, as was his later attempt to set up a screen on his North Sea flank against possible landings in Denmark, Belgium or the Netherlands.

Meanwhile, the Cork was inserted into the bottle and no marked reaction was at first discernible in the Bay. However, on D-day 40 U-boats rushed out of their pens, casting caution to the winds in their haste to reach the Channel and also to form a defensive line against possible landings on the Biscay coast. Of course we were waiting for them and in the first five days 23 surfaced U-boats were attacked. In spite of fighting back, six were sunk outright and five turned back to their pens. One aircraft sank two U-boats in 20 minutes!

It was a rout. After 10 June, the only U-boats that tried to reach the invasion Spout were the few fitted with *Schnorchels* and they were harried remorselessly by our aircraft and naval units. By mid-July the U-boat threat to the Invasion Flotilla had been completely liquidated. Altogether during these engagements in the North and South, the Command itself accounted for a total of 30 kills and shared five others with naval surface forces; 26 U-boats were also damaged. In the process, we lost 45 aircraft and their crews in action against the U-boats and another 24 from the hazards of weather. Of the hundreds of ships involved in the Invasion and its aftermath, only nine were sunk by U-boats.

While this battle was going on, the enemy surface craft tried to interfere, as had been expected. Three destroyers from the Brest area were attacked from the air on D-day and then shadowed so that our naval forces waiting to strike were able to deal with them and they were all immediately sunk or driven ashore. The E- and R-boats in the east fared no better. They were attacked by all our anti-ship aircraft, especially at night, and quickly became ineffective. Some Mosquitoes were armed with rocket projectiles and others with six-pounder cannon and were easily able to see off any convoys and mine-sweepers wherever they could be found in the Channel and along the Biscay coast.

Suddenly, there seemed no longer so very much for us to do! Our battle plans had borne the sweet fruit of success. Our aircraft and aircrews had performed magnificently and with great skill, determination and gallantry and a high degree of co-ordination had been maintained with the Royal Navy. The invasion had been safely launched and we could now easily 'hold the ring' against any future interference with the back-up supply sea traffic. True, several U-boats had managed to escape to Norway and later those with *Schnorchels* took up threatening positions around our ports in the UK to attack our shipping. But these were the enemy's last desperate measures. The U-boat construction yards were heavily attacked by Bomber Command and by the USAF, for the U-boats were now being built in pre-fab sections and assembled without great difficulty.

There was much early and well-founded rejoicing and self-congratulation among the headquarters staffs at Command and at the Groups whose control of their huge forces had been so successful. Immediate awards of KBEs, CBEs and OBEs decorated the operations air staff at Plymouth and at Chatham. But nothing had been done for the inventor of the Cork and I indignantly raised the point with SASO. 'Tired Aubrey' seemed surprised and asked me what James Perry had done to merit any honour? I was flabbergasted and reminded him who it was who had invented the whole set of patrols and timetables which had been such a resounding success. I was asked what I had in mind and replied that Perry deserved an OBE.

'Oh!' replied SASO, 'You have to do something really big for that!'

I explained that though Perry had only taken 48 hours to think it up and work out all the details, Cork was a work of pure genius and on its implementation innumerable awards had been made, including an immediate knighthood for the AOC No 19 Group! Even my colleague, Peter Canning, had been appointed a CBE on the strength of its success. Didn't its author merit recognition? 'Oh well,' SASO languidly conceded: 'you go and write it up and I'll see what I can do.'

I had already been told that the Air Ministry wanted me to be posted as Deputy Commandant and Director of Studies for the new Empire Air Navigation School (EANS) opening in September at RAF Shawbury under Air Commodore Philip Mackworth CB DFC. I was flattered he wanted me to serve with him again: we had been together in No 216 Sqn before the war. It would be great fun to be his deputy and to direct the technical studies.

When I said goodbye to SASO, I handed him a very strong citation for an OBE for Squadron Leader James Perry RAFVR, an overdue recognition of five years of very dedicated service and for brilliant inventiveness. Three months later, Perry was Mentioned in Despatches! In my humble opinion, that was nothing short of a gratuitous insult.

It had been a great experience for me to play a small part in such a great Command. Its activities were no less invaluable because they received such scant publicity, a necessary shroud for the many secret and unglamorous tasks in which it was engaged. Often the very monotonous and never-ending anti-U-boat task was fulfilled by simply registering a threatening presence. That Coastal Command did not receive its proper allocation of scarce resources was regrettable, leading to loss of life and of valuable ships and supplies. Moreover, its aircrews constantly flew beyond the normal limits imposed by the elements as well as against the enemy with inadequately-equipped and often unreliable aircraft.

Apart from the comparatively small force of flying-boats, the main force of land-based aircraft had not been designed for maritime operations. For that, the Command would have to wait another ten years – for the Avro Shackleton! The gallantry of the aircrew, in the face of such odds, was second-to-none and their persistence, coupled with that of their naval comrades, undoubtedly saved us from the disaster of total blockade.

I left for RAF Shawbury on 1 September and the Command had another nine months of maritime warfare to fight before the U-boats surrendered in May 1945. When, at last, the Allied Armies over-ran the U-boat bases and removed the threat of the already emerging, new and highly-dangerous advanced Mk 22 submarines, they brought to a final conclusion the almost six-year-long Battle of the Atlantic which the enemy had fought with great tenacity to the bitter end.

Cold statistics are not an appropriate medium for dealing with the sacrifice of war, but the sheer size of the continuous air maritime battle merits dispassionate consideration. During the period 1939 to 1945, Coastal Command on its own sank190 U-boats and 309 other enemy ships; damaged 278 other U-boats and 714 other enemy ships.

The Command's specialised photographic reconnaissance squadrons of unarmed, unpressurised high-altitude Spitfires, totally unaided navigationally and dependent on the courage, skill and tenacity of greatly-daring lonely pilots, successfully penetrated from the earliest days of the war deep into Europe and, what was even more important, somehow returned to base with vital photographic evidence of what the enemy was doing.

The graceful Spitfires were later supported by squadrons of unarmed high-altitude elegant Mosquitoes, whose pilots were supported by helpful air navigators. No 1 PRU at Benson produced essential strategic and tactical intelligence throughout the entire war for the commanders of all our forces, from Mr Churchill downwards. Its record was so highly regarded by the USAAF that they patterned their own efforts in gathering photographic intelligence upon the Benson experience.

The Command's resources also included ubiquitous air/sea rescue launches that plied the seas around us in all weathers, effectively saving one in every three aircrew who had ditched in the sea. It also provided daring daily meteorological flights to obtain weather data upon which to plan operational tactics.

In achieving its numerous aims, the Command lost more than 1,500 of its multi-crewed aircraft through enemy action and a great many more from a multitude of other causes. Altogether, 5,866 highly trained aircrew had sacrificed their lives, a seemingly modest total by comparison with Bomber Command's losses, but less so when taking account of the disparity between the numerical strengths of the two Commands and the very uneven priority accorded to their resources.

Numbers are not the last word in war. The stark reality was that the enemy very nearly succeeded in blockading our country and in cutting the lifeline of Allied supplies to Russia. Maritime air and naval forces could not of themselves have won the war; but they could either win the maritime battles or else lose everything.

Coastal Command's battle motto was *Constant Endeavour.* It just had to be!

Notes to Chapter XVIII

1 E-boats were high-speed, heavily armed launches; R-boats were motor mine-sweepers.
2 See *The Everlasting Arms: The War Memoirs of Air Commodore John Searby DSO DFC*; William Kimber, 1988.

XIX

Empire Navigation

RAF SHAWBURY is situated in the lovely rolling farmland of Shropshire and had originally been chosen as having good weather for an airfield. Like many other well-sited RAF stations, it enjoys a climate all of its own, shielded as it is by the Welsh mountains on the west from where clouds and rain mostly come. By the time the Atlantic air has climbed over the hills and been cooled in the process, it has shed much of its moisture; and as the air tumbles down the other side almost to sea-level again, it warms under the increasing atmospheric pressure and becomes even drier. The well-known phenomenon of a 'rain shadow' allows the sun to shine at Shawbury when, not many miles away, the country may be shrouded in low cloud and heavy rain. In 1944 the station enjoyed spacious pre-war buildings and a runway long enough for heavy bombers to use with safety. It boasted large hangars, specially-built workshops for electronic equipment, an operations room, pleasant offices with comfortable living quarters for all except married ranks, and a large Officers' Mess.

When the Commandant and I arrived on 1 September, it was occupied by the Central Navigation School, giving navigators and pilots advanced air navigation training. It still ran a six-month specialist navigation course and a 12-week course for staff navigators; 120 officers on staggered programmes worked in six utility wooden huts, each holding two classes and heated by free-standing cast-iron coal stoves.

We felt no need to upset this particular apple-cart and left the organisation to tick over while we bent our minds to its reconstruction into what amounted to a Service 'university of air navigation'. The Commandant lived in a generous-sized suite in the Mess with its own sitting-room and toilet on the first floor and I put myself into an adjoining bedroom of ample proportions. We breakfasted in his suite; went together to briefing sessions with the course commanders to discuss their planned flying exercises for the day in relation to weather and aircraft availability; then we retired to the Commandant's sitting room to discuss endless ideas and draft proposals.

Far from being clear about our official aims, we discovered that the three-month-old Air Ministry Directorate of Navigation (and Control) in the 'Air Box' had hardly found its own feet, let alone been able to work out what it wanted us to do. As the Director was unable to issue a precise directive, he suggested we not only draw up our own Charter but also write our own 'Establishment'. Such a *carte blanche* was very heady stuff indeed to us, accustomed as we both were, before and during the war, to trying to make both ends meet. So we let our imaginations run riot and, with the examples of the new Empire (*sic*) Flying School and the Empire (*sic*) Air Armament School to follow, formulated our own lavish educational plans. We decided to call our school the Empire Air Navigation School (EANS).

We decided our first aim should be to create a central repository of navigation knowledge covering every aspect of military aviation; secondly, we would build a common forum where the air forces of the Dominions and ourselves could study and research side by side; thirdly, we would aim to co-ordinate development of navigation from the user's point of view; fourthly, we would maintain a continuous liaison with the Dominions and Allies by frequent flying visits and by drawing our staff and students from the RAF, the Dominion and Allied air forces. We planned to forge a permanent relationship in the field of air navigation between the RAF, the air forces of the Dominions and our Allies too. Our draft Charter was accepted by the Director without a murmur. An Air Vice-Marshal had previously once said to me: 'EANS – is that a new Greek political party?' I now had a rather long answer ready for him!

But it was one thing to have a comprehensive and ambitious charter and quite another to have the means to implement it. Our next hurdles could therefore make or break us: we had to have the right framework of posts, the right staff to fill them and enough of the right types of aircraft to meet the flying implications of our stated duties. For day-to-day administration we came under No 25 Group at Market Drayton, whose AOC, A V-M Davies, was answerable to the AOC-in-C Flying Training Command at Shinfield Park, Reading. The early arrival of their Establishment Committee to approve our elaborate plans for jobs, staff ranks and aircraft was of very considerable concern to us at the embryonic EANS.

The Establishment Committee seemed to be completely out of their depth when asked to say what they thought was or was not necessary to set up such a Service unit as we now laid before them. True, they had to contend with a bright Commandant who had a very nice way with him and had earned a reputation for being persuasive and forceful without being aggressive. According to Air Marshal Sir Edward Chilton, who knew him well, Philip Mackworth could even explain things navigational to senior officers who were almost beyond comprehension in such matters.

We were ready to argue, but in the event spent two days diplomatically elaborating on what we planned to do, while the Committee listened wide-eyed and open-mouthed. One explanation of their ready agreement to our starry-eyed scheme was that they could feel the war was coming to an end and they could be indifferent to the future costs involved in such a piece of make-believe. To make sure, we laid on a guest night in the Mess and plied them with lubrication. Much to our relief, next day they agreed to everything we had proposed.

The organisation comprised an Air Commodore Commandant, a Group Captain Director of Studies, seven Wing Commanders, 25 Squadron Leaders and 38 Flight Lieutenants. The Training Wing was to be my baby and I had four Wing Commanders responsible respectively for a new nine-month Specialist Course; for eight 17-week Staff Navigators Courses and a four-week practical Post-graduate and Visitors Course; for the conduct of Testing and Development; and finally for Liaison and Investigation.

This prodigious mini-empire drew upon the resources of 12 specialised sections, namely Radar, Signals and Astro nav aids, Compasses, Instruments, Maps and Charts, Meteorology, Maths and Physics, Instructional Techniques, Briefing and Analysis, Intelligence, a Museum and finally Editorial. There remained three other branches of activity, the most important of which was the Flying Wing with 20 Wellington XIIIs and 20 Halifaxes, all earmarked for navigation training. It had a Liaison and Testing Squadron comprising two Avro modified Lancasters, a Mosquito, a Mustang, an Avro Anson and a Tiger Moth; to which were briefly attached new types entering the RAF whose navigation set-up had to be put under user scrutiny. Supporting this structure was an Administrative Wing and an extensive Aircraft Servicing Wing.

We now started combing the operational commands for their outstanding exponents of navigation. Until this point had been reached in WW2, it would have been unthinkable to expect our requests to be given a second thought. With the war in the bag, as we all believed, we met with no resistance at all and within a month had collected a distinguished and enthusiastic team of hand-picked pilots and air navigators, too numerous to name. Mention must, however, be made of the then Wing Commander David McKinley DFC AFC, a flying-boat expert and first captain of *Aries*, the modified Lancaster. Subsequently, he rose to A V-M and was an early President of the Aries Association. At Shawbury he had the task of implementing Liaison and Investigation.

Wing Commander Kenneth C. Maclure DFC RCAF was in charge of Testing and Development. He invented the so-called 'Grid' method of orientation in polar latitudes, first used on the pioneering trans-polar flights of *Aries*. After the war he became a Professor at Magill University and was appointed the Scientific Adviser to the Canadian High Commission in London. On our staff we also had Wing Commander 'Viv' Branch DFC who helped organise ICAO (the International Civil Aviation Organistion) after the war.

In the Training Wing, over which I presided, Wing Commander E. W. 'Andy' Anderson OBE DFC (later President of the Royal Institute of Navigation) ran Navigation Specialist courses. Wing Commander Jobbins organised eight staff navigators courses which had a frequent turn-over and required an arduous flying programme to be completed with longish sorties abroad. I must not forget to mention Squadron Leader Stephenson, the chief Education Officer responsible for instructing in teaching methods and lecturing technique and a most lively exponent of the piano for off-duty entertainment. He became Chief Education Officer for Essex after demobilisation. I have already mentioned Squadron Leader Robert Irving DFC and Bar who had joined the Training Wing. All our war veterans had to be highly articulate as behoved the staff of such a prestigious body. Wing Commander Alan A. Saw, an old friend and colleague from No 216 Sqn to whom I had acted as Second Pilot in the 'thirties and who was now a seasoned engineering specialist, commanded our vast Servicing Wing with great efficiency.

One night when the Commandant and I were still engrossed in detailed planning, a gale blew up while we were sound asleep. After breakfast we went to the usual daily briefing session at 8.30 to discuss plans for the day's flying programme. Wing Commander Jobbins, whose staff navigation courses were due to fly, was standing about looking a little vacant and, asked what his plans were, replied by asking us how we thought his students could fly? Pressed to explain this extraordinary statement, he replied that they had no flying kit left after the fire.

'What fire?' we asked. A look of utter amazement then spread over every face. Had nobody told us? One of the keener students had been burning the midnight oil in one of the wooden huts, swotting for a coming exam. It had been a cold night with a strong gale blowing and he had stoked up the stove accordingly; but when he left for bed he forgot to shut down the flue. The stove became white-hot in the gale and set the room on fire. Within a short time the neighbouring huts downwind had also caught fire: each had students' individual steel lockers holding flying kit, navigator satchels, log forms, manuals, air almanacs, air navigation tables, maps, drawing instruments and Gee charts (still on the Secret list). The whole lot had gone up in smoke and nobody had thought of waking either the Commandant or myself; not that we could have done anything more than had been set in motion in our absence. We hadn't heard the fire brigades arrive from Shrewsbury and Market Drayton, but they were too late to save three double class-rooms and their entire contents: for weeks to come, we were retrieving half-burnt Gee charts, blown by the gale all over the local woods and farms. An hour later, the Fire Officer from No 25 Group arrived to investigate and Mackworth and I both felt embarrassingly red-faced. It was as though we had been caught with our pants down.

Our new Specialist course turned out to be difficult to fill because the war was still very much alive and we were looking for entrants with reasonably high academic ability combined with extensive flying experience. Visiting speakers addressed the students on a variety of subjects chosen to widen their perspectives and the whole curriculum was put over on liberal university lines. A successful new departure was the introduction of the four-week course for post-graduates and visitors. This aimed at refresher training for Service navigators who had already had a smattering of advanced technology. It also offered an insight into navigation to those in the equivalent rank of Squadron Leader nominated by the other Services and by our Allies. Thirty hours of practical air navigation formed part of the tuition and culminated in a flight to Gibraltar, to Maison Blanche in Algeria or to Reykjavik in Iceland depending on the season, the weather and the offerings of the local produce markets, for which we had our own Customs-clearing procedures as agreed with HM Customs at Liverpool, of which more anon.

The Test and Development department carried out service trials of navigation equipment and examined aircraft layouts from the users' point of view. We were uniquely qualified in having an overwhelming number of technological 'nabobs' as well as plenty of 'guinea-pigs' available; this did not duplicate the work of Telecommunications Research Establishment at Malvern, the Farnborough Royal Aircraft Establishment or any experimental

RAF establishments and we reported directly to DNC (Directorate of Navigation and Control). Air navigation and air tactics had been acknowledged during the war as being inseparable and any new equipment prompted revisions of operational tactics which the EANS was well placed to devise. In this task we worked in close company with the Empire Central Flying School (ECFS), then at RAF Hullavington, whose Navigation Officer was Squadron Leader Frank Chichester, and also with the Empire Air Armament School (EAAS) at RAF Manby.

This was where Development began. The EANS co-ordinated and analysed the multitude of navigation techniques which had become such an important feature of air warfare. It was exemplified by the trans-polar flights of *Aries*. Maclure's Grid technique addressed the problem of orientation in polar latitudes and was developed by the staff and finally put to practical test in May 1945. A heavy programme of development was soon scheduled for attention.

The most interesting tasks involved Liaison and Investigation. Routine flights were planned to the Dominions and to both theatres of war, that is to say to Europe and Asia. But we kept an eye open for any important air force activity. Missions were directed by the Air Ministry and reported to the department of the Air Member for Training. They were led either by the Commandant or by myself. Advantage was taken of the opportunity for a record-breaking flight offered by one such official visit to the air forces in New Zealand, Australia and New Guinea by the Commandant and David McKinley who captained our converted Lancaster *Aries*. They went round the world *via* Montreal, Washington DC and the Pacific between October and December in the first British aircraft ever to do so.

The flight covered 36,000 nautical miles in 202 flying hours and the mission accomplished its primary tasks of updating Allied aircrews all round the world on the latest navigation techniques and of assessing the problems of long-range bombing operations against the Japanese. The process of discovering shortcomings in the transit organisations and faults in the aircraft instruments led to a host of new developments. In Seattle David had an instructive encounter with an inquisitive American aircraft operative who asked with genuine interest what uniform he was wearing. When told he was an RAF officer, the American was amazed and replied, 'Say! I thought the RAF had been disbanded after the Battle of Britain!' Seattle faces the Pacific and little real news about the war in Europe ever found its way into the US Press.

On 15 January 1945 I set off on a liaison mission sponsored by the

Air Member for Training to investigate the air navigational practices of air forces in South-East Asia. with particular reference to operational units and formations in that area and to report on navigation problems on the transit route and those confronting British air forces out there. One of the four experts on board with me was Squadron Leader C. W. B. Kelly DSO DFC who had been nominated by Bomber Command.

We flew a Wellington Mk XIII and reached Karachi in four days, having stopped off at Malta, Cairo and Shaibah. At Karachi we picked up our guide, Wing Commander W. T. H. Howell DFC, Chief Navigation Officer from Air Command South-East Asia, and proceeded to visit 16 units and formations in the next 17 days, a very taxing schedule. We interviewed operational air navigators, pilots and station, squadron and flight commanders and called on air headquarters in South-East Asia, including ACSEA and SACSEA,[3] commanded by Admiral Lord Louis Mountbatten at Kandy in Ceylon (Sri Lanka). We also went to Eastern Air Command and No 221 Group at Calcutta; No 222 Group, Colombo; No 224 Group in Chittagong and squadrons at Cox's Bazaar; No 225 Training Group, Bangalore and the HQ of the Combat Cargo Task Force at Comilla.

It was pleasant to encounter former No 216 Sqn buddies like my first deputy flight commander, once Flight Lieutenant now A V-M Donald Hardman at Comilla. In conjunction with the USAAF he was grappling with the air supplies for Chiang Kai-shek which had to be flown over the highly dangerous 'Hump' that led from Assam to Chungking.

At Cox's Bazaar the former adjutant of No 216 Sqn at Heliopolis was now the AOC of No 224 Group fighting the Japs in the Arakan. A V-M Paddy Bandon gave me a very warm welcome before sending me on to Akyab, the base of his bombing forces on the Burma front. Who should be one of the fighter/bomber squadron commanders but dear old Pat Meagher from No 4 FTS, Abu Sueir, now wearing a DSO and as laid-back as ever. He was able to give me the low-down and it was clear that by any standard the air operations were primitive in the extreme. To some extent this was due to the lassitude induced by the climate and the primitive conditions at Akyab. But they were suffering from the absence of appropriate OTU backing, the lack of reliable maps, poor 'Met' information, the excessive intensity of flying (crews logged up to 120 hours a month), poor flight planning, very little advanced training in squadrons, no attempt to practise serious air navigation and, above all, extremely poor communications, leaving everyone neglected and forgotten.

To make matters worse, there was no continuity of front-line experience because tour-staggering had not been achieved. As a result, squadrons suffered catastrophic 100% changes of aircrew on tour-expiry when the monsoon's arrival presented enormous problems to the uninitiated newcomers. It seemed to me that the few qualified navigation staff officers available were doing their utmost to raise efficiency but they had a thankless task when they were out of any organised touch with ACSEA.

We returned to Shawbury on 12 February, having visited HQ Middle East on the way and spent a night at Gianaclis, south-west of Alexandria, where Group Captain Revington was running a Staff Navigation school on the edge of a very hospitable vineyard. The flight back to EANS took us over the empty battlefields of Libya with a night-stop at Maison Blanche, Algiers, and another at Istres, in partly-liberated France. We also had an unusual experience flying through the 'Toulouse gap' when, in the lee of a westerly gale sweeping over the Pyrénées, our Wellington, flying in fairly clear but extremely turbulent air, proceeded to gain and lose 4,000ft in a few seconds no matter what we did with the flying controls. My very critical report, dated 20 March, ran to 49 foolscap pages of text with 15 pages of Appendices. Its 51 recommendations were designed to help plan an effective all-out war with Japan.

The Commandant then decided to visit Canada and I took over as Deputy Commandant. It seemed just my luck one morning, while I was dealing with station affairs, when the Station Adjutant announced the arrival of two high-powered visitors asking to see me. They were the Chief Customs Officer and his No 2 from Liverpool. My heart sank, for we had made arrangements with HM Customs to inform them of every flight that came from abroad, so that they could exercise their prerogative of sending their own officers to clear the flight. We had something like ten such flights a week and Customs usually deferred to our own organisation to do the job, we having appointed one of our staff to act as Customs-clearing officer and to render the formal manifest of dutiable items. This being more than a rather sensitive subject, we knew it would always be easy for someone unscrupulous to try to get away with murder.

Playing for time and after the usual pleasantries, I offered my visitors coffee or tea. Conversation dried up and I feared the worst but, to my great relief, the reason for their visit then came out. When their own officers cleared our flights, very seldom were any items found to be dutiable; but when we Customs-cleared ourselves, we always submitted a long list on which duty had been levied. They found this embarrassing and would be grateful if we realised they weren't a bit interested in things we brought from abroad so long as they were intended only for our own use. In other words, please would we not be so enthusiastic! I was then regaled with fascinating stories of smuggling which the Chief Officer had encountered in his long career. They eventually went on their way, assured that RAF Shawbury's Customs Officer would no longer upset their professional pride.

Plans were already being drawn up for testing Ken Maclure's polar Grid. Discussions had taken place with the Director of the Cambridge Polar Institute and it was decided to make a run for the North Pole from Reykjavik in April or May when the Sun and Moon were briefly both available for astro navigation and for use with a sun compass. The return could be made to an RCAF base in Labrador and a sortie from there could ascertain the position of the north Magnetic Pole. *Aries* would then fly west to Whitehorse in the Yukon and from Whitehorse it could fly non-stop on a great circle track, *via* the north Magnetic Pole before reaching Shawbury – plans that had to be only slightly modified in the light of events.

These flights caught the popular imagination and the Press were given every facility to publicise the RAF's pioneering efforts. They were invited to a guest night, together with Top Brass from the Air Box and Flying Training Command, on the night before the return flight was expected. A dozen temporary telephone lines were put at their disposal and everything was set for the Saturday afternoon touchdown. It was a moment of triumph which we shared with our guests. But at the crew de-briefing, all the Press could think to ask were trivial questions such as how the crew had felt flying over the snowy wastes of Greenland, or how their wives had taken this intrepid adventure.

Knowing the Press from previous contacts, we should not have been disappointed by the accounts which were carried in the national Sunday papers. All the reports had missed the point that aviators could henceforth fly safely on routes that went over the North Pole from where all directions are 'south'. Had Maclure been able to patent his system, he could have cashed in on the many transpolar flights that came to use it in commercial flying after the war, for the North Pole lies on the shortest path between Europe and many destinations on the North Pacific.

By now EANS had grown in stature and become something of a 'show piece'. VIPs representing the Dominions came to visit us, keen to reserve places on our courses and to participate in our activities. The war in Europe had been won in May and victory had been duly celebrated over two days with song and dance. There remained the Japanese. Philip Mackworth had launched the School and was now promoted to A V-M and posted as SASO to Transport Command. While deputising for him, I had had to send for the Honours and Awards Top Secret file to send forward citations for awards for several of our staff. To my great surprise – and no little embarrass-ment – the top document in the file was a copy of a citation for me as CBE. It had clearly been put together rather hurriedly and I wasn't at all surprised when it failed to produce!

In Mackworth's place came the suave Air Commodore N. H. 'Jimmy' D'Aeth CBE who sported the Polar Medal he had won on a pre-war expedition. With the surrender of Japan in August, the time seemed ripe to call a comprehensive conference at EANS for all the operational commands, the Air Box, the Ministry of Aircraft Production, ECFS, EAAS, RAE, TRE, A and AEE – in fact Uncle Tom Cobley and all! We sat down to discuss a huge agenda which lasted all day.

I began to feel it was time to move on, having been involved in air navigation for eight years, with a short break in No 502 Sqn. My career would suffer unless I moved to other 'General Duties'. As an escape route I therefore applied for Staff College which was then moving to Bracknell. Luckily, I was selected and decided to fly across to RAF Manby to say goodbye to colleagues at EAAS with whom I had developed a close working relationship. Before boarding the air-craft in my flying gear I went to draw a parachute from the store, still wearing my round hat with its scrambled egg. A young WAAF at the counter stared up at me blankly, not recognising the only Group Captain on the station, and when I asked for my parachute, replied, 'And who are you, Sir?' It was a question for me to savour for the rest of my life.

At Bracknell during the next six months, with 59 other substantive and acting Group Captains on No 16 War Course, I learnt how to think clearly for the first time in my life. I emerged crammed with knowledge, clear-headed, brain-washed and fine-tuned for whatever excitements lay ahead in 12 more years of Service and many more years of other activities besides. It seemed incredible to me in 1946 that I had ever been able to graduate in 1931, let alone publish AP1234 in 1941. But the population of war-hardened Group Captains, including stalwarts like 'Digger' Kyle and Douglas Bader, became so brassed off with the Bracknell management that, halfway through our studies, the Air Commodore Deputy Commandant was unceremoniously 'moved on'; and at the end of the Course the Air Vice-Marshal Commandant followed him into obscurity. Not many

Staff College courses have exerted such influence on their environment as we did.

All eyes anxiously scanned the Air Ministry Postings when the fates of the new psa annotees in the Air Force List[2] were finally announced. The grim contraction of the Services had begun and 'acting' ranks became highly vulnerable. I was delighted to see mine was to be secure as Group Captain Operations at HQME – the only Command still in action (in Palestine). I hurried out to Cairo, without embarkation leave, only to find the post already filled for six weeks by a namesake of identical rank, of whose existence I had been completely unaware.

By chance I had become the butt of an inefficient 'Air Box' personnel staff officer who, in a passing encounter years later, volunteered being the author of the mistake which he thought extremely funny! It led to my return to Nairobi as No 2 in HQ East Africa to administer a wide-flung parish with penny packets of RAF scattered from Juba in the Sudan, southwards over Uganda, Tanganyika, Northern and Southern Rhodesia; north-east to Mogadishu in Somalia, east to the Seychelles and south-east to Madagascar and Mauritius – two years packed with unusual experience which, in retrospect, I was highly privileged to have enjoyed.

It cost me three years' of paid acting rank and was certainly not the career the 'Air Box' had planned for me. But some you win and some you lose. It was not all fun, acting as a dreaded 'hatchet man'. The next ten years were equally unpredictable, with never a dull moment, and brought 25 years as pilot/navigator to a conclusion. I have gladly kept close links with a much-loved and uniquely youthful Royal Air Force.

I've been called a lot of things in my time and for some years answered to the name of 'Mr Air Navigation', a cap that no longer fitted my balding head. It's been said that 'Man is not Lost'; but that doesn't help! My accidental beginning, reported at the start of this story, only gives a clue to Why I am. I've tried not to become a mistake – but who knows? I fear, after almost 50 more years of toil and many varied and fascinating occupations since that Shawbury WAAF posed me such a searching question, when all's said and done I'll never know the answer. You must just take your pick.

*   *   *

Dickie Richardson retired from the RAF in 1958; he was made CBE in the 1959 New Year Honours and had been twice Mentioned in Despatches in 1944 and 1945. He died on 12 October 1995 in his 84th year and a Service of Thanksgiving for his life and work was held in the RAF Church of St Clements Danes on 7 November 1995.

Notes to Chapter XIX

1 Respectively Air Command South-East Asia and Supreme Allied Commander, South-East Asia.
2 Being annotated 'psa' in the Air Force List meant 'passed Staff College course'.

Index

Index

Index

271

Index